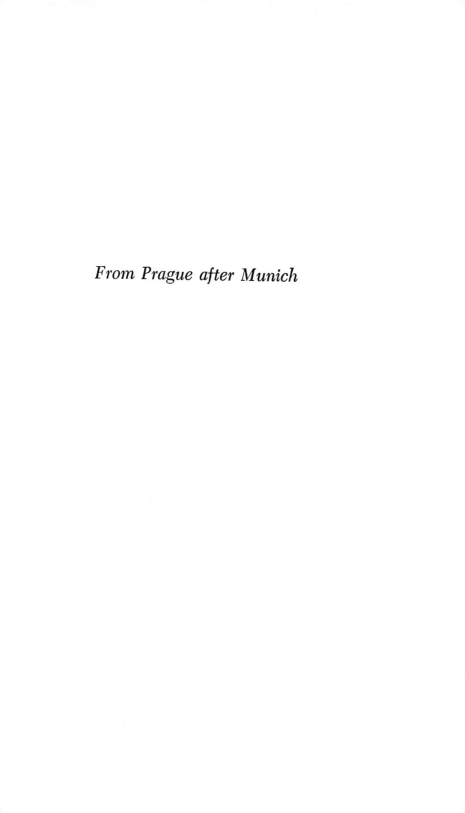

From Prague after Munich

From *Prague*
after
Munich

Diplomatic Papers
1938-1940

BY GEORGE F. KENNAN

PRINCETON, NEW JERSEY
PRINCETON UNIVERSITY PRESS
1968

Preface

When engaged, recently, in the preparation of memoirs covering some twenty-five years of experience in government, I encountered among my papers approximately 300 pages of papers I had written from Prague in the years 1938 to 1939. They were obviously too voluminous and too highly specialized to warrant reproduction as part of my general memoirs. On the other hand, it seemed to me—and others who knew more about Czechoslovakia than I did had the same impression—that they had some value as source material and should not go entirely unused. Out of this realization grew the thought of publishing them in a separate volume.

The circumstances in which these papers were written were as follows:

In August 1938, after serving for one year in Washington, I was assigned as Secretary of Legation at Prague. I arrived in Prague on the day of the Munich Conference. The following day I stood on the Vaclavske Namesti and watched people weep as the news of the disaster at Munich came in over the radio loudspeakers. Six months later I witnessed the entry of the Germans into the city. I was still there when war broke out, at the beginning of September 1939. Then I was transferred to the Berlin Embassy. But a lingering responsibility for the official American premises in Prague, plus an undiminished interest in what was occurring in the former Czechoslovakia, brought me back to the German-occupied city for occasional brief visits down to the end of 1940.

Throughout the period of my service in Prague my primary task, and—for the most part—my only task, was political reporting. Until March 1939 I pursued this function in my capacity as Secretary of Legation. When the Germans occupied the entire country, and our Legation was withdrawn, our government, seeing no one to whom I could suitably be accredited as a diplomatic official, left me there in the non-descript capacity of "foreign service officer," charged with custody of the official American diplomatic files and premises. The German occupiers, as inexplicably lenient about some things as they were ferocious about others, never objected to my presence in this noncommittal capacity; and I was allowed to pursue my reportorial activities without hindrance.

I had behind me, as I came to this assignment, a solid decade of experience with Eastern European and Central European affairs. I had studied the Russian language, and Russian history and literature, at the University of Berlin. I had served for some years in the Baltic countries and in Moscow. For a year, just prior to the Prague assignment, I had been in charge of the Russian "desk" in the Department of State. In addition to the years of study in Berlin, I had resided in, and performed normal foreign service duties, for considerable periods of time in both Germany and Austria. I was already entirely fluent in both Russian and German, and I found no great difficulty in learning enough Czech and Slovak to read the papers and, where necessary, to conduct conversations. Fascinated and enormously stimulated by the tragic but historic events taking place before my eyes from the day of my arrival in Prague, I threw myself into the study of the local scene, traveled extensively about the country, and poured forth my impressions in a series of official reports, personal letters, and diary notes. These, with certain minor exceptions, are published for the first time in this volume.

Within a period of days after the Munich crisis the great corps of Western correspondents that had descended on Czechoslovakia while the crisis was in progress had dispersed. Western opinion rapidly withdrew its attention from what was regarded as a lost country. This left me almost alone in the quality of a Western observer of, and commentator on, the post-Munich scene. There were one or two correspondents left, but their attention was inevitably concentrated on the happenings of the moment; they had little time for analytical reports. What flowed from my pen during that unhappy period has therefore today a certain uniqueness as a contemporary record of the initial experiences of the people of Czechoslovakia under German occupation and domination, as seen through the eyes of a Western observer.

This material was unavoidably in many respects unbalanced and inadequate. It reflected serious lapses in my own historical background, as well as in the range of my contacts in the Czechoslovak society of the time. The selection of subject matter was inevitably affected by the limitations on opportunities for reading, for travel, and for personal acquaintance. The quality of the reports improved with time, as experience and background accumulated, so that the hasty reader, who has time only for their casual perusal, will do best to start with the summary report of October 1940, which comes at the very end and is in my own opinion the best of the lot. But even taking into account this gradual improvement in authority, the papers will not serve as an exhaustive treatise on the situation and experiences of the Czechoslovak people in those unhappy months. They do not, in fact, even constitute the totality of the political reports submitted from the official establishment in Prague during the period in question, many reports having gone by the telegraphic channel and some having been written by other people. They are, on the other hand, source material and as such may be of some interest to a variety of historical scholars: to students of Czechoslovak history; to those interested in the history of the Nazi regime; to those concerned with the Second World War in general; and above all to those students of the political process who wish to examine the anatomy of an attempt by a militarily powerful country to dominate and control, under modern conditions, the life of a small and helpless but highly developed neighbor for whose national feelings, and claim to independence, it has only contempt.

For myself, the experiences reflected in these documents

were valuable in subsequent years as criteria for judgment on precisely this last point: the possibilities for great-power imperialism among the advanced countries of our time. It is my hope that this body of material, humble as it was in purpose at the time it was written, will help to illustrate for a modern public both the hideousness and the futility of the effort by one people to dominate another one, and to ride roughshod over its national feelings, in the circumstances of the modern age.

I have taken pains to include only such material as I know to have been written exclusively by myself and not significantly modified by any other hand. Many of the documents were signed by myself or remained, as diary notes, among my personal papers. Others, however, were usually signed, for form's sake and in accordance with official usage, by one or the other of the two men who were successively the senior officers of the official American establishment in Prague during the year of my service there: Minister Wilbur J. Carr and Consul General Irving N. Linnell. In one instance, the despatch was signed, in Mr. Carr's absence, by my good friend and colleague, Mr. Raymond E. Cox, who was then functioning as Chargé d'Affaires. In such cases, the one or the other of these gentlemen accepted responsibility for the content of the document, and it must continue to stand, in the formal and official sense, as his statement. I have taken care to indicate, on the face of each of the respective documents, the identity of the official authorship. I have Mr. Cox's kind consent to the inclusion of the body of his despatch. Neither Mr. Carr nor Mr. Linnell is now alive; but I am quite confident that neither would have objected to the publication of the documents in this context. In the case of Mr. Linnell, I was not a member of his consular staff. I did not work in his office. He would not have objected, I think, had I chosen to sign the communications personally. But, acting on my own initiative, in the interests of courtesy towards an older and more senior official serving at the same post, I took the drafts across town and submitted them to him for formal signature. I cannot recall that he ever suggested any changes or indeed that we ever discussed the content or wording of any of them.

In the case of Minister Carr, things were different. I was indeed a member of his staff. We were in daily touch. I benefitted in many ways by his wise and kindly guidance. Without his guidance, the reports would surely have suffered. I welcome this opportunity to record my indebtedness to him in this respect and my admiration for him as a great American gentleman of his day, experienced in the ways of both men and governments, whom I was fortunate to have as a chief.

None of these reports was written at the time for publication. All were written either for private purposes or for the confidential information of the United States Government. More than a quarter of a century has now elapsed since they were composed. They contain numerous references to individuals. Most of these individuals are no longer alive. Almost all of them met with a tragic fate. The references to them represented the best judgment I could form at the time on the basis of the information then available to me. In order not to impair the historical value of the documents, I have left these references unchanged. They should not be taken as representing the views I would hold today on these same individuals and their activities, if time and inclination permitted a scholarly reexamination of the record. It is perfectly possible, even probable, that some of these judgments may have been in error, or ill-founded. My apologies go out to those now alive, if this is the case. Actually, considering the perplexities with which all these people were faced, and the tragic miseries into which, almost without exception, they were then heading, I am inclined to feel sorrier for most of them today than I did at that time, and slightly ashamed of the flippancy with which, in 1938-1939, I sometimes treated their persons and their affairs. For this reason, I shall be particularly happy if these reports, fumbling and tentative as they were, will at least serve to shed some light on one of humanity's oldest and most recalcitrant dilemmas: the dilemma of a limited collaboration with evil, in the interests of its ultimate mitigation, as opposed to an uncompromising, heroic but suicidal resistance to it, at the expense of the ultimate weakening of the forces capable of acting against it. Everyone involved in the drama of post-Munich Czechoslovakia was tossed, one way or another, on the horns of this dilemma. It is the variety of their responses to it that form the meat of this story. All deserve to be judged in the light of the bitterness of the dilemma itself.

I am indebted to Dr. William M. Franklin, Director of the Historical Office of the Department of State, for his helpful attention to the problems of governmental clearance, and indeed to the Department of State itself for its liberality in permitting the publication of those of the documents which constituted part of its official files. To my friend Raymond E. Cox must go a word of special appreciation for his consent to the inclusion of excerpts from his despatch of January 12, 1939. I must record my thanks to my friend Howland H. Sargeant, of the Radio Liberty Committee, for his help in compiling the glossary of names of persons mentioned in the documents. Finally, I owe a debt of thanks to Professor Frederick G. Heymann, now of the University of Calgary, for his help in evaluating the historical significance of the documents which he has set forth in his epilogue. His great authority in matters of Bohemian history, added to the fact that he, too, was living in Prague through a good portion of the period to which these papers relate, give him exceptional qualifications for judging their historical value.

Relating as they do to this crucial period in the history of American foreign policy, these documents will serve as a supplement to the basic documentation on this subject published by the Department of State in the excellently-edited and highly useful series *Foreign Relations of the United States.* This later series is devoted more particularly to policy problems and communications with other governments, and its editors are able to include, for obvious reasons, only a small portion of the great mass of reportorial material that flows regularly into the Department of State. (Only one of the documents contained in this present volume, namely No. 28, is also published in that series.) For additional information on American relations with Czechoslovakia in the years in question, the reader might wish to consult *Foreign Relations of the United States*, 1938, Volume I, pages 483-739; 1939, Volume I, pages 1-130 and Volume II, pages 457-467.

Historical Introduction

The events of that time were so kaleidoscopic, so fleeting, and so impermanent in their effect that few readers could be expected to have them all now clearly in mind. For this reason a few words recalling the historical background against which they occurred may not be out of order at this point.

On October 5, 1938, five days after the Munich Conference, the Czechoslovak President Eduard Beneš, abandoned by the French and British, allowed to believe that his continuance in office would cause his country to be treated with even greater ruthlessness than otherwise by the Germans, and sickened by the further concessions made to Hitler at Czechoslovakia's expense in the final delimitation of the new border, resigned his position and retired to private life. The premier, General Jan Syrový, former Commander in Chief of the Czechoslovak armed forces, decided to remain as premier, to exercise *ad interim* the functions of the presidency as well, and to make the best of what possibilities might lie in an effort to collaborate with the Germans. This decision, reflecting no doubt the bitterness and despair of the moment, was one which would bring heavy retribution down upon his head in future years. But the choices of Czech political leaders at that tragic and excruciating juncture were neither obvious nor easy. By behaving in this manner, Syrový preserved, for the moment, a certain continuity of the Czechoslovak state and political system. A Czechoslovak government continued to exist albeit on a curtailed Czechoslovak territory. It continued to be recognized by the Western powers, including the United States, as the legitimate government of Czechoslovakia.

The Munich Agreement had envisaged primarily only the cession to Germany of those areas of predominantly German-speaking population that rimmed the saucer-shaped region of

Bohemia and Moravia. The cession of these areas was in itself a crushing loss to the Czechoslovak state. Not only did they contain the great fortifications on which the Czechs had expended so much labor and substance over the course of many years, and without which the country was really quite helpless, but they also were the seat of a large and important portion of the country's industrial potential. Nevertheless, the settlement left ostensibly intact the inner core of the "Historic Provinces" of Bohemia and Moravia, including Prague and its environs, as well as the outlying provinces of Slovakia and Ruthenia; and within these areas, as the French and British understood it and as the Czechs themselves were led to believe, the Czechoslovak government was to be able to carry on in the exercise of its sovereign powers. Its freedom of action was limited, so far as the letter of the Munich Agreement was concerned, only by the obligation to exempt all Sudeten Germans from military service, to liberate those then in prison, and to come to better terms with the Hungarian and Polish minorities (this last being only an implicit requirement). No other servitudes were specified. Hitler himself was liberal with avowals that he wanted no Czechs in the Reich and had no further claims on the Czech nation. It was even stipulated in the Munich Agreement that once the new arrangements with the Hungarian and Polish minorities had been concluded (nothing was said in this connection about border changes), Germany and Italy would join with France and Britain in guaranteeing the new frontiers of the country.

This was, ostensibly, the situation at the time when the first of the documents reproduced in this volume was written. Reality, unfortunately, was destined to take a different course. The dramatic spectacle of Czechoslovakia's abandonment by her allies, followed by her humiliation and partial dismemberment at the hands of Germany, had unleashed ulterior forces that were now scarcely to be contained. The Poles and Hungarians began at once to rend coveted bits of territory by force of arms from the flesh of the stricken country. Slovak and Ruthenian chauvinists, impressed by the Hitlerian example, proceeded to seize local power in their respective regions and then, exploiting the tragic plight of the Czechs, to demand in each case an autonomy little short of independence—an autonomy which, in the Slovak case, was even conceived by those who demanded it as a prelude to an early and complete separation from the Czechoslovak state.

Of even greater importance, in the undermining of the ostensible outcome of Munich, was the development of the Führer's own plans and calculations. Notwithstanding the impression he had contrived to convey to the British during the Munich negotiations, the fate of the Sudeten Germans was never the source of his main interest in Czechoslovakia. The Sudeten Germans served for him, as the Slovaks, too, were soon to do, only as willing pawns in a much larger game, and one which was to lead to their own ruination. What Hitler had in mind at Munich was the ultimate creation, on a very broad scale, of a new order in Eastern Europe generally—a new order in which the Czechs would have no greater role to play than any other Slavic people, which meant no independent role at all. If, at Munich, he had appeared to content himself with the annexation of only a part of Bohemia and Moravia, this was because the complete destruction of the Czechoslovak state appeared to him at that moment premature, difficult, and not urgent. The French and British, he had assumed, could be nudged only gradually, in easy stages, along the path that would lead eventually to their own undoing; they must not be frightened into a vigorous resistance to his purposes before he had had time to destroy every serious possibility of military opposition in the East. But beyond that, he had no desire, as of September 1938, to occupy the whole of Czechoslovakia with German forces; this would merely disperse German strength and tie down troops that might be needed elsewhere. Yet to occupy the Historic Provinces and not Slovakia would be, as he then thought, to abandon Slovakia to annexation by the Hungarians or partition between the Hungarians and the Poles. He appears to have labored, at the time of Munich, under the impression that the general weight of Slovak opinion favored reunion with Hungary, and that such reunion would inevitably ensue if Czechoslovakia ceased to exist. Reunion with Hungary, or partition between Poland and Hungary, meant the establishment of a common Polish-Hungarian frontier, the erection of a solid Polish-Hungarian *cordon* along the eastern border of the Reich, and a narrowing of his political choices in that area. The German military leaders, in particular, were emphatically adverse to it. A Slovakia tenuously attached to a weak Czech state was therefore better, in Hitler's eyes, than one cast adrift and allowed to gravitate to Hungary. These considerations clearly favored the continuation, for the time being, of something at least resembling a Czechoslovakia.

In the tempestuous course of events that attended and followed the Munich Conference, however, these assumptions began to undergo rapid change. Hitler's concern for British and French reactions was, in the first place, diminished by the astonishing weakness the statesmen of these countries had exhibited at the Godesberg and Munich meetings. One needed, apparently, no longer to fear any strong reaction on their part. ("I have seen these miserable men at Munich," he was later to say, contemptuously, as he confidently planned further acts of aggression.) The reactions of the Hungarians, Poles, and Slovaks, on the other hand, seemed to suggest that it would not be so easy as he had originally supposed to leave the rump Czechoslovakia for long in the state envisaged at Munich. The demands of the Hungarians for reincorporation of Ruthenia and Slovakia were stormy and insistent to a degree that began to constitute, for Berlin, a major diplomatic embarrassment. At the same time, these demands, together with the mutinous behavior of the new autonomous regimes in those two provinces, provided the government in Prague not only with an excuse but with an indisputably valid reason for continuing to maintain armed forces on a scale which Hitler found irritating and undesirable. He and his generals had been disagreeably surprised to discover the modernity and strength of the Czech fortifications in the areas already taken under German control. True, these fortifications were now in German hands. The country was in grievous disarray and relatively helpless. Still, Hitler was nervous about the prospect of any sort of Czech armed force being maintained, particularly one that still maintained ties with the Western powers. At the same time, he was surprised to learn from the many subterranean contacts which his aides developed with the new Slovak leaders, and particularly from a long talk Ribbentrop had with Tiso and Durčansky in Munich on October 19, that what the Slovak fascists wanted was not union with Hungary but a complete nominal independence, in return for which they were perfectly willing to accept German leadership and to subordinate their foreign policies to German purposes.

These realizations materially altered the picture, as it then presented itself to Hitler. If Slovakia were nominally independent, there would be no common Hungarian-Polish frontier, in that area at least, and there would be no need for any Czech protection or policing of Slovakia. The Czech armed forces could then safely be eliminated. Nor would the Germans have to occupy all of Slovakia. Faced on all sides with greedy or resentful neighbors and wholly dependent on German protection, the Slovaks would have no choice but to toe the line. Germany could content herself with whatever military facilities on Slovak territory might be useful for the outflanking and intimidating (and if worst came to worst, for the attacking) of the next victim—in this case, obviously, Poland. But if a Czechoslovakia was no longer required as an anchor for the Slovaks, then why retain it at all? The territory of Bohemia and Moravia already lay virtually as an enclave in the German Reich. Hitler would have to make military use of it, anyway, in the forthcoming showdown with Poland and Russia. Why, then, permit it to have independent relations with the Western powers, and an independent armed force?

Once these realizations had sunk in (and they were all ones that were absorbed in the days immediately following the Munich crisis), Hitler lost no time in laying his plans for the early destruction of the rump Czechoslovakia to the existence of which he had just agreed. On October 21, two days after Ribbentrop's meeting with the Slovaks, he issued a directive to the military high command to the effect that while another directive would be issued later, defining "the future tasks of the Wehrmacht and the preparations for the conduct of war resulting from these tasks," the armed forces must meanwhile be prepared for several eventualities, one of which was the "liquidation of the remainder of the Czech state."[1] The exact timing of this operation was a matter on which, quite obviously, Hitler proposed to continue to reflect and with regard to which he would leave himself, for the moment, a free hand; but that this objective would be accomplished sooner or later was something of which, even from the final days of October 1938, there was never any doubt in his mind.

It was against this background, then quite unapparent to the author of the documents presented here, that the autumn of 1938 wore on, in the capital of the rump Czechoslovakia. In response to Slovak and Ruthenian demands, Czechoslovakia was changed, by constitutional amendment, from a unitary to a very loose federal state. Meeting at Vienna in early November, Ribbentrop and Ciano arbitrated the Hungarian-Slovak frontier differences and allotted portions of both Slovak and Ruthenian border regions to Hungary. In Prague, the members of the Czechoslovak government, strug-

[1] *Documents on German Foreign Policy, 1918-1945*, Series D, Vol. IV, *The Aftermath of Munich*, U.S. Government Printing Office, Washington, D.C., 1951, p. 99.

gling wretchedly to adjust themselves to the new situation, begged repeatedly for some sign of help and encouragement from the German side. But as the weeks went by the German attitude became increasingly evasive and ominous. The Germans resisted all suggestions either from the Czechs or the French and British that they should make good on their undertaking to guarantee the frontiers of the rump Czechoslovak state. They gave the Czech leaders no help in their pathetic effort to make the new Czechoslovakia a good neighbor to the Reich. And when, finally, in late January, the Czechoslovak Foreign Minister, Chvalkovsky, came to Berlin for an interview with Hitler, he found himself showered with complaints, reproaches, accusations, and new demands —treatment only too reminiscent, in the light of history, of that which had been heaped upon the unfortunate Austrian Chancellor Schuschnigg, a year before, when Austria had been ripe for annexation.

Meanwhile, the Slovak and Ruthenian autonomous regimes, both in close contact with the Germans, continued to make every sort of trouble for the central government in Prague. They resisted every attempt by the central authorities to exert influence in their affairs. They defied, in their own political conduct, the principles of democracy on which the Czechoslovak Republic had been founded. They conducted relations with other powers, primarily Germany, clandestinely, behind Prague's back. They spent money with wild improvidence on the consolidation and outward decoration of their own dictatorial authority. They neglected their own economies, yet demanded angrily of Prague that it take responsibility for the resulting financial deficits. The situation, as some of the documents in this volume serve to illustrate, was rapidly becoming an impossible one. But when Prague, driven to desperation, endeavored, in late winter, to reassert at least its financial and military authority in these two regions, the local regimes put up violent resistance. Exploiting this as an excuse, though really guided by the timetable of his developing action against Poland, Hitler chose the Ides of March as a time for action. On March 15, 1939, as recounted in these documents, the Germans proceeded to the occupation of the rump Bohemia and Moravia, including Prague, and the complete destruction of the Czechoslovak state.

The decision to take this action involved a parallel decision as to the disposal of Slovakia and Ruthenia. In the case of Slovakia, the answer was obvious: the nominal independence under German "protection" for which the Slovak leaders were calling. But this change in Slovakia's status was bound to unleash new pressures from the Hungarians for the satisfaction of their territorial demands. Ruthenia presented even greater difficulty. It was inconceivable that an occupied Prague, separated from Ruthenia by an independent Slovakia, should continue to take responsibility for that remote province. The Germans themselves recognized, on the other hand, that Ruthenia could not conceivably be viable as an independent state. They had no desire to occupy militarily a distant province to which they had no direct access and possession of which would constitute a financial as well as a military liability. The decision was therefore taken—and it was communicated on March 13 to the Hungarians, to the great delight of the latter—to toss this bone of a province to Hungary. True, this created, albeit in a narrow area, the common Hungarian-Polish frontier which the German generals did not in principle want. It also involved the sacrifice, for the moment, of the "Ukrainian idea"—the idea, that is, of someday exploiting Ukrainian nationalism against Moscow. Ruthenia, linked linguistically to Galicia and the Ukraine proper, was thought of, after all, by professional Ukrainian patriots as the "Piedmont" of a future independent Greater Ukraine; and it was by this dream that the pro-German autonomous regime in Ruthenia had lived over those troubled weeks from Munich to the Ides of March. But supporters, in the eyes of such as Hitler, were expendable. The acquisition of Ruthenia would console the Hungarians for the frustration of their desire to reincorporate Slovakia. And whatever inconveniences it might involve could be made good at a later date, when the realization of grander designs would cause all these minor problems to fall into place.

Such were the ingredients of the changes of March 1939 described in these documents. What emerged from them, geographically and politically, will be seen from the third of three maps included in this preface. Ruthenia was now a part of Hungary, its previous "Ukrainian" masters having been obliged, at least in part, to take to the hills. Slovakia was nominally independent but subject, by special treaty, to German "protection" and obliged to harbor certain German military facilities, particularly in the valley of the Vah River. The remnants of Bohemia and Moravia, as they had existed after Munich, now became officially a "protectorate" of the Reich, occupied by German forces. A Czech government of sorts carried on, but only under the authority of a "Reichs-protektor" (initially the former German Foreign Minister, v. Neurath). Czechoslovak armed forces now ceased to exist; the Czechoslovak "government" was deprived of its ministries of War and Foreign Affairs. Every branch of Czech political life was now subject to German interference and domination.

Most of the men who manned this "protectorate" government, including outstandingly the elderly president, Emil Hacha, accepted the responsibility with good intentions, though with heavy hearts, believing that their activity in this capacity would at least mitigate the catastrophe that had overtaken their people and would help to assure that the Germans would continue to recognize the Czechs as a nation and permit Czech culture to survive, in some form, to a better day. Whether this calculation was correct is a question that surpasses the purpose of this brief summary. Suffice it to say that as the wartime years went by the Germans heaped upon these men humiliation after humiliation, frustration after frustration, indignity and disappointment of every conceivable

Czechoslovakia before Munich

Czechoslovakia after Munich and until March, 1939

Czechoslovak Region after March, 1939

sort. The ministers of the Protectorate nevertheless struggled on through the war, in growing helplessness and agony, to an ending so ignominious and obscure that it has not been easy even to discover what became of them, individually, in the general debacle of 1945. Of those who later faced trial as collaborators, some were wholly exonerated, some punished lightly, some punished with great severity. Hacha, whose plight was the most pathetic and tragic of the lot, was granted by Providence the mercy of dying naturally in prison before he could be tried.

In Slovakia, of course, a somewhat different situation prevailed. The Slovak leaders were much more heavily involved with the Germans than were the Czechs. They accepted gladly and eagerly the collaboration with Hitler's Germany to which their Czech confreres submitted reluctantly and with the heaviest of hearts. In addition to serving as instruments of Nazi foreign policy, they embraced, and applied against their own people, many of the internal principles of German National Socialism. In all of this, they incriminated themselves far more than the Czech leaders had done. An uprising against their authority in 1944 provoked a bloody and—for them—humiliating German intervention. This was followed shortly by the entry of the Soviet armed forces. In the final great sweep of the war, the situation now wholly outside their control even on the territory to which their ambitions and authority ostensibly extended, the Slovak leaders came, almost without exception, to tragic and ignominious ends.

Of the documents reproduced here, only the first nine deal with the period from Munich until the occupation of Prague in March 1939. The bulk of them were written in the further five and a half months that elapsed from the March events to the outbreak of the Second World War in September. One, the last, was written after a visit to Prague in the autumn of 1940 and constitutes a review of the entire first year and a half in the experience of the "Protectorate of Bohemia and Moravia."

GEORGE F. KENNAN

CONTENTS

Contents

Contents

From Prague after Munich

1. Personal notes on the
Munich crisis, written in early
October 1938

Prague could never have been more beautiful than during those recent September days when its security hung by so slender a thread. The old streets, relieved of motor vehicles by an obliging army, had recovered something of their pristine quiet and composure. Baroque towers—themselves unreal and ethereal—floated peacefully against skies in which the bright blue of autumn made way frequently for isolated, drifting clouds. In the sleepy courtyards, sunshine varied with brief, gentle showers. And the little groups of passers-by still assembled hourly in the market place, as they had for centuries, to watch the saints make their appointed rounds in the clock on the wall of the town hall.

Yet rarely, if ever, has the quaint garb of this old city seemed more museum-like, more detached from the realities of the moment, than it did during these strange days. The world had taken final farewell, it seemed, of nearly everything that these monuments represented. Gone were the unifying faith and national tolerance of the Middle Ages; gone—in large measure—was the glamour of the Counter-Reformation, the outward manifestation of the wealth and power of Rome; gone indeed were the gay dreams of the empire of Joseph II and Maria Theresa: the laughing voice of Vienna, the spirit of Mozart. A sterner age was upon us; and it was only in the gaunt spires of the Tyn Church— those grim reminders of the century-long struggle of a stubborn and rebellious Bohemia against the united power of western Europe—that there was something vitally connected with the problems of this day. The ghosts of Jan Hus and the Bohemian Brethren stalked again through "blacked-out"

3

streets which could not have been darker in the fifteenth century itself. And again a remarkable little people, whose virtues and whose failings are alike the products of adversity, found themselves standing out in lonely bitterness against what they felt to be an unjust and unsympathetic Europe.

These days, so tragic for the Czechs themselves, have been anything but pleasant for their friends. It is easy to point out the mistakes of the past; but it is not easy to comfort people for what they regard as twenty years of misplaced endeavor, betrayal by their friends and the loss of the dream of centuries—a dream that seemed, only a short time ago, so tantalizingly close to realization.

No one can deny the efforts the Czechs have put forth to develop their territories and to lay the foundations of a permanent, healthy state. No one can look at their beautifully prepared atlases or follow the excellent Sokol foot-trails through the Bohemian forests without sharing their grief at the rude smashing of the clay which they tried so hard to mold into a sound and enduring vessel. It is impossible not to agree when they tell you that they were not responsible for the presence of three million Germans within the natural strategic and economic frontiers of Bohemia, and that they feel themselves to have been, despite their lack of experience in government, more considerate hosts to their own racial minorities than many of those who have now, with such sudden flutters of indignation, gathered non-Slavic minorities under the maternal wing. It is not easy to tell them why, after they have worked so hard to make their country a bulwark in central Europe of those virtues which the Western democracies professed to cherish, they should be punished with an arrangement which to many of them spells the virtual end of their political and economic independence. Finally, it is impossible to object when they now turn as bitterly on their erstwhile liberalism as they have on the alliances which supported it, and set out to show the world how well they too can play at the game of authoritarian government, if the only alternative be failure and isolation.

Fortunately, one does not need to share this despair in order to understand it. In this crowded heart of Europe, where neighborly jealousies run so high, there can never be any solution of the ills of the day which will satisfy both Jack and Tom alike. It is comforting to reflect that if no good wind can fail to blow ill, no ill wind can fail to blow good. Change will always involve suffering, but one can at least hope that such changes as occur will lead in the direction of greater economic security and greater racial tolerance for people sadly in need of both. And while recent events, to be sure, have done no immediate service to either of these goals, there is hope that their ultimate results may lead in this direction.

Czechoslovakia is, after all, a central European state. Its fortunes must in the long run lie with—and not against— the dominant forces in this area. It is generally agreed that the breakup of the limited degree of unity which the Hapsburg Empire represented was unfortunate for all concerned. Other forces are now at work which are struggling to create a new form of unity where individualism and sectionalism have held sway for two decades. To these forces, Czechoslovakia has been tragically slow in adjusting herself. It is idle at this late date to attempt to apportion the blame for this fact between the country's own statesmen and its foreign advisors. The adjustment—and this is the main thing—has now come. It has come in a painful and deplorable form. But it has relieved the Czechoslovak state of liabilities as well as assets. It has left the heart of the country physically intact. Finally, and perhaps most important of all, it has preserved for the exacting tasks of the future a magnificent younger generation—disciplined, industrious, and physically fit—which would undoubtedly have been sacrificed if the solution had been the romantic one of hopeless resistance rather than the humiliating but truly heroic one of realism.

The story of Czechoslovakia is not yet ended. There is no use in minimizing the dangers and trials that lie ahead. But if there is any lesson to be learned from the tortuous history of this continent, it is that strength, courage, and perseverance—qualities which the Czech people now possess in greater degree than ever before—have never been permanently suppressed and have never failed in the end to win their just place in the surging, changing movement of political life.

This thought will not comfort the Czechs in their present mood of bitterness and frustration; but it may well be a source of consolation to those outsiders who have followed their past struggles with sympathy and admiration and who have never ceased to wish them well for the future.

". . . word came that the German troops had already reached the palace"

"A crowd of embittered but curious Czechs looked on in silence"

". . . hundreds and hundreds of vehicles plastered with snow . . ."

". . . the soldier . . . nervously fingering the trigger of
his machine gun as he faced the crowd"

These photographs of the dramatic entry of
the German forces into Prague on March
15, 1939, were obtained from a private independent source. Not taken in any connection
with the account of that event which appears
in this volume, they will nevertheless serve
to convey something of the atmosphere of
that tragic and harrowing day.

". . . the occupation was complete and the people were
chased off the streets . . ."

2. Excerpts from a personal letter of December 8, 1938

I wonder whether it is possible for anyone who has not been here to conceive of the chaos which the Munich catastrophe created in political life and political thought in Czechoslovakia.

Everything which had any powers of cohesion went by the boards. Nothing was left in the popular mind but bitterness, bewilderment, and skepticism.

Every feature of liberalism and democracy, in particular, was hopelessly and irretrievably discredited. I spent week ends in the country where the guests did nothing but toss down brandy after brandy in an atmosphere of total gloom and repeat countless times: "How was it possible that any people could allow itself to be led for twenty years by such a *Sauhund*—such an international, democratic *Sauhund*—as Beneš? Such a people doesn't deserve to exist. It ought to be annihilated," etc. To realize the full significance of this, one has only to recall that but little over a year ago on the occasion of Masaryk's funeral here, seemingly the whole nation was united in an outpouring of grief and devotion to the state and the policies which he had inaugurated, which of course included the foreign policy of Beneš.

Complete fascism is scarcely any more popular than democracy. The Czech people are not, in the main, highly emotional, along German or Italian patterns. They are now less than ever before inclined to place great confidence in any single leader. The radical fascist group has always stood in bitter feud with the army generals and the legionnaires, who are still a power. So fascism, too, as an internal program, offers no commonly acceptable solution.

The Catholic Church, which might—and in past times

would—have profited by the occasion to offer a real unity to the people did nothing but stand timidly aside and watch to see which way the cat would jump. With Hitler on the right of them and Hitler on the left of them, the Catholics doubtless dreaded the thought of assuming any open political responsibility. They are apparently pleased enough that President Hacha[1] has kissed the bones of St. Wenceslas and deported himself as a highly pious Catholic (with one eye cocked at the devout and troublesome Slovaks) and that no one has yet made any threatening gestures toward their extensive real-estate holdings or other worldly belongings in Czechoslovakia.

Thus it was—all in all—terribly difficult to find any real rallying point for political activity, and order was maintained through October and a good part of November only by the ponderous calm of General Syrový, the discipline of those Czechs who were in the armed forces and the apathy and discouragement of those who were not.

In these conditions, it is not surprising that the birth of a new form of government should have been a hard one. There were even some tense days, at one time, when it looked as if Adolf—who was after all the father in a sense—was getting impatient and was about to take a direct part in assisting the delivery—a development which might have produced a lusty child with commendable promptness but would have been hard on the mother.

All this, however, has passed. Things have been fixed up after a fashion—for the time being. Thanks largely to the hopelessness and indifference of the public in a beaten country, a new group—whose only common bond is really necessity—has managed to assert itself, and its members will probably cling to power for some time, until internal dissension gets the better of them or international politics takes a sudden turn and cast them on the junk heap the way it did Beneš.

[1] See glossary-index.

8

As for the new regime itself which prevails in Prague and the historic provinces: to me it bears an ominous resemblance to the Schuschnigg regime which I knew in Austria in 1935. There is the same disapproval of democracy, the same distrust and alienation of the labor element, the same Catholic piety, the same moderate and decorous anti-Semitism, the same futile hope of building up—without resorting to serious intimidation—an enthusiastic national movement in a section of Europe where the dominant political reactions are incredulity, jealousy, and distrust. However, the Schuschnigg regime was not a bad thing for Austria; and only the insoluble problem of its relations to Nazi Germany led to its fall. Here, relations to Germany are simpler for the very reason that the Czechs are Slavs and not Germans. I have seen no indications of any desire on the part of Hitler to make Germans out of the Czechs. Their role is that of a vassal—and the vassal's role has always been easier to execute than that of the independent younger brother.

Slovakia and Ruthenia are, of course, another story. Neither people has the prerequisites for an independent political existence. Their leaders have been completely won over by the Germans through flattery, cajolery, and display of force. They are making awful fools of themselves; dressing up in magnificent fascist uniforms, flying to and fro in airplanes, drilling comic-opera S.A. units and dreaming dreams of the future grandeur of the Slovak or Ukrainian nations. Everything that the Czechs have tried to teach them during these twenty years they have flung back into the Czechs' faces. They are momentarily happy in a false autonomy which is rapidly destroying every possibility of a real national self-determination for decades to come.

3. Excerpts from a personal letter
of January 6, 1939

There have been few outward changes here since I last wrote you, but very interesting things have been going on behind the scenes. It is evident from a number of indications that the Germans have not yet made up their minds what to do about Bohemia and Moravia. As one Czech put it to me yesterday, they are dangling Bohemia over the abyss. Local businessmen who have dealings with Germany find it impossible to pin the Germans down to any long-term arrangements. They have the definite impression that the people in Berlin with whom they deal are waiting for some sort of decision from above and are reluctant to make any commitments until this decision is issued. The local Nazi Germans have also been extremely circumspect. They will not define their attitude toward the present Czech government and are obviously doing their best to keep their hands free to support it or oppose it at a later date, as their instructions may read.

Here in Bohemia a silent but intense battle is taking place in every corner of the country and in every section of society between the old ideology and the new. If this is the death struggle of democracy in Bohemia, as many fear, it can at least be said that democracy is dying hard. The government, to be sure, desires to be strong and authoritative and wants to put an end to a political system which was built on a large number of petty, selfish party groups. It wants to be able to speak with sufficient authority to satisfy Hitler's insistence that he will not deal with semi-responsible parliamentary regimes. Above all, it wants to avoid anything which might be offensive to Berlin. I do not feel, however, that it wants to subordinate everything to the interests of the state, to detract from the dignity of the individual, to instigate pogroms against the Jews, or to force cultural life into a real strait jacket. After all, two of its members were former Rotary Club leaders and seven are members of Masonic lodges. Most of them, furthermore, are specialists in their respective fields and are forced by this very fact to reject any form of political fanaticism.

All this, of course, is a source of extreme irritation to many of the youthful elements in the new government party of National Unity. At a meeting of these young people which was held a few evenings ago, many of them appeared in the uniform of the Czech fascists and took a very prominent part in the proceedings. Their leader, General Gajda, was on the platform. To all recitals of the government's accomplishments in the building up of a new political system the fascist hecklers shouted that it was not nearly enough and that things must go much farther.

These young Czech fascists deserve, perhaps, as much as any others of their ilk, the lovely definition of National Socialism which has been current here: "Austrian efficiency and Prussian charm." They profess disappointment, just as the Austrian Nazis used to, at the lack of support they get from Berlin, and they will tell you with long faces that the Führer is misled by his immediate environment about the situation in Czechoslovakia. Should the Germans ever decide, however, that Bohemia is ripe for Nazism, the function of these Czech fascists might become a very important one. I suppose that Gajda regards his role in the National Unity Party as similar to that of von Papen in the Herrenclub in Berlin before the advent of National Socialism.

I have been much intrigued by the behavior of the local Nazi Germans. They are demanding for themselves what amounts to a complete system of extraterritoriality, with virtual jurisdiction over all persons of German nationality in Czechoslovakia as well as over all German social and cultural activities. Just as the precedents for so many other modern developments have to be sought in the Middle Ages or the period of the early Renaissance, so one has to go back to the early history of the system of capitulations in the Near East in order to find anything like a precedent for present German demands concerning German minorities in other countries (excepting Italy). The Germans have the same proprietary feeling toward Germans abroad that the people in Moscow have toward communists, and for the Czechs to intercede in Berlin in behalf of a Bohemian German would doubtless occasion the same pain and displeasure as did our intercession in Moscow in behalf of Madame Robinson-Rubens.[1] The local Germans have been told that they must "remain at their posts" in Czechoslovakia and not return to the Reich (an order which may have its own special significance). They must be completely subservient, even in questions of their personal life, to the local German Nazi leader. The Slovaks even struck a snag when they endeavored, under the impression that they were faithfully copying German Nazi examples, to set up a single and all-inclusive state-controlled labor union. They were reminded very sharply that the Germans in Slovakia would of course have to have their own Nazi labor union and could not be members of the Slovak organization. It is interesting in this connection that German university students from the Sudeten areas recently incorporated in the Reich were forbidden to attend Reich universities but must study in Prague. When they arrived here they were taken in charge, body and soul, by the local Nazi organization, which even assigns their living quarters and marks out the channels of their social life.

The Slovaks have continued in general to have a riotous time playing at fascism. Their open hostility to the Czechs has been somewhat tempered of late, partly by their desire to lure Czech tourists and Czech capital back to Slovakia and partly because their difficulties with Hungary have made

[1] The reference here is to a lady, evidently a person with intimate Communist connections, who, although the bearer of an American passport, disappeared in Moscow in the late 1930's.

them hesitate about slamming the door too demonstratively in the faces of their Bohemian brothers. I am still puzzled about the reasons which led them to undertake a sudden and energetic campaign for the revision of the borders laid down in the Vienna award. It is being said that the Germans have only recently realized how seriously the cession of Užhorod and Mukačevo and certain portions of Slovakia to Hungary complicated the construction of effective ways of communication in a lateral direction across Czechoslovakia. These communications are of high importance just at present in German eyes and the inference is that the Germans, with this in mind, are encouraging Slovak irredentism against Hungary and thus trying to keep the question open for the time being. In view of the extent of German influence in Bratislava it would hardly be expected that the Slovaks were acting entirely independently in a matter of such importance. On the other hand, the relations between the Slovaks and the Germans have not been all sweetness and light during the last two or three weeks. There was not only the question of the labor union mentioned above, but the Slovak government annoyed the local German Nazis seriously by slipping one over on them and taking an unannounced census of the population on December 31. The Germans, who were not prepared for it and did not have time to import Germans into Slovakia from all directions for the event, were furious, and I doubt that the poor Slovaks will even be permitted to publish the results of their labors. In general, there is something deeply shocking to the popular mind in this part of the world about the idea of an impartial and unprepared census, and there is a general feeling that the Slovaks have not observed the rules of the game.

Severe anti-Semitic measures are expected in Slovakia as soon as the new Slovak Diet meets, which should be within the next few weeks. One of the Slovak ministers recently announced that in the free professions there would be no *numerus clausus*: there would be a *numerus nullus*.

4. Report on conditions in Slovakia, written in January 1939

It is well known that when, at the end of the World War I, the Slovaks succeeded with the help of the Czechs in gaining their independence from Hungary, they were almost totally lacking in an intelligentsia. They had neither administrators or educators of their own tongue. They were—and have remained—largely a rural people. Their cities were mostly Magyar in character and even the Jews, who constituted a good part of the urban population, were in large part educated in Hungarian institutions and spoke Hungarian rather than Slovak in all their public dealings. The Slovak dialect was at the outset not even sufficiently developed to serve as a language of public administration. It thus fell to the Czechs, who had a far larger educated class, who were politically more mature, and whose spoken tongue is almost identical with Slovak, to provide a small army of administrators and educators and to assume extensive responsibility for the development of the Slovak population.

This task the Czechs cheerfully assumed, and it is characteristic of them that they carried it out with more zeal and efficiency than tact. For twenty years Czech officials worked industriously in Slovak communities, accomplishing a good deal for Slovakia in comparison with some of the former masters of that country, but constantly antagonizing the more easygoing and imaginative Slovaks with their aloofness, their suspiciousness, and their schoolmasterish attitude. Above all, they failed (and it is idle now to attempt to apportion responsibility for this failure) to do what they were originally expected to do: namely, to train and make way for a new and indigenous Slovak intelligentsia.

This situation—rightly or wrongly—provided the soil for

the bitter Slovak autonomous movement which grew up and identified itself with the Hlinka People's Party. As long as the old leaders of this party were active, the movement remained fairly reasonable and moderate in character. But with the death of Hlinka and the unwise incarceration of Tuka, control of the movement passed to younger elements whose loyalty to the Czech state was slight and whose knowledge of the outside world was even slighter.

These elements provided an easy field of penetration for the Poles and Germans in their efforts to break up the Czechoslovak state. There is little doubt that for years preceding the Munich Agreement some of the present leaders of the Slovak government worked closely with Berlin and Warsaw in order to bring to a fall the Beneš-Masaryk regime and the principle of Czechoslovak centralism which that regime incorporated.

There is nothing succeeds like success; and as long as the Prague government stuck to its guns and put up a bold front to its foreign enemies, the Slovak Autonomists remained a minority in Slovakia. The bulk of the Slovak population still felt that the best chances of advancing their national interests lay in cooperation with Prague and participation in the Czech parliamentary system. But the collapse of the Beneš regime after the Munich Agreement, followed by the territorial demands of Hungary, cut the ground out from under the feet of the moderate leaders. It became an easy matter for the Hlinka extremists, in the face of the general bewilderment and helplessness of the centralists, to seize the reins and to extort from a totally powerless Prague government the autonomy to which they had always aspired. By October 6 the Prague government was already forced to agree in principle to Slovak autonomy and to turn much of the local power over to the Slovak leaders. By the end of November, as a result of a ruthless exploitation by the Hlinka leaders of the catastrophic difficulties of the Czechs and repeated threats of complete secession, the Slovak Autonomy Bill had been passed and implanted into the Czechoslovak Constitution. A regional Slovak government was set up, with a prime minister and several ministers, and began to exercise complete control over practically all phases of public life except military affairs and the administration of the customs.

Entrusted with the exercise of power, the Slovak leaders have found themselves richer in enthusiasms than in definite purposes. Their ideology is not replete with ideas for the future development of Slovakia. They are devout Catholics and in their mixture of nationalism and religion they resemble the Sinn Feiners of Ireland. They are strongly anti-Semitic and anti-democratic. They have a predilection for swastika methods in internal politics. In foreign affairs, they are for the moment anti-Czech, anti-Hungarian, wary of the Poles and friendly with the Germans. They have vague hopes of developing their country economically, but little idea of how to go about it. In short, they are—even literally speaking—all dressed up, and have no definite place to go.

Their accomplishments since their assumption of power have not been many. They have demonstrated their popularity by conducting the election of a parliament—in true totalitarian fashion—from a single list of candidates. They have fitted out their more youthful followers in fine fascist uniforms and taught them a greeting which—symbolically enough—is a halfhearted compromise between a friendly wave and a full-fledged fascist salute. They have permitted an unsavory but apparently short-lived pogrom in a number of places and promised far-reaching anti-Semitic legislation for the near future. They have frightened the Czech and Jewish capital out of the country and the foreign visitors out of their mountain resorts. They have continued to flirt with the Germans over the heads of the Prague government and have entered upon a violent irredentist feud with the Hungarians. They have expelled thousands of Czech officials and pedagogues and created a serious shortage of trained personnel in a number of fields of activity.

The relations of the Slovaks with Germany stand, of course, in the center of all their problems and have held the greatest interest for the outside world. There is no doubt that Berlin's influence in Slovakia is great—greater, indeed, than that of Prague. Much of it is dictated by sheer geographical fact, and the Slovak Prime Minister's efforts to minimize it to me in conversation carried little conviction when one could look out of his office windows in Bratislava across the frozen Danube and see considerably more German territory than Czech. But there are other reasons as well. One is a sense of appreciation—it is dangerous to speak of gratitude —for the services rendered by the Germans to Slovak autonomy. Another is the fact that the German minority in Slovakia —some 150,000 strong—are scattered throughout the country and are not concentrated in any compact mass as are the Germans of the Sudeten regions. Thus there is no such strong linguistic prejudice as in Bohemia, and German is spoken freely in the streets and public places without arousing hostility. (They say that the Czech Minister of Agriculture, Dr. Feierabend, was somewhat nonplussed, on the occasion of a recent visit to Slovakia, to have a German waiter coolly refuse to serve him because he declined to speak German.) Finally, there is the prevalent anti-Semitism and anti-liberalism mentioned above, and the consequent admiration for many of the features of National Socialism.

The results of all this have been obvious. Bratislava— only 40 miles from Vienna—swarms with unofficial envoys and agents from the Reich, whose sense of power and prosperity is anything but concealed in their demeanor. The leader of the German minority, in reality a Nazi official, is an "undersecretary of state" in the Slovak government. The *Stürmer* and the *Völkische Beobachter* grace the newsstands in quantity, and the German Arbeitsamt in Bratislava —the center of German Nazi activity—has an air of bustling and mysterious importance.

The Slovak leaders are possibly sincere when they deny that they consider themselves under Nazi domination. They are a robust lot; their nerves are strong; and they do not look unnecessarily far into the future. They believe that they are playing a smart game and exploiting the favor of the Reich to their own advantage wherever it suits them. They have recently been bold enough to annoy the local German faction by firing Germans out of public jobs and by conducting an unannounced census which caught the German minority unawares. It is even said that there is a certain reaction in the Slovak government against the pro-German tendencies and that Durčansky, the Minister of Communications, who has been the chief protagonist of the pro-German alignment and the outstanding contact-man with Berlin, is soon going to be sent into diplomatic exile as Czechoslovak envoy to the Vatican.

All this, however, will be of no avail. The Slovaks, whether they realize it or not, are completely in German power and such autonomy as they enjoy exists only through the grace of Hitler. All the Germans need do in present circumstances is to withdraw their opposition to a common Hungarian-Polish frontier, and a good part of the Slovak state will be taken over by Hungary within a week. Nor are the Slovaks entirely safe from direct German revisionism. Their capital city of Bratislava, now almost surrounded by German territory, already has a German element numbering around 40 percent of the total population and this percentage is growing daily, due partly to new arrivals and partly to rapid "conversions" of nationality on the part of fainthearted Czechs. Thoughtful Slovaks are already contemplating the prospect of having to move the capital to some small town in the interior of the country.

With regard to the Czechs, the official Slovak attitude is that they wish for good relations founded not on sentimental phrases about blood brotherhood but on a friendly recognition of mutual equality. Actually, there is no getting around the fact that they have been rough on the Czechs during the last few months, exploiting their difficulties without mercy, enlisting German support against them wherever necessary, and creating an atmosphere in their own country which has made most of the expelled Czech officials quite content to leave. In constitutional matters their demands have gone so far and been pressed so ruthlessly that it is not facetious to say that in Czechoslovakia everyone now has autonomy except the Czechs. All this the Czechs have accepted with remarkable equanimity, dismissing the Slovak behavior outwardly as the pranks of a headstrong child who has been given a new toy. But the bonds of the republic have undoubtedly been loosened. While Czech military units are still stationed on the Slovak external frontiers and still engage in border skirmishes in those districts, their martial spirit derives mostly from the natural pleasure which any normal Czech would experience at being able to train a rifle on a Hungarian or a Pole, and I doubt whether the majority of the Czechs, even if their position at home were sounder, could work up much enthusiasm any more for a real defense of the frontiers of Slovakia as such.

Relations with the Poles started out in a friendly fashion, but have subsequently deteriorated seriously for a number of reasons. Contact with the Polish government had been maintained for years by Sidor, now a minister of the Slovak government and one of the most important figures in Slovakia. Before Munich, he was always welcomed in Warsaw, where he made repeated visits; but since then I understand that the Poles, having got substantially what they want from the Slovaks, have given him a cool reception. The Polish occupation of certain Slovak territory in the Beskid mountains was a blow to the Slovak leaders, who thought that it had been firmly understood between them and the Poles that the latter would take territory only from the Czechs. Polish advocacy of a common Hungarian-Polish frontier and the consequent encouragement given to the Hungarians to bite off still further chunks of Slovak territory completed Slovak disillusionment.

The Poles are now said to be suggesting a deal between Hungary and Slovakia whereby some of the most important Slovak towns, particularly Košice and Užhorod would be restored to Slovakia, in return for which the Hungarians would take the remainder of Ruthenia. At the moment, the Slovaks are turning a deaf ear to these enticing suggestions from Warsaw. Not that they would particularly mind selling out their Ruthenian cousins; but the step would be sure to arouse the most serious displeasure in Berlin, and that—for the time being—is decisive.

The severe losses of territory to Hungary through the Vienna Award constituted a bitter shock to the Slovaks, who had reckoned with the breakup of Bohemia but had not envisaged the loss of some of their own most valued lands and cities. They could do little else, however, than to accept Berlin's assurances that the Vienna arrangement constituted the best bargain that could be made for the moment. If they were to lose Berlin's support, after all, it was obvious that the Hungarians, who were being spurred on by the Poles to take most of eastern Slovakia, would go still further. For six weeks following the Vienna meeting, the Hungarians were the restless party, and the Slovaks took the defensive, relying entirely on their German protectors. The Germans repeatedly warned the Hungarians and the Poles that when fascist states came to an agreement among themselves that agreement was meant to stay and that it would be dangerous to press for any alteration of the Vienna Award. Toward the end of December, however, the Slovaks surprised foreign observers by themselves unleashing an energetic campaign for an alteration of the Vienna decision and for the recovery of certain of their cities from Hungary. The official Slovak explanation for this is that the Hungarian treatment of their new Slovak minority has been so cruel that the Slovaks in the homeland can no longer tolerate the prospect of many of their blood-brothers remaining indefinitely under Hungarian rule. Actually, of course, there is more to this than meets the eye, for the Slovak action could hardly have been undertaken entirely independently of German opinion.

The details of German-Slovak relations are a state secret for all concerned, but from certain hints let fall by various Slovaks in their conversation, I suspect that the situation is substantially as follows. Germany is interested in Slovakia chiefly as a line of communication toward the east. While the Germans were doubtless aware at the time of the Vienna meeting of the high strategic importance of Košice and certain other ceded cities from precisely this point of view, the general diplomatic situation at that particular moment was such that they were unable to insist, in the face of Italian opposition, on the retention of these cities by Slovakia. Within a few months' time, the situation—if German hopes mature—will have changed. Italy will be more in need of German support than vice versa and the German minority in Hungary will have been developed a full-fledged nuisance value which can be used to extort other concessions from the Hungarian government. Thus there is a possibility, in the German view, that these cities may be recovered for Slovakia at some future date. For this reason it seems to have been suggested to the Slovaks from Berlin that while any immediate revision of the Vienna Award was out of the question, no harm would be done for the time being if they were to keep alive the grievances of the Slovak population in the recently ceded areas. The gusto with which the Slovaks have proceeded to give effect to this suggestion has aroused displeasure in

Berlin and the Germans are now beginning to wonder—particularly in view of the recent border incidents—whether they have not started a ball rolling which will not be so easy to stop.

In internal affairs it is the anti-Semitic program which has aroused the most comment abroad and which seems indeed to be the only definite and positive factor in the Slovak government's internal program. According to the latest government calculations, the number of Jews in Slovakia is only 39,158. These calculations, however, were based on the 1930 census, which was notoriously incomplete insofar as it listed as Jews only those who declared themselves as such. Those affected by the government's anti-Semitic policies will doubtless be all persons of Jewish blood, within substantially the limits of the German Nuremberg definitions, and their number—now swelled by the émigrés from other countries—should be estimated at a figure closer to 100,000 than to 39,158.

The Slovak resentment of these Jews is deep-seated. To a large extent it is founded on the same reactions which are prevalent in the remainder of the Jewish zone of eastern Europe. The Slovak Jews are mostly of the poorer orthodox type. They are small merchants, saloon keepers, druggists, lawyers, etc. They undoubtedly play a dominant part in a number of these lines of activity, partly no doubt through their superior intelligence but partly—the Slovaks feel—through their trickiness and unscrupulousness, through the successful evasion of any and all inconvenient restrictions, and through an incurable clannishness and nepotism. To these grievances, which are common to many of the non-Jewish peoples in eastern Europe, there is added a very serious one of a local character, which perhaps also has its parallel in other countries. The Slovaks feel that the local Jews have always allied themselves with Slovakia's enemies.

When the country was under Hungary the Jews, according to the Slovaks, made common cause with the Hungarians in exploiting the Slovaks; when the country fell to Czechoslovakia the Jews joined with the more liberal Czechs in opposing Slovak autonomy. However accurate this view may be, it seems to be a fact that most of the anti-Jewish disorders which have thus far occurred in the new Slovakia were caused by just this feeling. Some 15,000 of the Bratislava Jews, for example, convinced that Bratislava was doomed to fall to the Hungarians, endeavored to enlist in advance the benevolent disposition of the Hungarian authorities by presenting to the local Hungarian Consulate a formal petition pleading for the incorporation of the city into Hungary. This step immediately became known to the Slovaks, who regarded it as a particularly invidious confirmation of what they had always said about the disloyalty of the Jews to Slovakia. The result was the expulsion—under very cruel circumstances—of a large number of Jews who were found not to be entitled to Czechoslovak citizenship, and a certain amount of disorder on the part of the rowdy young Slovak element in the town. Similar events, on a smaller scale, are said to have taken place, during the period when the territorial question was acute, in other communities where word got about that the Jews were supporting the territorial pretensions of the Hungarians.

Outside of these occurrences, which seem to have pretty well ceased since the occupation of the ceded territories by the Hungarians was completed, little is known to have happened in Slovakia thus far which would justify the extremely alarming reports circulating in Jewish circles in Prague and elsewhere about conditions there. The government, however, has made it evident that it proposes in the very near future to put into effect anti-Semitic legislation approximating in drasticness that which is in effect in Germany. Despite press reports to the effect that these measures would have to be closely coordinated with those taken in Prague in order to prevent a mass migration of Slovak Jews to Bohemia, the Slovak Prime Minister told me that they doubtless would be more severe than the measures which would be adopted in the Historic Provinces, where the Jewish problem had a different and less serious character. He also assured me that there would be in Slovakia no such excesses—particularly of the type involving physical cruelty—as those which had recently occurred in Germany. While it is quite possibly the honest intention of the Slovak government to prevent brutality, it is hardly to be anticipated that they will in all cases be able to restrain the more hotblooded of their young supporters, whose sense of political responsibility is singularly limited and who have been deeply impressed by the worst German examples.

In economic life, the Slovak leaders are facing difficult problems. The capital invested in Slovakia was almost exclusively Czech or Jewish. Considerable amounts of it are said to have been already withdrawn, and certainly very little fresh money is flowing into economic enterprises in Slovakia. German interests are said to have recently acquired one chemical plant in Bratislava, and it is rumored that the Dresdener Bank is quietly buying up control of all the German banking concerns in the territory. But apparently neither Germans nor Slovaks want Slovakia to be incorporated entirely into the German economic orbit just at this time. The Slovaks hope that by attracting foreign capital and developing trade with the non-totalitarian states they will be able to create for themselves a profitable position as broker between Germany and certain other countries with which Germany, as a result of difficulties with credit and exchange, is unable to trade to the extent that she would like. They are particularly anxious (and in this they doubtless have the full support of the Germans) to attract capital from the Slovaks in America, and are sending a special envoy

. . . to the United States to attempt to correct the impression said to be current in American-Slovak circles to the effect that the present Slovakia is a "Nazi show."

These hopes, of course, are less indicative of the economic future of Slovakia than they are of the ignorance and naïveté of their holders. As long as present conditions obtain, little foreign capital other than German is going to flow into the Carpathian districts. Meanwhile, economic life is stagnating. The Carpathian mountain resorts, in particular, which were once a fruitful source of income, are now in a state of desertion which brings to mind the plight of the Sudeten-German resorts before Munich and the sorrowful witticism: "Ein Reich, ein Volk; ein Gast!" It is this situation which makes many of the Czechs confident that, unless the Germans are willing to commit themselves much more heavily in Slovakia than they have done thus far, Prague needs only to wait until the prodigal son returns repentant and offers to recognize paternal authority in return for paternal support. It is said that the Federal Finance Minister, Dr. Kalfus, who has recently been in Bratislava for the purpose of discussing financial matters with the Slovak leaders, has already had considerable success in bringing the Slovaks into line with the economic and financial policies of the Prague government. Thus it is quite possible that the Slovaks may be successfully retained within the Czech economic orbit; but this, of course, is itself an uncertain conception. If Bohemia should be swallowed up economically by the Reich, the ultimate effect on Slovakia would be no different than if that province were to seek its economic Anschluss over the head of the Prague government.

In cultural matters, as in economic, the endeavors of the new Slovak government have produced more negative than positive results. The only guiding principle has been linguistic chauvinism in its most petty and shortsighted form. The elimination of Czech pedagogues has left certain sections of the higher learning establishments almost depleted of competent personnel. It is characteristic that the government has contrived to find as chief of its propaganda office one of the few literate persons in the vicinity whose linguistic accomplishments are limited entirely to his native Slovak, and he is installed in office in a capital city where the majority of the population speak other tongues. It is equally characteristic that one of the principal accomplishments of the new regime in the cultural field has been the issuance of an order whereby performances at the Slovak National Theatre, which have heretofore been conducted alternately in Czech and Slovak, shall now be conducted exclusively in Slovak. This much-bruited change, the significance of which is confined principally to the fact that the "r"s will no longer be syllabicated nor the common word "*cho*" pronounced as "*tao*," is expected to lead to a considerable increase in attendance on the part of the local Slovaks, who profess to have found their sensibilities offended by sitting through performances of Czech, every word of which they understood without difficulty. In general, therefore, Slovak cultural policy shows a concentration on form rather than content—a concentration which promises to isolate Slovakia still further from her immediate neighbors and to aggravate the existing linguistic rivalries which already constitute the curse of central Europe.

In essence, what is now happening in Slovakia is little more than a repetition of the old story of central Europe: local aims and jealousies being exploited with ease by outside forces, for purposes which have little to do with the interests of the persons concerned. In accepting German aid against the Czechs, the Slovaks—like Shakespeare's Englishmen—have sold the pasture to buy the horse, and the pleasure which they gain from the transaction will, I fear, be short-lived. It is evidently Slovakia's immediate destiny to be a relatively helpless satellite of the German Reich, under whatever sovereignty may suit German convenience. Its capital city will probably fall sooner or later entirely to Germany and the remainder of the country become a base, of sorts, for the pursuance of German military aims in eastern Europe. Its native leaders are so sadly lacking in experience, in imagination, in breadth of view, and in depth of purpose that they cannot hope to maneuver successfully for very long amid the powerful national and ideological currents which are playing all around them in central Europe.

Slovakia's brief achievement of autonomy was only an incidental and temporary outcropping of the slow shift of power in the central European area from Vienna and Budapest northwards to Berlin. Its loss of autonomy, when it comes, will have to be regarded as an inevitable reversion to the natural state of affairs.

5. Excerpts from a despatch of January 12, 1939, from Mr. Raymond E. Cox, Chargé d'Affaires at Prague, to the Department of State, concerning German-Czechoslovak relations

The real circumstances concerning Czech-German relations are surrounded by much secrecy and neither Germans nor Czechs seem willing to discuss them in any considerable detail, even in confidence. The principal question involved is that of the intentions of the Germans, since the latter have it in their power to carry out practically any program they may eventually adopt for the future of the remaining Bohemian territory. The real key to future relations between Prague and Berlin consequently lies chiefly in Berlin.

Viewed from this point of view, there are two main conclusions which can be arrived at today. The first of these is that Germany is not entirely satisfied with the way things are going in Czechoslovakia, and that there are certain points on which it has not yet proved possible to find a community of views between the two governments. This is evidenced by the fact that the Czechoslovak Foreign Minister, Dr. Chvalkovsky, has not yet found it possible to make the trip to Berlin which he has hoped and planned to make at various times throughout the last month.[1] The reason for this is probably that he is unable to take with him to Berlin the assurances which the Germans desire and without which, from the German viewpoint, there can be no question of find-

[1] It is reported in this morning's press that this visit is now finally to take place on January 21.

ing a permanent and satisfactory foundation for Czech-German relations.

It is suspected in well-informed circles here that one of the most important bones of contention is the character and the role of the Czech army. It is rumored that the Germans are endeavoring to establish a widespread control over Czech military policy and that with this in mind they are pressing for the despatch of a permanent German military mission to Prague.

It is only natural that such a program would meet with strong opposition on the part of the higher army officers in Czechoslovakia. These men are for the most part members of the Czech Legion (an organization which has been consistently loyal to Masaryk and Beneš), moderate in their political views and no friends of Hitler Germany. They do not wish to carry out the role of a foreign legion for Germany. They enjoy enormous prestige among all the patriotic elements in Bohemia and continue to command the overwhelming bulk of the armed power of the country. The humiliation of the Munich capitulation still rankles in their minds, and the fact that they have had to give up their defenses without resistance is all the more reason why they are not inclined to yield their internal position without a fight.

It is not surprising that the Germans, as is frequently reported, should be doing everything in their power to eliminate the influence of these older Czech military leaders. It is said that the Germans are demanding the establishment of a purging commission which would eliminate most of the higher command. They are also reported to be working hard on many of the younger officers and endeavoring to convince the latter that they have nothing to lose by throwing in their fortunes with the Germans and that they might even have the satisfaction of going against the Poles and the Hungarians with German backing and recovering some of the territory ceded in such humiliating circumstances.

That the Germans have had a certain success in these

efforts is probable but the Military Attaché of this mission doubts that they have yet succeeded in winning over a really serious number of officers. The older generals appear to be holding their ground stoutly and to be showing no sign of yielding to German pressure. There is reason to suspect that the recent action of the President of the Republic in appointing a "Legionnaire" and French-trained officer—one of the very group which the Germans resent—as one of the three ministers of the new Ruthenian regional government, has been regarded on the German side as an attempt on the part of these conservative Czechoslovak army circles to assert their independence and authority.

The position of the Czech army is not the only cause of German discontent. Neither the foreign nor the internal policies of the present Czech government are entirely satisfactory to the Reich. The Germans would like to see Czechoslovakia break entirely with her former foreign policy and her former friends and to seal this break by adhering to the Anti-Comintern Pact. They would like to see the two-party political system abolished and a completely totalitarian regime established along Nazi lines. They would like to see strong measures taken to eliminate the last vestiges of the influence and prosperity of the liberal and Jewish elements in Bohemia. They would like to see the treatment of the German minority in Bohemia improved. They feel that the time has come for the Czech government to stamp out the antipathy toward the German language and German culture which the Czech inhabitants of Bohemia take so little pains to conceal. Finally, they would doubtless like to see eliminated much of the influence of Czech industrial circles who fear inclusion in the German economic orbit and who see their only future in a retention of the economic ties that bound the former Czechoslovakia with the non-totalitarian countries.

If it is clear in Prague, however, that the Germans are dissatisfied with the present state of affairs in Czechoslovakia,

it is equally clear—and this is the second of the two conclusions mentioned above—that they have not yet made up
their minds what to do about it. An air of impermanency
hangs over everything connected with Czech-German relations at the present time.

Little or no attempt is being made, apparently, to develop
the Fifth Zone boundaries into a permanent frontier. As
far as the Legation is aware, no permanent customs houses,
railway junction facilities, passport control offices, etc., are
being erected. On the contrary, the Germans seem to be
doing everything in their power to play down the importance
of the existing frontier. It was recently announced that the
usual international documents are no longer required for
motorists with Czech or German licenses who wish to cross
the frontier.

There is nothing in the attitude of the Reich toward the
remaining German minorities in Czechoslovakia which would
indicate that Berlin regards the role of these minorities as in
any sense completed. Every effort is being made to prevent
the Germans of Czechoslovakia from returning to the Reich,
and indeed the German authorities seem to be doing their
best to increase the number of persons in the historic provinces or in Slovakia who are willing to declare themselves to
be Germans. A member of the Legation staff who was recently in Olomouc was informed that German representatives
there are paying 200 crowns a head to Czech unemployed
for going to the German Arbeitsamt and registering themselves as Germans. Similar efforts to swell the ranks of the
German minority are apparently being made in other communities as well, particularly in Bratislava and other cities
which lie near the German frontier and already have large
German elements. University students from the areas recently ceded to the Reich are forbidden to study in Reich-German
universities and are compelled to continue to come to
Prague. Some two or three thousand of them are to be en-
rolled in the coming semester in the German institutions of

higher learning in this city. They enjoy no independence whatsoever in either their academic or their personal lives. All their activities are "organized" by the local Nazi leaders, who even assign them their living quarters and control their personal associations.

In economic matters, similar uncertainty seems to be prevalent. Czech businessmen who have dealings in Berlin report that it is impossible to pin down their German friends to any long-term arrangements. Nor have the German officials shown themselves willing to commit themselves to any clear policy in commercial relations between the two countries. They obviously cannot see their way clear to a complete customs and currency union at the present time. I am informed on good authority that many of the acts of the present Czechoslovak government are dictated by the aim of demonstrating to the Germans how unfavorable such an arrangement would be to the interests of the Germans themselves. As the Department is aware, pressure is being exerted on the Czechoslovak government in the direction of moderation by the British, who are withholding the greater portion of their promised loan until the situation here has been clarified. On the other hand, there seems to be a strong feeling in German circles that some form of special status will have to be worked out for Czechoslovakia in this country's economic relations to Germany. The nearest thing to a definition of official German views on this subject was perhaps the statement of the Chief of the Economic Division of the German Arbeitsamt in Prague, Dr. Kieslinger, who said in the course of a recent lecture here: "If common sense is applied in economic matters it should be possible for Germany and Czechoslovakia to find a solution somewhere between the minimum of most-favored-nation treatment and the maximum of a customs union." The hindrances to such a solution, he added, were only emotional and selfish and could be overcome. But no German official will take the responsibility of defining the possible solution in any great detail, and here, as in other matters, everything seems to be waiting for some major decision from Berlin.

All in all, it is not probable that the present situation can be maintained for any great length of time. Either the present government will have to alter its policies in ways desired by the Germans or it will have to make way for another and more totalitarian group of people. Should either of these alternatives meet, as is possible, with any determined resistance on the part of the higher army circles and the other moderate elements, the independence of the country may very well again be seriously jeopardized.

6. Excerpts from a despatch of February 1, 1939, from the Honorable Wilbur J. Carr, American Minister at Prague, to the Department of State, concerning German-Czechoslovak relations

The tenor of the talk which took place between the Czechoslovak Foreign Minister, Dr. Chvalkovsky, and Reichskanzler Hitler on January 21 was reported in my telegram under reference, and such information as has subsequently become available has merely confirmed that version of the conversation. Hitler demanded prompt and radical anti-Semitic legislation, a fargoing reduction in the size of the Czech army, a "neutral" foreign policy if not an actual adherence to the Anti-Comintern Pact, and a certain degree of adaptation of the Czechoslovak economic system to that of the Reich: an arrangement which would give Germany the predominant control over Czechoslovak foreign trade and national finances without going to the extreme of a customs and currency union. Until these demands have been fulfilled, Hitler is not prepared to agree to a guarantee of the Czechoslovak frontier. In other words, he is still dangling Czechoslovakia over the abyss of military occupation and using this threat as a means of influencing the policies of the Czechoslovak government.

As was to be expected, Dr. Chvalkovsky's report to the Czechoslovak Cabinet concerning this conversation stimulated the government to action along a number of lines. There were several matters in which the government had evidently planned to take measures agreeable to the Germans, but had been prevented from doing so by strong opposition on the part of the liberal and democratic forces in Czechoslovakia. The new impetus given by Mr. Hitler's remarks to Dr. Chvalkovsky was evidently sufficient to enable the government to overcome much of this internal resistance.

Among the events which followed Dr. Chvalkovsky's return from Berlin were the following:

(1) All the communist labor unions were dissolved and the government issued a decree which will make possible the liquidation of the influential communist cooperative societies.

(2) The newspaper *Narodni Osvobozeni*, the organ of the Czechoslovak legionnaires, which was edited by Dr. Lev Sychrava, was suspended. Dr. Sychrava was a close personal friend of Beneš. The police are also reported to have suspended the *Hlas Mladych*, which is allegedly the periodical of the socialist and communist and young socialist elements tending towards communism.

(3) The Prime Minister, Mr. Beran, and the chairman of the United National Party, Deputy Černy, made public speeches pointing out that the dangers confronting the Czechoslovak state were by no means overcome and warning the left elements that any further sabotage of the government's program for the realization of a totalitarian state might lead to catastrophe.

(4) The Czechoslovak government accorded *de jure* recognition to the Franco government in Spain.

(5) An agreement is reported to have been concluded between Czechoslovakia and Germany for a mutual non-stop train service over Czechoslovak and German territory respectively. It is understood that this agreement will permit Germany to carry out troop movements by rail without hin-

drance over the Czech "bottleneck" through Brno and Přerov and that the Czechs may follow a similar course through Zwittau, Hohenstadt, and Lundenberg.

(6) The Czech Minister of Interior is reported to be prepared to permit the establishment in Czechoslovakia of a German National Socialist party. It is presumed that this would mean that the flying of swastika flags and the wearing of the swastika in public would also be permitted.

(7) The government has decided to take certain administrative action with respect to the Jewish question. It is understood that all civil servants, both of whose parents are Jews, are to be pensioned off without delay. Furthermore, all naturalizations of Jews which have taken place since 1918 are to be subject to revision, the purpose presumably being to deprive at least a certain portion of these Jewish émigrés of their Czechoslovak citizenship and thus to force them eventually to leave the country. It is understood that Jews who were resident in the country in 1910 will not be subject to any discriminatory treatment, at least not at the hands of the central government. Some special regime will presumably be worked out, within the limits of the general legislative measures dealing with the Jewish question which are now in the course of preparation, for those who came to Czechoslovakia between 1910 and 1918.[1]

In addition to these measures of the central government, the Slovak government is at work preparing certain anti-Semitic legislation of its own, which will probably go farther than that envisaged for Bohemia.

There is no question but that the German demand for anti-Semitic measures in Bohemia has met with stubborn resistance in a good part of the Czechoslovak population.

---

[1] The government has also recently issued a decree strengthening the police registration and control of the population in the large towns and making it possible to deport persons from the urban areas who have come into the country since January 1, 1938. This measure may also be applied in such a way as to affect particularly some of the Jewish elements.

This would explain Dr. Chvalkovsky's flat statement, reported in my telegram under reference, to the effect that Czechoslovakia could never adopt the same policy toward Jews as has been adopted in the Reich. The Jew has never had as much influence or attracted as much resentment in the Bohemian villages as he has in Slovakia and the territories farther east. The Czech explanation of this is that in Slovakia and Sub-Carpatho-Russia the Jews have been usually Hungarian in sympathy and have spoken Hungarian and therefore not been loyal to the interests of the Slovaks. Furthermore, in commercial transactions they have gained the advantage over the less efficient Slovaks. On the other hand the Czechs claim that they have had no difficulty with the Jews because they have been able to hold their own with them in a commercial, professional, and social way. The Czech intelligentsia, and the wealthy land-owning society, furthermore, are very extensively bound up with Jewish society through intermarriage. It is being constantly reported with respect to nearly everyone of the present leaders that he has Jewish blood or is related to Jews by marriage, and many of these reports are doubtless true. The President of the Republic, Mr. Hacha, whose daughter was married to a Jew, is said to be exercising a strong influence in the direction of moderation in the government's attitude toward the Jewish question.

Such action as is taken in Bohemia by the present government will probably be confined, therefore, to the Jews who have come to Czechoslovakia during recent years. In addition to this, however, it is anticipated that the Aryan lawyers, doctors, professors, etc., will take advantage of the situation to eliminate the competition of most of their Jewish colleagues by forcing them out of the profession. This can be done by the action of professional boards such as the Bar Association, etc., and the government, in present circumstances, will scarcely dare oppose it. This process has already begun to operate on a serious scale.

(8) Mr. Kundt, the leader of the German minority in Czechoslovakia and the virtual satrap of Herr Hitler in Bohemia and Moravia, was received by the Foreign Minister and discussed with him at length the question of the position of the German minority in this area. A special commission has been set up to work out a sort of charter of liberties for the German minority. Thus it is expected that within a very short time legal form will be given to the system of extra-territoriality which the German Nazis and their adherents already enjoy in this country.

(9) The Economic Committee of the Cabinet has been working hard on plans for the coming commercial negotiations with Germany. It is believed that this work has consisted principally in the preparing of lists of German goods which Czechoslovakia could conceivably accept in return for exports to Germany. The Czechoslovak Minister of Commerce, Mr. Šadek, has just visited Berlin and it is announced that his visit will be followed at a later date by that of the Minister of Finance, Dr. Kalfus. These visits will undoubtedly be the occasion for a serious attempt to effect the special commercial regime which the Germans have in mind for Czechoslovakia but which they have heretofore been unwilling to define in detail.

With respect to German demands for reductions in the size of the army, there is no record of any action having been taken in this direction thus far. It is estimated that there are at least 10,000 army officers now on active duty in Czechoslovakia. Most of these officers are men for whom the army has been a career and a profession. They are not adapted to civil life by training and to force them into it without proper preparation would be beneficial neither to the men themselves nor to the economic life of the country.

The demand for a smaller Czechoslovak army would seem to indicate that the Germans were no longer laying emphasis on the hope of using the Czech army against the Poles. The

Deputy Prime Minister, Mr. Sidor, recently mentioned this scheme in a newspaper interview as something which could now (presumably since Hitler's talks with Beck and Chvalkovsky) be ruled out. This may well be a result of the conversations which have taken place between Colonel Beck and German leaders during the last month. It may also have been the result of moral resistance encountered within the ranks of the Czech army. It is not to be supposed that the Germans have forgotten the unhappy outcome of Vienna's efforts to use the Czech troops for its own purposes during the world war.

There is no indication that Germany has exerted any direct pressure on Czechoslovakia to join the Anti-Comintern Pact. The official Slovak press, however, which could scarcely be expected to take the initiative in such a matter without prior consultation with German officials, has now raised the demand for such adherence, and the influence of the Slovak leaders will presumably be exerted in this direction. One cannot avoid the impression, therefore, that the Germans feel it below their dignity to solicit Czech adherence to the pact, but are trying to bring pressure to bear through the back door with a view to inducing the Czechs to take the initiative themselves.

The burning question of Czech-German relations is, of course, whether these concessions on the Czech side will be sufficient to alleviate the dissatisfaction with the tempo of reconstruction of Czechoslovak life which Mr. Hitler has undoubtedly experienced in recent weeks, or whether Germany will feel herself compelled to seek a more radical form of satisfaction.

There seem to be very few people here who are convinced that the present situation is permanent and who do not fear that the outcome, sooner or later, will be a German occupation. These fears arise naturally from the state of suspense in which the country is being kept, the failure of the Germans to guarantee the frontiers, and the continual statements attributed to German officials in the Sudeten territory to the effect that: "Es wird sich bald alles ändern" (Everything will soon be changed).

And, indeed, the present system seems to be on anything but a firm basis. The natural inhibitions which stand in the way of an indigenous totalitarian regime in Czechoslovakia are truly formidable. If Hitler presses the Czechs too hard the result may well be the failure and breakup of the present government. President Hacha himself is reputed to be only too ready to resign from his position if German demands become much stiffer. It is difficult to imagine who could replace the present government, should it fall, except the Germans themselves. A regime of any of the Left parties would be totally intolerable to the Germans and is out of the question. Any other group of moderate conservatives such as that now in power would find itself in much the same position as the present government and there would be little point in its undertaking to assume responsibility. The Czech fascists are numerically weak and sadly lacking in administrative experience. All in all, it is quite possible that a resignation of the present government would lead to such confusion in Czech political life that a complete German occupation of Bohemia and Moravia would appear as the natural answer.

On the other hand, it should not be forgotten that there are very good reasons for Hitler's obvious reluctance to take this step. While the Department doubtless has more authoritative information on this point from other sources, the reports which trickle in here from the Sudeten regions and from Austria do not indicate that the process of digestion of these areas is in any sense complete. The remaining portion of Bohemia, with its stubborn alien population and its independently organized economic life, would be an even harder nut to crack.

Furthermore, if Bohemia is to be occupied, what is to become of Slovakia and Ruthenia? They are both, in their present situation, deficit areas and none but the most extreme alarmists could suppose that Germany, in the face of its present economic difficulties and after including Bohemia among its undigested acquisitions, could be interested in adding these further liabilities at once to the balance sheet of the Reich. On the other hand, these provinces could scarcely stand alone in present circumstances and would almost surely be swallowed up by Hungary and Poland if they were not to be part of some other large political entity.

Until recently, Germany has stoutly opposed all efforts of Hungary and Poland to form a common frontier. The Beck-Ribbentrop conversations, to be sure, appear to have brought about a certain change in this respect. It is commonly agreed that all thought of a German initiative in the Ukrainian question has been abandoned for the immediate future (in any case for the coming spring), and there are signs that German interest in Ruthenia, in particular, is on the wane. But the Germans, regardless of their immediate plans for expansion in eastern Europe, would doubtless think twice before taking a step, namely the occupation of Bohemia, which would put them in a position of having to take direct responsibility for Slovakia or to turn the bulk of it over to Hungary.

In summary, it may be said that the situation in Bohemia is still precarious. The Germans would evidently like to see the territory remain nominally independent for the immediate future, but only on conditions which make it extremely difficult for any Czech government to operate. There is a limit to what any Czech regime can do for Germany, and sooner or later the Germans will have to choose between continuing to tolerate in their midst an independent Czech state which can never identify itself entirely with the National Socialist ideology, or proceeding to an occupation of Bohemia and endeavoring to cope with all the new problems which this step would bring in its train.

*7. Excerpts from a despatch
of February 17, 1939,
from George F. Kennan
(as Secretary of Legation at Prague)
to the Department of State,
on the Jewish problem
in the new Czechoslovakia*

The number of Jews in Czechoslovakia, as far as revealed in the official statistics, is shown by the following table:

	IN FORMER CZECHOSLOVAKIA		IN PRESENT CZECHOSLOVAKIA	
	By declared nationality	*By confession*	*By declared nationality*	*By confession*
Bohemia	12,735	76,301	8,844	55,000
Moravia and Silesia	17,267	41,250	12,480	32,000
Total for the Historic Provinces	30,002	117,551	21,324	87,000
Slovakia	65,385	136,737	39,158	91,000
Ruthenia	91,255	102,542	65,828	73,500
Total	186,642	356,830	126,310	251,500

These figures are of course incomplete. In the case of the nationality statistics this is amply demonstrated by mere comparison of the number of those who declared themselves to be Jewish nationals with the number of those who declared themselves to be of Israelite confession. The nationality figures might better be taken to indicate those who spoke Yiddish in the home. The statistics by confession come nearer to giving an accurate picture, but they too are quite incomplete. Interest now centers around the Jewish problem in Czechoslovakia from a racial rather than a religious point of view, and to get an idea of the number of people who are apt to be affected by anti-Semitic policies it is necessary to take into consideration not only the members of the Israelite faith but also a considerable number of persons—in whole or in part non-Aryan—who belong to other churches or to none at all. Finally, the figures in the above table are not the result of any direct count but have been arrived at only by calculations based on the 1930 census. Thus they fail to take into consideration the influx of refugees from Austria and Germany which has been taking place during the last six years, as well as movements of population resulting from other causes. More recent figures are available, as will be seen below, in the case of Slovakia, but these are also not particularly illuminating, since they cling to the same principle of voluntary declaration, and Jews are now less than ever before inclined to go on record as being of Jewish rather than Slovak nationality.

In general, the number of full-blooded or nearly full-blooded Jews in Czechoslovakia may be estimated to be somewhat in excess of 300,000 at the present time. This means that the Jews constitute roughly three percent of the population, for the country as a whole.

The various aspects of the Jewish question vary considerably in the three principal sections of the Republic, and these variations are reflected in the attitude of the authorities. Since each of the three regimes—Prague, Bratislava, and Chust—has its own field of competence in which it can take action affecting the position of the Jews, it is necessary to review separately the situation prevailing in each of these capitals.

The Jewish question in Bohemia is just about as old as the Bohemian state. The cities of the Historic Provinces have had their Jewish merchant colonies since the early Middle Ages. The first wave of anti-Semitism, curiously enough, appears to have been introduced by the Germans who came through Prague at the time of the Crusades on their way to the Holy Land. When they had gone, anti-Semitic feeling continued to remain high among the local population, and many Jews began to make plans for departure. It has a distinctly familiar ring when we read in a recent history of the city of Prague that the Bohemian king, upon learning that the Jews were planning to emigrate, had the Jewish quarters attacked and plundered in the most cruel fashion. "They shall leave this country as poor as they came into it!" he is said to have exclaimed on this occasion.

Actually, of course, they did not leave, but remained and continued to do business, their protracted periods of prosperity being punctuated—particularly in times of social unrest—by anti-Semitic outbreaks on the part of the Gentile population. After the inclusion of Bohemia in the Austrian Empire many of the Jews, who were German-speaking, found favor, in contrast to the nationalistic Czechs, with the Germanic ruling element and enjoyed in general the protection of the Austrian authorities.

It has been characteristic of the situation in Bohemia that the Jewish colonies have always been concentrated in the larger cities. The industry and shrewdness of the Czechs as petty traders and artisans have been such that the Czech village has never presented such attractive possibilities for the Jew as have the villages of Slovakia or Ruthenia. The Bohemian Jews have for the most part been wealthy merchants, intellectuals, professional men, and administrators. More recently, there has been considerable intermarriage of Jews with the upper-class Bohemian society and many Jewish families have become quite assimilated. These Jews now enjoy considerable silent support in influential Czech circles. Indeed, it is characteristic of Bohemia, where nationality is a matter of language rather than of blood, that

44

speech rather than origin is the distinguishing characteristic of friend or foe. Such resentment of the Jews as exists in Bohemia thus centers largely on the German-speaking Jews—particularly those who have come to Bohemia since the war.

Among the Czechs themselves, there is comparatively little anti-Semitism. Only the small Czech fascist groups and certain sections of the nationalist-conservative element are anti-Semitic. This applies particularly to the younger element in the New National Unity Party, which is being organized as a government party. All these elements together, however, make up only a small minority of the Czech population. The mass of the people appear simply to have very little interest in anti-Semitism.

The present talk of anti-Semitic measures and the general anxiety of the Jewish population is due principally to the pressure which is being brought to bear on the Czech government by Berlin in the direction of an anti-Jewish policy. There is no doubt of the existence of this pressure. It is sufficient to note that this was one of the principal points mentioned by Hitler in his conversations with the Czech Foreign Minister, Dr. Chvalkovsky. The official German attitude toward the Jews in Czechoslovakia has been defined as follows by the German leader in Prague, Herr Kundt, in an article written for the Berlin *12-Uhr-Blatt* (quoted in the Prague *Narodni Politika* on January 4, 1929):

"Our devotion to National Socialism explains our attitude toward the Jewish problem. It is only natural that we, as German National Socialists, fully recognize and advocate the racial policy of the Third Reich. In Czechoslovakia, the Jewish problem has vital significance because the Jews in the large cities exercise influence not only on the theaters and the press, but also among the physicians and lawyers. Moreover, they have succeeded in gaining influence in the parties and public offices and it would appear that so far their influence in that respect has not yet been eliminated.

An unusual characteristic of Czechoslovakia is that the Jews have interfered after a fashion in the political issues between Germany and Czechoslovakia and steered Czech policy to a point where the situation became intolerable. The so-called Beneš policy was in fact the work of Jews and free masons. We trust that after this past experience the Czech nation will obtain a clear and true picture of the Jewish problem. I assume that a solution of the Jewish question in Czechoslovakia will help to clarify the problems still pending between Germany and Czechoslovakia."

Thus, German pressure has been applied continuously during the last few months for anti-Jewish measures in Czechoslovakia, on the official pretext that the Jews disturb the relations between the Czechs and the Germans.

Opposed to this German influence there has been not only the quiet resistance of influential Czech circles, who feel that they have troubles enough without creating new ones, but also pressure from the British and French in the direction of moderation. As has already been reported, the British have endeavored to make it a condition of the granting of financial assistance to Czechoslovakia that there be no radical action taken against the Jews in this country. The Czechs have thus found themselves torn between the conflicting desires of the Germans and the Western powers, with their own instincts inclining them toward moderation.

Very little has happened in Prague thus far to justify the panicky atmosphere which has prevailed in Jewish circles here since the Munich Agreement. The vast majority of the Jews in Bohemia and Moravia have remained up to the present quite unmolested both in their private lives and in their economic activities.

There has been no legislation whatsoever bearing directly on the Jewish question. The only legislative acts which are commonly regarded as directed primarily against Jews (and in this case only against certain limited categories of Jews) have been the two decrees of January 27, 1939, calling for a review of the naturalization proceedings through which certain persons obtained Czechoslovak citizenship and for the deportation of certain aliens. These decrees apply, of course, not only to Bohemia-Moravia, but to the country as a whole. They provide, in general, that the naturalization proceedings of all persons of non-Czechoslovak nationality who have acquired Czechoslovak citizenship since 1918 shall be subject to reconsideration by the local authorities, who shall have complete and final discretion in deciding whether these people shall still be considered as entitled to Czechoslovak citizenship. Those who lose their citizenship in this fashion can then be compelled to leave the country. It will be seen that the effect of these decrees, the purpose of which is obviously to permit the state to get rid of a number of refugees from Germany, will depend entirely on the manner in which they are administered by the local authorities. It is not anticipated that they will affect more than some 20,000 to 30,000 people, of whom not all are Jews, and of these only a certain proportion will presumably be deprived of their citizenship. It is even doubtful whether the number of Jews forced to leave the country by virtue of these decrees will be much greater than the number who would find means of emigrating in the normal course of events, during the period in question.

In addition to these measures, the position of the Jews has been somewhat affected by administrative practices of the government. Here the most important item is the government's policy, evidently adopted two or three weeks ago, of removing the Jews from all positions in government service. The effect of this policy is not as serious as it sounds. For one thing, it is being applied only in the case of full-blooded Jews. Persons of whom one parent was Aryan are not affected. The number of full-blooded Jews in government service seems to be very small. Government jobs, during the lifetime of the Republic, have been given almost exclusively to Czechs, except in the minority institutions. It is estimated that probably not more than 1,000 people in all will lose their occupations in this manner. And even these people will not be deprived of their means of existence. For the first three years after their dismissal they will continue to receive their basic salaries (which are smaller than the salaries they receive when on active duty). After three years they will be pensioned off. It should be added that these people are not being summarily dismissed on the ground that they are Jewish. They are being advised to leave voluntarily; if they fail to do so their jobs are often abolished as a part of the drive for government economy. The same thing is being done with certain categories of Aryans whose presence in the state service is offensive to the Germans and therefore embarrassing to the government.

It is, of course, not surprising that in all Germanic institutions supported by the Czech state Jews are being eliminated completely. This has applied particularly to the German section of the Charles University in Prague, where some 45 German-Jewish professors were pensioned off. The same principle has been applied in the German schools throughout the country. The Jews who were engaged in the German theatrical establishments have all lost their jobs, and a certain "purging" has taken place in the German newspaper offices. It is understood that a good deal of this purging has been carried out at the direct personal instigation in each individual instance of Herr Gregory, the press attaché of the German Legation, who is known to be the special representative in Prague of the German Ministry of Propaganda.

The government has also taken steps to prevent Jewish refugees from the Sudeten areas from establishing themselves in commercial activities or in the free professions in Bohemia. A decree of November 8, 1938, enjoined the competent authorities to grant permits for the establishment of a trade or profession or other enterprise, and to issue licenses for the conduct of business, only in the event that no objection could be raised thereto from considerations of public interest. The decree further provided for a reconsideration of all permits and licenses issued subsequent to March 1, 1938.

In the free professions there has been a certain amount of unrest, but very little real action. An association of Aryan lawyers has been founded and a certain amount of agitation started in the local bar association for the elimination of German-speaking Jewish lawyers and the application of the *numerus clausus* to the Czech-speaking ones. There is no unanimity, however, even within the Aryan section of this association, with regard to the desirability of such measures, and so far none have been adopted. In medicine, Jewish doctors are being forced out of their jobs in the sickness and accident insurance institutions and presumably out of all state-controlled clinics, but most of these doctors have private practices as well, which have not yet suffered interference. The question of anti-Semitic measures seems to be more acute in the legal than in the medical profession.

This more or less exhausts the list of the hardships to which Jews, as far as the Legation is informed, have been and are being subjected at the hands of the Prague authorities. The local Germans, who presumably speak for official Reichs-German circles, profess dissatisfaction with the moderation which the government has shown and insist that far more radical measures should be taken to eliminate Jewish influence. No one knows, however, just how far this dissatisfaction goes in Berlin or whether serious pressure will be applied for the adoption of a more extreme policy toward the Jews. It seems to be a fact—and the Germans are doubtless well aware of it—that the present Prague regime, including President Hacha—would hardly be prepared to go much farther than it has already gone on the path of anti-Semitism. Thus German insistence on a more radical policy might very well necessitate readjustment in the Prague government. I believe it to be questionable whether the Germans would wish just now to take responsibility for such readjustments, which could not be made without bringing to a head a number of most delicate and difficult questions of Czechoslovak politics.

So much for the policies of the Prague government and the situation in Bohemia-Moravia. In Slovakia, other conditions prevail. Here the percentage of Jews, in the first place, is higher than in Bohemia.[1] The Slovak Jews are not only prominent in the cities but, in contrast to the situation prevailing in Bohemia, are scattered in large numbers throughout the countryside and play a conspicuous part in the economic life of the Slovak village. They are the object of widespread resentment on the part of the Slovak population. Their dress, their manners, and their habits are conspicuous and—to many Slovaks—offensive. As noted in an earlier despatch, they are prominent in the villages as money-lenders, lawyers, saloon-keepers, druggists, merchants, etc. In the larger cities they form a wealthy class which makes up a good part of the "intelligentsia" and controls a very large proportion of the capital of the country.

Many of the educated Jews are Hungarian-speaking and have always looked to Budapest for cultural inspiration. A smaller but by no means insignificant number have had a German cultural orientation. This doubtless explains to a large extent the feeling prevalent in many Slovak circles to the effect that the Jews have always sided with the oppressors of the Slovaks, against the native population.

The present Slovak autonomous regime grew out of the Hlinka movement, which had been subject to extensive and direct German influence for some time before the Munich Agreement. It is not surprising that it should have come into

[1] As was seen above, calculations based on the 1930 census showed a total of 39,158 Jews in Slovakia, by nationality, and 91,-000 by confession. The "surprise" census taken by the Slovak government at the end of December 1938 showed lower figures: 29,928 by nationality and 87,487 by religion, but these differences doubtless reflect "the flight from Jewry" stimulated by the anti-Semitic statements of the Slovak leaders. The actual number of Jews in Slovakia must be upwards of 100,000.

power with an out-and-out anti-Semitism as one of the principal planks in its platform. There is no point in reciting here the various statements of Slovak leaders with respect to the Jewish question. There have been many statements of this sort and their tenor has all been more or less the same: that the influence of the Jews in the political and economic life of Slovakia would have to be eliminated, and that the Slovak government would not shy at extreme measures in pursuing this purpose. These views were confirmed . . . by the Slovak Prime Minister, Dr. Tiso, in a personal conversation. The Prime Minister stated that the Slovak government intended to take measures toward the solution of the Jewish question independently of Prague and that these measures would probably go farther in scope than any that might be taken by the Prague regime. He also stated the intention of his government to avoid irresponsible excesses and physical cruelty, but I suspect that this statement was made largely for the sake of effect and that the policy of the Slovak government in this point will be governed primarily by considerations of expediency.

An important factor in the attitude of the Slovak authorities toward the Jews is the attitude of the Roman Catholic Church. Dr. Tiso is himself a priest and the regime is strongly Catholic in character. Thus far, the Church has not seemed to be doing much to moderate the attitude of the government on the Jewish question. The Church's attitude was recently defined in detail by the Provincial of the Jesuit Order in Slovakia, Father Rudolph Mikuš, who granted to the semi-official Bratislava newspaper, the *Slovak*, what was evidently a carefully prepared interview on this subject. A full translation of this statement, which must be presumed to represent the attitude of the Church not only in Slovakia but in other European countries as well, is enclosed.[2] It will be seen that the Church, according to Father Mikuš, favors the segregation of the Jews and the elimination of their influence in political

2 Omitted here.

and economic life in Slovakia. He would limit the scope of action of the authorities in attempting the "solution" of the Jewish problem only in instances where the marriage rights of baptized persons under canonical law might be effected. He made it clear that the Church cannot refrain from baptizing Jews who were sincerely converted to the Catholic faith and cannot, once having baptized them, discriminate against them on the grounds of nationality. His attitude toward other Jews, however, was sharply negative, and it is evident that the Slovak leaders will encounter little opposition from the Church in the promulgation of an anti-Semitic policy.

In Slovakia, as in Bohemia, the Jewish question is largely the football of foreign influences. The Germans, through their local German minority, press for action against the Jews, on the grounds that the Jews exercise a disturbing influence on their relations with the Slovaks. On the other hand, severe financial pressure operates in the direction of moderation. A large proportion of the fluid capital in Slovakia is Jewish, and considerable amounts of this have been withdrawn from the province in recent months as a result of the anti-Semitic attitude of the Slovak authorities. The absence of Jewish visitors has contributed in no small measure to the unhappy plight of the Slovak health resorts. The Slovak government is in dire need of capital from without, to boost its own revenues and to keep the wheels of its economic life in motion. It has hopes of attracting such capital not only from Prague but also from other countries, including the United States. Its members are now beginning to understand that these hopes stand less chance now of realization if an anti-Jewish policy is to be pursued. There seems to be little doubt but that the appreciation of this fact has led to differences of opinion among the Slovak leaders and their followers, and constitutes one of the most difficult and important problems of Slovak political life at the present moment.

Thus far, in Slovakia as in Bohemia, relatively little hardship or inconvenience has been suffered by the Jewish population. Immediately after the political changes in the beginning of October, when local power was largely in the hands of more or less irresponsible units of the Hlinka Guard, there was a certain amount of disorder and molestation of Jews, labelling of shops, etc. A particularly unpleasant situation arose in October in Bratislava, where the feelings of the Slovak population were aroused by a report—apparently not without foundation—that representatives of some 15,000 Bratislava Jews had approached the Hungarian authorities with the request that the city be included in Hungary in the final territorial settlement which was then anticipated. This step was viewed in Slovak circles as proof of the disloyalty of the Jews. The result, in addition to a certain amount of public disorder, was that the local Slovak authorities routed out 200 or 300 *staatenlos* Jews who were found to be living in Bratislava, and put them across the line on the Hungarian frontier. The Hungarian authorities refused to admit them, and these miserable people, among them over 100 women and children and a number of persons in poor health, were forced to camp out for weeks in the fields between the two lines. Representatives of the Jewish organizations in Bratislava endeavored to provide them with food, clothing, and shelter. But the authorities were not always cooperative and there was evidently considerable real suffering before the Hungarian authorities finally took pity and accepted the refugees.[3] A similar shunting around of refugees, many of whom were Jewish, took place at other points on the Slovak-Hungarian frontier, but on a smaller scale. The fate of two Jewish children, who were found frozen to death in an open truck in the course of these operations, appears finally to have made an impression on the authorities on both sides, and to have

[3] A number of other incidents occurred on the borders of Bohemia and Moravia where groups of Jews were left without shelter between the lines. These incidents have not been recounted here because the initiative in all these cases, to the Legation's knowledge, came from the German rather than the Czechoslovak authorities.

led to a greater observance of some of the elementary principles of human decency.

Since November, there has been comparatively little anti-Semitic activity in Slovakia. A few signs are hung around in the cities, admonishing the populace not to destroy or damage Jewish property because "we will get it in the end." Physical violence and offensive behavior toward Jews seem to have ceased entirely for the time being.

Meanwhile, the government has appointed a commission, under the leadership of Sidor, head of the Hlinka Party and Deputy Prime Minister in the central government, the function of which is to work out decrees dealing with the Jewish question. It is understood that the labors of this commission are practically at an end, and the results should become known in the near future. It is difficult to predict these results. Members of the commission have let it be known that such action as will be taken will be a compromise between the "racial" and the "Christian" conceptions of how the Jewish question should be solved. The measures will probably put forward the *numerus clausus* principle in the free professions and cultural life, and impose certain restrictions on retail commercial operations by Jewish firms.

In addition to these contemplated measures, there is no doubt that discrimination against the Jews will continue to take place in Slovak administrative practice. Insofar as the new decrees of the central government concerning the revision of naturalization proceedings are to be administered by the Slovak authorities, it can be viewed as almost certain that such administration will be particularly severe. The Slovak authorities have already let this be known officially.[4]

---

[4] It has also been announced that the Slovak government will issue a special decree of its own dealing with the citizenship of Jews in Slovakia. The Legation is at a loss to understand just what the nature of such a decree could be. The decrees issued by the Prague government are, as noted above, valid for the entire Republic, and as long as a general Czechoslovak citizenship exists, the federal government would presumably remain competent for its regulation.

Instances have already occurred in which the authorities have openly discriminated against Jewish firms in the allotment of government purchase orders. The Jews, however, are said to have countered such discriminations quite effectively through charges of bribery and corruption on the part of the officials concerned; and it is possible that the financial difficulties of the Slovak government, which are just now presenting themselves in all their ugliness in connection with the passage of the Slovak budget, will make it necessary to accept the proffered cooperation of the Jews in respect to government purchases.

There remains the question of Ruthenia. Here the attitude of the government is obscure. The Ruthenian Prime Minister recently informed a Ruthenian Jewish delegation that he "appreciated all respectable and religious Jews quite as much as he did other respectable citizens." He is said to have added that "the Constitution secures the rights of all citizens. Our internal order shall be based on the Constitution, which we have neither amended nor wish to amend. In the face of the law all citizens are equal." He is further said to have assured the delegation that his government would endeavor as far as possible to meet Jewish cultural demands, and that in economic matters it wished to observe the principle of honest and free competition but would naturally take precautionary measures against harmful elements. Minister Revay, of the Ruthenian Cabinet, has just recently given renewed assurances that no radical solution of this question was contemplated.

All the larger Ruthenian cities have been lost, so the Jews who remain are mostly villagers. Their number (roughly 75,-000) is relatively large: they constitute 12 percent of the population and are officially stated to control 95 percent of the economic life of the province; but this monopolistic position in economic life makes it almost impossible for the government to take measures against them without thereby damaging the economic life of the province and adding to the already fantastic economic difficulties with which it is faced.

The Ruthenian Jews seem to have made little or no effort to dispute the predominance of the ruling "Ukrainian" group in cultural or political matters or to influence the "foreign policy" of the Ruthenian regime. As in Slovakia, they are commonly suspected of disloyalty, and it is scarcely surprising that their attitude towards all the factions interested in Ruthenia—Ukrainians, Hungarians, Czechs, Poles, and Germans—should be one of a wary and disillusioned skepticism. But the present Ruthenian regime, despite the extensive German influence to which it has been subjected, has found its Jews in some respects too much and in others too little of a problem to be tackled at this time, and has thus far been content to leave them pretty much alone.

As will have been seen from the above discussion, the Jewish question in Czechoslovakia presents a highly confused picture. The Jews themselves fall into many different categories, varying from the highly cultured intellectuals of Prague to the pious and primitive orthodox Jews of the Slovak and Ruthenian villages. They are divided among various cultural tendencies: Yiddish, German, Hungarian, Polish, and Czechoslovak. The attitude of the Aryan population toward them varies again, between city and country, between the various classes and professions, between the different provinces. In these circumstances, it is scarcely to be expected that any clearcut policy or attitude on the part of the responsible authorities will emerge. It seems evident that if Czechoslovakia existed in a vacuum the Jews, despite their considerable number, would not present any problem which could not be solved with relatively humane and painless methods. The country does not contain in itself the basis for a really serious and widespread anti-Semitic movement.

But the present disturbing conditions in neighboring countries cannot, as long as they prevail, fail to have repercussions on the relations between Jews and others in Czechoslovakia, and the situation may be further complicated, at any time and to an unpredictable extent, by direct German pressure.

8. Report on conditions in Ruthenia, written March 1939

In ordinary circumstances the fate of half a million primitive Slav peasants in the foothills of the Carpathians would hold little more than academic interest for most people in other parts of the world. When these same peasants, however, become the potential keystone of Germany's eastern policy, normal conditions can no longer be said to prevail. It is this development—the attempt by Germany to create out of Ruthenia the Piedmont of a future Greater Ukraine— which makes it necessary to give serious attention to certain matters which might otherwise be, at best, a subject for humorous treatment.

The Ruthenians are the descendants of Slav tribes which penetrated southward across the main crest of the Carpathians, encountered more warlike peoples on the plains to the south, and were forced to make their homes in the foothills and the southern slopes of the Carpathian range. There, for centuries, they have eked out a scanty existence as peasants and woodcutters.

To those who inquire whether (and this has long been one of the central questions of Ruthenian political life) these peasants are Russians or Ukrainians, there is only one answer. They are neither. They are simply Ruthenians. Their dialects (for there are a number of them) are closely related to the dialects of Galicia, and are thus nearer to the Ukrainian than to the Russian, but are far from being identical with either. Inasmuch as they are hill people, their habits of life and thought are doubtless equally distant from those of the Russians and the Ukrainians, both of whom are—in overwhelming majority—plainsmen.

To the Ruthenian peasants the question whether they belong to the Russian or the Ukrainian cultural sphere is one of singularly little importance; but to the small class of educated Ruthenians, afflicted with a sense of strangeness and inferiority in the face of the more highly developed cultures of neighboring states, this question has meant everything. If they were to hold their own with Czechs, Magyars, and Germans, they could not rely merely on the folklore of the native valleys; they had to seek support in some larger and related cultural entity. But which to choose? The Ukrainian was linguistically the nearer; the Russian incomparably the richer. The result has been a split of long standing between the Russophile and the Ukrainophile Ruthenian intellectuals —a split which has been recently exploited by larger states in their efforts to gain influence over the province.

For decades before the World War, the Great-Russian tendencies were kept alive in Ruthenia, despite all the suppressive talents of the Hungarian authorities, by the Russian pan-Slavists. After the cession of the province to Czechoslovakia it was, curiously enough, the Hungarians who gave extensive support to the pro-Russian[1] element, in the hopes of weakening the Czech hold on the territory. The Poles did likewise. One of the principal protagonists of the Russian cultural tendency was a Hungarian-born editor and local political figure by the name of Brody. He had his own little political party, with purely local—Ruthenian—support. He was apparently financed throughout the last few years mainly by the Hungarians (which does not mean that contributions from other foreign governments were not also forthcoming at times). His principal competition in the pro-Russian field came from a Ruthenian deputy to the Prague parliament, Fenčik, who likewise had his own local party and whose

---

[1] The term "pro-Russian" as used in this connection refers solely to those who favored the Russian cultural alignment within Ruthenia. It does not signify any predilection for Russia—least of all Soviet Russia—in matters of foreign policy.

funds appear to have come at one time from the Poles and later from the Hungarians. In addition to this foreign support, the Russian cultural tendencies in Ruthenia were vaguely connected, during the parliamentary days of the Czechoslovak Republic, with the conservative nationwide parties, particularly the Agrarians.

The Ukrainian tendencies became powerful chiefly after the World War, when the province had already gone to Czechoslovakia. Philologists, who established the similarities between the Ruthenian and Ukrainian tongues, contributed extensively to their origin. They were supported by refugees from Polish Galicia. They found favor among the clergy of the Uniate (Greek Catholic) Church. This Church, to which the majority of the Ruthenians belong, preserves the rites of the Eastern Orthodox Church but recognizes the primacy of the Holy See and is administratively subservient to Rome. Its leaders doubtless saw in the Ukrainian tendencies among the Ruthenian intelligentsia an instrument for weakening the influence of the Russian Orthodox Church, which still commanded the adherence of a large and important minority throughout the province, and which in general supported Russian cultural traditions.

The Ukrainian tendency seems never to have found expression, during the pre-Munich period, in any political party of its own. Its followers had their cultural societies, cooperatives, etc., as did the adherents of the Russian alignment, but their votes went largely to the nationwide Czechoslovak parties of the left and center, particularly the communists, the Social Democrats, and the Šramek People's Party.[2] A number of the leading figures in the present fascistic "Ukrainian" regime in Ruthenia are thus former communists and Social Democrats. Julian Revay, now a minister of the Ukrainian Regional Government, was formerly a Social Democratic deputy in the Prague parliament. Vološin, the present regional Prime Minister and the only other Ruthenian

[2] A nationwide Catholic party.

member of the cabinet, was formerly a member of the Šramek People's Party. He is said to have received a total of only 7,000 votes in Ruthenia as a candidate for Parliament in the last elections before the collapse of the Prague parliamentary system.

During the years which elapsed between the founding of the Czechoslovak Republic and the Munich Conference, all good Ruthenians who had education enough to be interested in politics clamored for the granting of the autonomy which had been promised to them by the Constitution when the Republic was founded. The Czechs steadfastly refused to accede to these demands, on the grounds—by no means unfounded—that the Ruthenians were not yet capable of running their own affairs. When the Czechs were left helpless by the September catastrophe, the Ruthenians had as little difficulty as the Slovaks in obtaining Czech consent to the establishment of an autonomous regional government, and eventually this autonomy was defined and sanctioned, as in the case of Slovakia, by a special constitutional act of the Prague government. The Russian tendency being regarded as the stronger of the two, Brody was first appointed Prime Minister by the Prague government, with one pro-Russian and one pro-Ukrainian minister to assist him. Fenčik was given an important job as Ruthenian delegate for the settlement of frontier questions with Slovakia.

During the month of October, however, changes began to occur in Ruthenia with great rapidity. Foreign agents began to descend upon the more or less footloose province from all sides. Most prominent among them, in numbers and in seriousness of purpose, were the Germans and their Ukrainian-émigré protégés. German Nazis, attracted by the greater-Ukrainian conception, had long been interested in the Ukrainian tendencies among the Ruthenians, and we must assume—political practices in that part of the world being what they are—that German money had been finding its way into the pockets of pro-Ukrainian politicians. Now, in the hysteria of success which followed Munich, the hopes of certain party circles in Germany appear to have grown apace. If an autonomous "Ukrainian" regime could be established in Ruthenia, the Ukrainian elements in Poland and Rumania could—it was reasoned—be stirred to the point of open revolt. A Ukrainian state could soon be established in Eastern Europe under German hegemony, and this state would provide the point of departure for the conquest— through propaganda or through arms—of the rich expanses of the Soviet Ukraine. Thus the German dreams of commanding the resources and markets of the vast fertile territory which stretches from the Carpathians to the Caucasus would be realized.

In the face of these ambitious plans, it is only natural that Poland should have hastened to forestall the threat to her own territory by offering vigorous support to Hungarian irredentist claims on Ruthenia, and by pressing for the complete elimination of any autonomous "Ukrainian" regime in that part of the world through the achievement of a common Hungarian-Polish frontier. Thus Ruthenia became, for a time, the object of a diplomatic tug of war between Germany, on the one hand, and Poland and Hungary, supported by Italy, on the other.

The decision of the arbiters who met in Vienna at the beginning of November to determine the new Hungarian-Czechoslovak frontiers brought the Ruthenian question to a very difficult pass for all concerned, including the Germans themselves. One still hears speculation concerning the motives which prompted the Germans to agree to a territorial settlement which left Ruthenia just about as useless to themselves as to the Czechs. The award of Užhorod and Mukačevo to Hungary effectively cut the only lateral rail connections between Ruthenia and Czechoslovakia and within the province itself, thus decreasing its value as a German corridor to Russia. The award, furthermore, so crippled the economic life of the province as to render it an irremediable financial burden to any state—save possibly Hungary—which might find itself responsible for the conduct of its affairs.

Despite this discouraging situation, German interest in the territory appears to have continued undiminished throughout the fall. But since Germany was not in a position to preserve order and hold things together there, her policy was to make the Czechs do this for her. Whenever the weary Czechs, already overburdened with their own pressing problems, showed signs of a desire to wash their hands of the whole business and abandon the province to the Hungarians, German pressure—I am told—was applied in Prague to force them to continue their efforts to keep things going. But in general the Czechs seem not to have been particularly averse to their allotted role. However strange it may seem to us, considerations of prestige still play a prominent part in their mental processes, and what they have objected to most strongly thus far has not been the financial burden but the lack of control over the civil administration.

Thus it was the Czech army which evacuated the regional government from the ceded city of Užhorod to the inland village of Chust. Rail communications being severed, the army established an elaborate system of motor truck transportation over the single primitive road which connected Chust with the remainder of the province. It has continued to supply the whole territory with food and other necessities in this manner up to the present time. Czech troops fought to protect the borders of the province from the irregular marauders whom the Poles and Hungarians—anxious to create conditions of disorder which would justify military intervention—repeatedly sent onto Ruthenian territory. And since the Ruthenian regional authorities had no money, the cost of all this, together with the costs of the current administration, also had to be borne exclusively by the Czechs.

Meanwhile, Czech influence over the political life of the province grew weaker and weaker. At German insistence, the government was reorganized in such a way as to leave in it no one who was not under German influence. The Prime Minister, Brody, was arrested on the occasion of a visit to Prague and thrown into prison on charges—by no means difficult to substantiate—of disloyalty.[3] Fenčik, reading the writing on the wall, fled to Hungary. Vološin was appointed Prime Minister. The only other minister was, for the time being, Revay. Both of these men had by this time been won over entirely to the German-Ukrainian camp, perhaps by German material assistance but mostly through cajolery and flattery and rosy descriptions of the future which awaited them in the Greater Ukraine which was to come. Since that time, they have become little more than puppets in the hands of back-stage German agents.

After the reorganization of the government, the "fascization" of the province was carried forward as intensively as could be expected in the circumstances. The peasants were too primitive to provide good fodder for totalitarianism and the numerous Jews who play so prominent a part in the life of the villages were even less promising material. But these elements were at any rate passive and raised little opposition to the establishment of a totalitarian regime founded on the tiny strata of educated or semi-educated Ruthenians and on a large number of imported Ukrainians. A single "Ukrainian" party was established along Nazi lines and other parties were forbidden. A semi-military organization, obviously modelled on the S.A., was set up by Ukrainian officers whom the Germans had sent in. The members of this organization, commonly referred to as the Sich,[4] were fitted out with fine grey uniforms and genuine Hitler-Jugend side-arms. Extensive political propaganda was undertaken among the Ruthenian population and among neighboring Ukrainian elements in Poland. Concentration camps for the accommodation of polit-

[3] He has recently been released on the strength of a general political amnesty.

[4] The term "sich" is not an abbreviation, but means "owl" in the Ruthenian language. The organization is parallel to the Slav Sokol.

ical opponents appeared in two or three places. Money was spent freely for political purposes and a good time was had by all those who called themselves supporters of the Ukrainian idea. Questions of the economic life and finance of Ruthenia itself were relegated to a convenient background.

All this was naturally a severe strain on the Czechs, who were not only feeding and protecting the province, but financing it as well. The Ruthenian authorities continued to squander on politics whatever sums they could get out of the Czechs for purposes of current administration. For some time, the Prague government put up with the situation without serious protest. Finally, however, in January two things happened which strained its patience. In the first place, it was discovered that sums which had been granted to the Ruthenian regional government by Prague for purposes of urgent road construction had been used almost exclusively for purposes of propaganda, much of which, incidentally, was of a sharply anti-Czech character. Then Ruthenian irregulars, apparently stimulated by false hopes for the recovery of their lost cities, provoked a border incident in the suburbs of Mukačevo which developed into a full-fledged battle between regular army units on both sides, resulted in a number of casualties and some damage to property, and seriously embarrassed the Prague government in its relations with Budapest. The Czechs thereupon decided that they could no longer hold responsibility without authority, and proceeded to appoint a Czech army officer, General Prchala, who had formerly commanded the armed forces in that area, as the third minister of the Ruthenian government.

The "Ukrainian" regime at Chust went into tantrums of indignation over this appointment. The "Carpatho-Ukraine," they maintained, was to be for the Ukrainians. Indignation meetings were held; people talked of accepting Prchala "over our dead bodies"; the officially inspired press breathed resentment and defiance. A delegation sent to protest in person to Prime Minister Beran of the Prague government, who was then in Bratislava, carried out its mission so vigorously that its members had to be ejected bodily from his hotel room. Urgent telegrams were despatched to Berlin. For a time it looked as though a crisis was brewing which would force the Germans either to permit the Czechs to have authority over Ruthenia or to take direct responsibility themselves for the future fate of the province.

Actually, the Germans temporized, and managed in this way to stave off any real solution of the problem. The Chust "Ukrainians" found only lukewarm support in Berlin and were forced to swallow Prchala, on the face-saving condition that he keep out of Ruthenia's "foreign affairs." They accepted him for the time being—with a maximum of ill-grace. He was received like the representative of a hostile power. But his appointment signifies a serious attempt on the part of the Czechs to reestablish a certain amount of control over the regional government. And the Germans, it is interesting to note, have not offered any serious opposition to this endeavor.

At the present moment, political conditions in Ruthenia are in a strange state. General Prchala, during the time he spends in Chust, lives and works in one room in the Czech military headquarters. The building is closely guarded by his own soldiers, and I doubt if he often appears on the streets. His relations with his colleagues are of the most formal character. They appear, in fact, to be restricted to occasional exchanges of courtesy calls in connection with the numerous arrivals and departures (all the ministers do a great deal of travelling), and to the regular cabinet meetings. As far as the latter are concerned, it is easy to see that Prchala can always be outvoted on any matter of real importance.

The two Ukrainian ministers, as was seen above, are largely figureheads. Their actions are inspired—if not entirely controlled—by German agents. Real power appears to be held by a clique of outsiders—Ukrainians—who have established themselves in Chust as correspondents for foreign Ukrainian papers, as political secretaries to the Ruthenian leaders, as instructors and officers of the Sich, etc. These men doubtless work in close contact with the recently appointed German Consul and with the head of the local German minority, Olfredi, who enjoys the title of Undersecretary of State in the Ruthenian government and has his offices in the government building together with the Ukrainian ministers.

Neither Vološin nor Revay appears to have any great understanding of—or interest in—economic matters. Their thoughts are evidently concentrated on the Greater Ukraine, which they expect to come into existence in the near future, and the current exigencies of Ruthenian economic life seem to them to be of secondary importance. This is the main cause of the discontent which they have aroused among the Czechs, and it may be assumed that the latter will do everything in their power to get them out.

The value of the two Ruthenian ministers to the Germans lies in their unimpeachable status as natives of the province—something relatively rare today among influential figures in Chust. But whether this advantage will permit them to continue to enjoy German support for any great length of time seems questionable. Natives or no natives, some of their foreign advisors are evidently getting sick of them. Chust reeks with intrigue, and the government newspaper is speaking ominously of the need for a firm hand, for a Ukrainian Mussolini, for "someone from the outside," etc., to guide Ukrainian destinies. Thus Revay and Vološin might easily find themselves junked in the near future in favor of some outsider, quite possibly a military figure from the Ukrainian emigration. (I suspect that General Kurmanovich, a well-known Ukrainian military man who was active in the civil war in Russia, is a likely candidate.)

The new Ruthenia has now elected a parliament: the so-called "Soim." The election was in reality not secret, and was from a single list of candidates, so that its political significance is minimal. However, the body is now scheduled to meet in the near future; the government will then presumably submit a formal resignation and recommendations will be made to the President of the Republic by the Soim for the future composition of the Cabinet. It is possible that this will be made the occasion for a reorganization of the government, and the retention of the present Ruthenian Cabinet members, as well as of General Prchala, will doubtless come up for consideration at that time.

The principal issue at stake between the Prague authorities, as represented by General Prchala, and the Chust regime is that of the economic and financial future of the province. Its financial situation is discouraging in the extreme. Since the end of October, the Prague government has continued to meet the current administrative expenditures. The budget of the regional government for the coming year is now under consideration. Expenditures are estimated at something over 400,000,000 crowns. Revenues ought theoretically to be around 60,000,000, but the actual situation is such that they are hardly expected to exceed half that sum. The reason is that the favorable time for the collection of taxes has, through the neglect of the Ruthenian authorities, been passed. The standard of living of the peasants is primitive in the extreme. What little cash they accumulate in normal circumstances they have only in the early winter, after the completion of the season's labors. This is also the only time when many of them can be found at home. By spring their tax capacity has reached a low ebb.

The estimated figure of 400,000,000 crowns of expenditures does not include the costs of the maintenance of the military establishment through which the province is now being supplied. This item, which is also being borne by the Prague government, cannot be small. The army is probably operating between two and three hundred trucks daily over the road from Prešov to Chust, and performing other services as well for the well-being of the population. Thus, altogether, it can be estimated that the mere maintenance of the province as a part of the Czech state is now costing the Prague government between $50,000 and $100,000 a day.

The estimated expenditures also fail to include sums necessary for investment in economic improvement. If anything were to be done to build up the economic life of the province and to increase the government's revenues through taxation, investment would be necessary. Roads should be built; a railway connection with the remainder of the country should be provided; enterprises should be constructed for at least the primary processing of the territory's leading raw materials. But it is not apparent where money could be found for these purposes at the present moment.

The Prague government has plenty of financial difficulties of its own and it is not plausible to suppose that it could make available any great amounts for capital investment.

The Ruthenian Cabinet members claim to have offers of capital from various foreign sources: German, Belgian, Italian, and Jewish. But these claims fail to ring true. The chances are that if such offers have been made they have either not come from serious and responsible parties or have been surrounded by conditions which would make their acceptance scarcely within the realm of possibility.

The Ruthenian leaders also profess to lay great hopes on financial assistance from Ukrainian circles in other countries, particularly in the United States. They are said to have already received a sum of some $5,000 to $6,000 from persons in the United States, in addition to shipments of clothing for the Ruthenian population. But it is commonly believed that such sums as have been received up to the present time have also gone for political purposes (sometimes for subversive propaganda in neighboring countries) rather than for economic development. And the amount of such sums would have to be vastly in excess of anything which has been even thought of so far, before they could have any material effect on the economic development of the province.

There is, of course, always the possibility that the Germans themselves, if they really want the province to be a workable proposition as part of the Czech state, will finally decide to put up capital for its development. It can only be said that so far there have been no indications of any readiness to do this on the part of the German government. German money has apparently been available for propaganda and for political purposes, but for little else. As far as can be judged from this end, it is only the German Propaganda Ministry and certain party circles that are really interested in Ruthenia. German economic circles have shown little enthusiasm and the Reichswehr authorities are said to be skeptical as to the value which the territory might have for Germany in a military sense. It is commonly believed in well-informed circles that Colonel Beck's recent talks with Hitler have led to a definite slackening of German hopes for the realization of the Greater Ukrainian plan in the near future; and this, if true, should not increase German readiness to tie up money in Ruthenia's development at the present time.

Actually, it is questionable whether any conceivable investment of capital would make the province in its present boundaries a paying proposition for the Czechoslovak state within the foreseeable future. The principal resource capable of exploitation at this time is timber. A secondary role is played by the large salt mines which have been developed at two or three places. Both of these products are bulky ones, and their transportation by rail over long distances is not profitable. The natural outlet for the timber is Hungary. All the Ruthenian rivers flow down to the Hungarian plain, and this is the natural destination of timber flotations. For products which are shipped by rail, the advantageous position of Hungary is obvious from the fact that every one of the remaining railway lines in the province now leads into Hungary.

During the years preceding the Vienna Award, a certain

advantage could be derived for Czechoslovakia from Ruthenia due to the fact that the rail connection was in Czech hands and preferential rates could be granted which made possible the distribution of Ruthenian products in Czechoslovakia proper. At the present time, the cost of transportation by rail via Hungary to Slovakia and Bohemia is very high. The Hungarians are charging 2,500 crowns (something over $80) per carload, payable in Swiss francs, for transit over Hungarian territory on this route. This makes shipments of timber and salt commercially unprofitable. Negotiations are now being conducted in regard to these rates, and the Czechs will probably obtain a certain reduction, but it is questionable whether this will be sufficient.

A certain quantity of Ruthenian products is now being disposed of in Hungary. This movement of freight amounts at present to about one hundred carloads a day. If normal circumstances were to prevail over a long period of time, if proper business connections could again be established, and if the attitude of the Hungarian authorities were favorable, this might prove to be an important alleviating factor in Ruthenian's economic difficulties. But conditions are still upset; the restrictions on international trade and payments are still formidable; and it remains to be seen whether the Hungarians, who have by no means abandoned their hopes for the return of the province to Hungary, will wish to favor a development which would smooth Ruthenia's path as a portion of the Czechoslovak state.

In the past a considerable portion of the revenues of the Ruthenian peasant came from labor performed during the summer months on Hungarian farms. If this source of income could be revived, this too might have a beneficial effect on the economic life and the finances of Ruthenia. The Germans are talking of taking thousands of Ruthenian peasants for brief periods of labor service in Germany, and a good deal will depend on the extent to which these plans can be realized.

Another potential source of revenue is the tourist indus-

try. In natural beauty, the territory certainly has the prerequisites for considerable development along these lines. This,
however, would require extensive investments and the building up of a whole class of competent personnel. There is at
present not a single comfortable hostelry or first-class restau-
rant in the entire province. In view of the present restrictions
on the transfer of foreign exchange all over this part of the
world, a tourist industry in Ruthenia would have to depend
primarily on Czech guests. In this respect it would have to
compete with the highly developed and more favorably
situated Slovak resorts, which are themselves now finding
great difficulty in attracting trade.

Thus, any real economic improvement in Ruthenia could
take place only in the face of formidable obstacles. In any
case, it could be realized only after years of careful and
businesslike management, and through extensive capital investment. Present political conditions are not such as to
indicate that either the management or the capital will be
forthcoming. We can only assume, consequently, that for
the immediate future—and that means at least the next two
or three years—the province will remain a serious financial
liability to the Czechs.

What of the future?

The entire regime in Ruthenia now rests on two main
factors: German political interest and Czech financial support.
If either of these factors were to disappear, the entire situation would be changed.

No one knows, of course, how long German support for
the present Ruthenian regime will continue. While many believe Germany's interest to have waned since the Hitler-
Beck conversations, it has obviously not been entirely abandoned. My own impression is that the Germans would probably be glad enough to pull up stakes and allow the Czechs
to have more of a free hand in the province, but that they find
this difficult to do. They have got the bear by the tail. They

have established in power a lot of excited and desperate Ukrainians and have encouraged them to believe that they are participating in the foundation of the Greater Ukraine. If they wash their hands of these people too suddenly and too demonstratively, they will ruin their own prestige in the entire Ukrainian movement, and the demoralized Ukrainians will fall prey completely to the intelligence services of other interested states which are already busy enough in the Ukrainian organizations. Thus, while the Germans have no immediate use for Ruthenia, they have an interest in seeing their Ukrainian friends continue to keep happy by playing with its political affairs as long as possible. And they are presumably anxious to see it preserved for them under the sovereignty of Prague until they are themselves in a position to make better use of it. For these reasons, they can be expected to endeavor to preserve the status quo, or something akin to it, for the immediate future.

How long the Czechs will be able or willing to continue to pay the bills for this white elephant is another question. The answer to it depends to a large extent on the economic arrangements which may be arrived at between Prague and Berlin. It also depends on the extent to which the Czechs may be permitted to control the expenditure of the funds which they put up.

Here the Germans are faced with a dilemma—one of the many which they have created for themselves through the breakup of Czechoslovakia. If they allow the Czechs to reestablish control over the province, they let down their Ukrainian friends. If they refuse to allow the Czechs to reestablish such political control, they run the risk that the Czechs may find it impossible in the long run to cope with the economic problems of the territory and that conditions may arise which would easily justify Hungarian intervention.

Whether the Germans will find a satisfactory way out of this dilemma, I doubt. For the moment, their diplomatic power is sufficient in this part of the world to maintain more than one manifest absurdity. But it seems to be the common impression of foreign observers who visit Ruthenia—and it is one which I share—that somehow or other, and in the not too distant future, the unwieldy remnant of what was once Ruthenia will find its way back to the economic and political unit in which it most naturally belongs, which is Hungary.

9. Excerpts from despatch of March 9, 1939, from Minister Carr to the Department of State, on Slovak-Czech relations

I have the honor to report that relations between the Slovak leaders and the Prague government have recently again shown signs of considerable strain and have given rise to a number of somewhat alarming rumors to the effect that Slovakia was about to secede from the Republic. No official explanation has been offered either in Prague or in Bratislava of the reasons for this renewed tension, and the press in both capitals, being under governmental control, has been obliged to keep silence on this point.

There can be little doubt of the main practical issues in dispute between the two capitals. They are, as in the case of Ruthenia, the two requirements of state administration which are beyond the resources of the regional governments: finance and defense.

The Slovak budget for the coming year envisages a deficit of approximately 1,155,316,600 crowns. This sum constitutes 38.5 percent of the total expenditures, which are estimated at 3,015,746,800 crowns. There is no possibility of this enormous deficit being made good by the Slovaks themselves. They are at present engaged in endeavoring to cover some of it by mobilizing private financial reserves through a state loan on the German pattern. Large amounts are being

(This despatch contained other portions drafted by Minister Carr and by Secretary of Legation C. Burke Elbrick. The portion reproduced here was drafted by George F. Kennan.)

contributed by insurance companies, etc. But the amount that can be realized in this way will not even begin to make up the sum of over a billion crowns needed to balance the Slovak budget. This money can be obtained only from outside.

The Prague government has from the outset taken the position that if it is to put up money to cover the deficits of its autonomous provinces it must have some control over the way in which the money is to be spent. Both Slovakia and Ruthenia, however, have shown a tendency to spend for propaganda sums granted them for purposes of administration or economic improvement, and the Slovaks are out to see that they continue to get Czech money with no strings attached to it. Last week two of the Slovak ministers proceeded to Berlin where, according to the official announcements, they were received by General Goering and discussed with him and with other high officials of the Reich the economic relations between Germany and Slovakia. It is not apparent just what these Slovak ministers could do to improve trade between Slovakia and Germany, when matters of customs tariffs, exchange control, import licenses, currency, and commercial treaty negotiations are supposed to be in the hands of the central government at Prague. The probability is that their visit to Berlin was partly for the purpose of making clear to the German leaders the predicament in which they find themselves vis-à-vis the Czechs, and possibly also for the purpose of impressing the Czechs with the fact that they have powerful friends elsewhere to whom they could always appeal.

With respect to the matter of defense, the Slovaks have been pained and embarrassed since the granting of their autonomy by the fact that their territory has continued to be defended by Czech troops. They have long been demanding that Czech soldiers and officers be removed from Slovak territory and that Slovakia be garrisoned by armed forces composed exclusively of Slovaks, although paid for, of course, by the central government. It is believed that the Prague government would not be averse to adopting a policy which would

76

keep the rank and file of Slovak recruits largely on Slovak territory, but the military authorities make the point that there are not sufficient higher officers of Slovak origin in the Czechoslovak army to man these forces. To this argument the Slovaks have countered with the demand that Slovak officers of lower rank be simply promoted to high positions in the army over the heads of their Czech colleagues, a demand to which the higher army circles can be expected to present the most strenuous resistance.

It is not clear why these two questions, namely of finance and defense, which have been chronic causes of conflict ever since the inception of the new political system in Czechoslovakia, should now suddenly have led to a minor crisis in the relations between the regional and the central governments, accompanied by threatening hints of complete secession of Slovakia from the Czechoslovak republic. Some observers are inclined to suspect that the real reason is that the Czechs, who were compelled by the magnitude of their reverses on other frontiers to play more or less a passive role throughout the fall and early winter, have now gained courage and are talking to the Slovaks as well as to the Ruthenians in a much more vigorous and confident tone. In doing so they doubtless have reason to believe, or to suspect, that there is a certain amount of bluff involved on both sides in the relations between the Slovaks and the Germans and that Berlin is not actually going to raise any serious objections if the Czechs insist on increased political control in Slovakia as a condition for their financial support.

If this supposition is correct, it is not difficult to understand why the most radical wing of the present Slovak regime, composed of people who are still hostile in the extreme to the Czechs and to the idea of a Czechoslovak state and have consistently advocated the complete independence of Slovakia, should have taken alarm in no uncertain way and begun to cry out that Slovakia must secede at once or the Czechs would soon reestablish their domination. This applies particularly to Professor Tuka and to Slovak Propaganda Chief Mach, together with their hot-blooded followers in the ranks of the Hlinka Guard.

In any case, talk of complete independence became rife in Bratislava last week just at the time when the deliberations of the Slovak ministers were in progress in Berlin and in Prague. This talk was given active encouragement in the Slovak broadcasts of the Vienna radio. Fuel was added to the fire by an incident at Piešťany, where differences arose between a crowd of Hlinka guards and certain Catholic priests who had been forbidden to wear the Hlinka Guard insignia. The Germans made so much of the incident that the Vienna *Völkischer Beobachter* had to be banned for one day in pro-German Slovakia.

On Saturday, March 4th, the Slovak government, evidently concerned over the number and strength of the rumors which had grown up at home and abroad about a pending Slovak secession, announced that the Slovak Cabinet, after having received the reports of the ministers who had visited Berlin and Prague, was determined that Slovakia's future status, whatever it might be, would be worked out on the basis of the Žilina agreement of October 6, 1938. This meant that whatever might happen, Slovakia would remain within the framework of the Czechoslovak state.

Mr. Karol Sidor, accompanied by the Slovak Finance Minister, Dr. Teplansky, is arriving in Prague today to negotiate with the Prague leaders on behalf of the Slovak government. It is announced that he is bringing with him definite proposals for the establishment of the future relationship between the two parts of the country.

While no details have been made public, I consider it highly probable that what the Slovaks are proposing is a revision of the present constitutional arrangements, designed to make Slovakia a federative rather than an autonomous part of the republic. This would imply the final disappearance of the central Parliament, and the substitution in its place of a Diet for Bohemia-Moravia similar to these which have been recently elected in Slovakia and Ruthenia. It is assumed that under this arrangement Foreign Affairs, Defense, and Finance would continue to be dealt with through some sort of central organ. Such an arrangement would have the virtue of creating clarity in a political system which is now conspicuous for its vagueness and its contradictions. Slovakia and Ruthenia are already organized for such a federal status. It has been in Prague where the greatest unclarity still exists. No one can say with certainty when the Prague cabinet and the Czechoslovak parliament (which still exists in theory) are representing the republic as a whole and when they are representing the Historic Provinces.

The stumbling block, however, in any such federative arrangement would doubtless be the demand of the Slovaks and the Ruthenians for proportional representation in the federal organs. In view of the generally lower standard of education and political experience in Ruthenia and Slovakia, this is a demand which the Prague government would find it difficult—and in some cases quite impossible—to grant.

The conversations which are beginning today in Prague are expected to last two or three days. Before their results take definitive form, the Slovak ministers will probably have to return to Bratislava and report to their government. Thus the outcome of the conversations will presumably not be known before the beginning of next week.

10. *Personal notes,*
dated March 21, 1939,
on the March crisis and the
final occupation of Prague
by the Germans

On Thursday, March 9, I decided to leave the following morning for Spindlermühle, in the Riesengebirge, to spend the weekend and to bring Annelise and Grace—who were there skiing—back to Prague. We knew that important negotiations with the Slovaks were being undertaken in Prague that day and that a small faction in Bratislava was pressing for complete independence. We considered the Slovak situation to be one which could not endure for any great length of time without important changes. But we thought it probable that the negotiations between Czechs and Slovaks would drag out for several days and that the Slovak delegation would return to Bratislava and report to its government before any decisions would be announced. So I had few compunctions in going off for a long-sought weekend.

Thursday was a raw, dark day. There was a formal luncheon at the Egyptian Legation. Chvalkovsky was there, genial and unperturbed. Syrový, with the usual black band over his sightless eye, had the portly self-assurance of the commander-in-chief of a great army.

I took a long walk in the late afternoon. Darkness was falling and the lights were gleaming in the state chambers of the building opposite the Wallenstein Palace, where the Council of Ministers was in session with the Slovak delegates.

On the street below, two individuals were scuttling toward the entrance of the building, bearing trays full of glasses of excellent Prague beer, and I comforted myself with the assurance that over this conciliatory beverage no fatal steps could be taken. I underestimated the Slovak ability to separate business and pleasure.

On Friday morning we got off in good time by car. Riley, the Military Attaché, accompanied me, likewise three-year-old Joan Elisabeth and her nurse. The weather was still bad: a gusty March wind and flurries of futile snow which disappeared when it hit the earth. After two and a half hours' drive we reached the first frontier, and Joany showed her indifference for international boundaries by disappearing into the sentry box with her nurse, the latter bearing a mysterious parcel done up in brown paper. The sentry discreetly stayed outside until this additional border formality had been completed in leisure and dignity.

After a few miles of Germany, we emerged again into Czechoslovakia for a while, showing our papers at every turn. Then we got onto German territory for good. After Hohenelbe, the road suddenly became snow-covered, and we followed the valley of the Elbe—here only a modest mountain stream—up to Spindlermühle. By afternoon we were already plodding over the forest trails of the Riesengebirge, on top of a good meter of snow.

Saturday, March 11, was spent skiing. In the evening, I happened to see the front page of a *Völkische Beobachter*. "Czechoslovakia in Turmoil." "New Government in Slovakia." The next morning, Riley and I lost no time in getting back to Prague. We reached there in the early afternoon. For the first time, swastika flags were flying from some of the Prague windows. All the necessary telegraphing had been done, but I spent the afternoon going through newspapers from Slovakia and Ruthenia as well as from Prague.

Monday morning, the 13th, I got up early and walked over to the office. The bad weather was holding on: a damp, nasty wind, low clouds, flurries of snow. The morning's news was as foreboding as the weather. The Sidor government, which had just been set up in Slovakia by the Czechs, was obviously having hard sledding. Its enemies, who were some of the most popular figures in the Hlinka Guard, had either been clapped into jail or had fled to Germany and were denouncing the new government in Slovak over the Vienna radio. In either case, their plight boded no good for the prospects of a peaceful political development in Slovakia.

The afternoon brought the news that ex-Premier Tiso, who had just been removed from office by the Czechs, was going to Berlin for an interview with Hitler. This confirmed what seemed to many of us a disconcerting lack of clarity in German policy. No one understood at that time that a trap was being prepared which was designed to bring about the end of Czechoslovakia.

We had guests to dinner that night. They all thought that Slovak independence was probable. We speculated on what would become of Ruthenia. During dinner the Minister phoned. The Slovak Parliament had been summoned to meet at 10 a.m. Tiso was to attend. Slovakia would almost certainly declare its independence.

Two of my guests left hastily to encode telegrams. I phoned a friend who did all-night service in a government office. He said that there would probably be important news before midnight, and told me to keep the radio going. But the radio had nothing to offer and we sat around speculating until midnight.

After the guests had left, I went to the Legation, where they were finishing the telegrams. Elbrick and I walked home together in the early morning, with a feeling of extreme uneasiness.

Around four o'clock that morning, my friend from the censor's office phoned me to tell me that there had been no official announcement, but that they had news of German troop movements through Dresden and Salzburg.

Another gray day dawned (Tuesday, March 14). We were all over at the office early. Everyone was a little tired.

We puzzled over the troop movements. Both Czechs and Germans insisted that these were no more than the ordinary movements of troops into the large towns for the parades which were to be held. This was quite possible. All Central Europe was nervous and things frequently got exaggerated in the telling.

We learned on good authority that the Germans were demanding—as had been rumored the night before—the independence of Slovakia, a cabinet reorganization, and further guarantees for the treatment of the German minority in Bohemia. The last was a new and menacing note. The German minority had been living off the fat of the land for the last four months—in a peace and security which amounted to sheer extraterritoriality. The revival of the tales of its mistreatment could come only from ulterior motives.

The Slovak Parliament was in session from ten o'clock on until into the afternoon. The session was a secret one, and the secrecy was observed in true parliamentary tradition, which meant that we in Prague, over two hundred miles away, knew of its decisions before it had even adjourned. It was true: Slovak independence was to be declared. This meant the final breakup of Czechoslovakia, the loss of Ruthenia as well as Slovakia, and some sort of new order for Bohemia and Moravia. Vienna, furthermore, reported by telephone that the morning papers were screaming about the mistreatment of Germans in Brünn and Iglau, and we thought it probable that the German-language islands in the bottleneck of Moravia would be taken over by Germany in the form of a fat corridor between Austria and Silesia, the territory to the east of them assigned to the Slovaks as compensation for their treachery, and the mutilated remnants of Bohemia and Moravia left to preserve the fiction of an independent Czechoslovakia and serve as a source of foreign exchange and raw materials to Germany. This view, incidentally, was shared by the best-informed observers in the city.

The Minister and Elbrick went to a luncheon at the

Brazilian Legation. To everyone's amazement, the Foreign Minister, for whom the luncheon was being given, appeared punctually and made the rounds of the guests with complete composure—a remarkable performance for a man whose country was known to have just lost one-half of its territory and to stand in imminent danger of losing still more. His stay, however, was brief. After the first course, he excused himself and withdrew. Two hours later, he was on the way to Berlin.

The news that the President and the Foreign Minister had gone to Berlin left us no wiser than we had been before. In view of the events of the day, it was no more than natural. But it set the tongues to clacking and the rumors to coursing like wildfire through the city.

We went to the opera that evening with the Minister. Nazis were demonstrating farther down town, but the streets leading to the opera were quiet. The performance had been intended as a gala one, under the auspices of the President. It turned out to be a performance of the gloomy Slav fairy-tale "Rusalka." The President had called off his attendance only that morning, and we know now that while we watched the opera, he was attending a performance equally fantastic but only too grimly real, in another city. But at the time we knew nothing definite, and the members of the diplomatic corps buzzed in and out of each other's boxes during the entr'actes, exchanging rumors and conjectures. I felt that it would have been more appropriate if they had put on Tchaikovsky's "Evgeni Onegin," where the doomed tenor, waiting for his duelling opponent to arrive, stands in the snowy Russian dawn and sings:

> What has the dawning day in store for me?
> What is it that my eyes seek in vain to discern?

After the opera, there was an interminable wait for the car. An icy wind howled along the river bank, and the crowds in evening dress shivered while they waited for their chauffeurs to appear in the long line of vehicles under the portico.

We coded again, after the opera, until late at night. Then we went for a drive through the town, to see whether there were any more demonstrations. But the streets were quiet. Only before the Deutsches Haus the police were pushing along a small group of jeering adolescents.

At four-thirty in the morning, Wednesday morning, I was awakened by the cook, who said that the telephone was ringing. The shaky voice of a terrified acquaintance told me that the German troops would begin the occupation of Bohemia and Moravia at six o'clock. I phoned the Military Attaché and asked him to get confirmation from the military authorities. Then I called the Czechoslovak Press Bureau, where a depressed female voice told me that the report was true. Determined that the German army should not have the satisfaction of giving the American Legation a harried appearance, I shaved meticulously before going to the office. The wind was howling and the snow was falling in the dark streets as I made my way to the Legation. A light was on in the Italian Legation. The cop on duty outside looked at me strangely, and I wondered if he knew what was up.

The Minister was already at his desk in the Legation. The staff gradually assembled, and we got off a cable. It began to get light. Two dishevelled men, ashy-pale with fear, came up to ask for asylum. They had been Czech spies in Germany, they said, and they were known to the local Gestapo. Their faces were twitching and their lips trembling when I sent them away. They were followed by two German Social Democrats, fugitives from the Reich. They seemed almost dazed with terror. They seemed to accept my statement that I could do nothing for them, but they wouldn't leave. They refused to believe that they had to leave that building, where they still could not be touched, and go out into the streets, where they were no more than hunted animals. A Jewish acquaintance came. We told him that he was welcome to stay around there until he could calm his nerves. He paced wretchedly up and down in the anteroom, through the long morning hours. In the afternoon, he decided to face the music and went home.

About seven o'clock, I took a ride around town. A full blizzard was blowing, by this time, and the snow was staying on the streets. The downtown section was crowded, partly by the normal early-morning traffic of people going to work but partly by people running about and making last-minute preparations of all sorts. The news was widely spread by this time, and many of the women were weeping into their handkerchiefs, as they walked.

At home for breakfast, I found that I myself had a refugee, a Jewish acquaintance who had worked many years for American interests. I told him that I could not give him asylum, but that as long as he was not demanded by the authorities he was welcome to stay there and to make himself at home. For twenty-four hours he haunted the house, a pitiful figure of horror and despair, moving uneasily around the drawingroom, smoking one cigarette after another, too unstrung to eat or think of anything but his plight. His brother and sister-in-law had committed suicide together after Munich, and he had a strong inclination to follow suit. Annelise pleaded with him at intervals throughout the coming hours not to choose this way out, not because she or I had any great optimism with respect to his chances for future happiness but partly on general Anglo-Saxon principles and partly to preserve our home from this sort of an unpleasantness.

Back to the office after breakfast. A stream of desperate persons was by this time arriving at the Legation and we had to post a man down at the gate to turn those away whom we did not know well. But even the others were only too numerous.

About ten o'clock, word came that the German troops had already reached the palace. Parry and I set out in my car to verify this, for the palace was only a short distance away.

Driving up the hill on the Nerudova, just before my own apartment, we met a German armored car stopped in the middle of the narrow street. The driver was evidently trying to find the German Legation and had stopped there, by the Italian Legation, to ask the way. A crowd of embittered but curious Czechs looked on in silence. The soldier in the turret sat huddled up against the driving snow, nervously fingering the trigger of his machine gun as he faced the crowd. It seemed to me that the two famous eagles on the baroque portico of the Italian Legation had a distinctly startled air as they witnessed this scene, like one who was prepared to say something very important and has had the wind unexpectedly taken out of his sails.

For the rest of the day, the motorized units pounded and roared over the cobblestone streets: hundreds and hundreds of vehicles plastered with snow, the faces of their occupants red with what some thought was shame but what I fear was in most cases merely the cold.

By evening the occupation was complete and the people were chased off the streets by an eight-o'clock curfew. We drove through the town around midnight. It was strange to see these Prague streets, usually so animated, now completely empty and deserted. Tomorrow, to be sure, they would fill with life again, but it would not be the same life that had filled them before; and we were all acutely conscious that in this case the curfew had indeed tolled the knell of a long and distinctly tragic day.

11. An undated letter, drafted in the last days of March 1939, signed by Mr. Irving N. Linnell, Consul General at Prague, and addressed to the American Chargé d'Affaires at Berlin, concerning efforts of the "Ukrainian" elements in Ruthenia to enlist foreign support against the Hungarians

I am enclosing copies of two rather curious communications which were received at the Legation in this city, prior to the closing of that office, from persons purporting to represent the government of the Carpathian-Ukraine.

These communications are indicative of the unsuccessful efforts made at the last moment by the "Ukrainian" Ruthenians to enlist foreign support against the advancing Hungarians.

The first was written by Julian Revay, who, it will be recalled, had been dismissed only shortly before by the Czechs from his ministerial post in the Ruthenian regional government. Mr. Revay stated that Ruthenia had declared its independence and had asked for the protection of the Reich. The communication was dated March 14, and was thus presumably drafted before any official information was available concerning Hitler's intention to apply the "protection" formula to Bohemia, Moravia, and Slovakia. It looks, consequently, as though German intentions were already known at that time to certain of the anti-Czech factions in Ruthenia.

The second communication, dated March 18, set forth that the territory had been invaded by the Hungarians, that a Ruthenian delegation had gone to Budapest and had attempted to reason with the Hungarian government but that its efforts had been in vain and that the Hungarian troops had continued their invasion. This communication made no mention of any possibility of support or protection from the Germans but appealed to "the civilized world" to compel the Hungarian government to settle its difficulties with Ruthenia by peaceful means. One cannot avoid the impression, therefore, that the Germans, during the period between March 14 and March 18, refused a direct appeal for protection from the Ruthenian "Ukrainians" and told the latter to settle their differences with the Hungarians as best they could—a cynical bit of advice which could only mean the abandonment of Ruthenia to Hungary.

I am afraid that in the excitement of the last fortnight most observers have failed to notice the significance of the failure of the Germans to support the so-called Ukrainian regime in Ruthenia which they themselves had set up and which they had inspired with such high hopes for the future.

The fact is that in recent years the greater part of the underground Ukrainian nationalist movement had come to place its hopes almost exclusively on German support, and the new "Ukrainian" Ruthenia became during recent months the crystallization point of all this feeling. It was to be the Piedmont of the future Ukrainian state. Ukrainians from all over the world sent their donations to help keep the regime going. Many of the most active and determined of the Ukrainian émigrés went to Chust and participated, with the most intimate German support, in the development of the "Carpatho-Ukraine."

All these people have now been let down in the crudest

sort of way. The Germans, who had troops within two or three hundred miles of the vicinity and would have encountered no opposition at all in moving them eastward, stood passively by while the Ukrainian Sich units, clothed in German uniforms and wearing Hitler-Jugend side-arms, were driven back and finally routed entirely by the Hungarian regulars. The officers and men of the Sich formations were in a particularly difficult position because, in the first place, they had always taken a violently hostile tone toward the Hungarians and could expect no quarter from that side, and on the other hand they had been encouraging subversive movements among the Ukrainians in Poland and Rumania (many of them, in fact, were political émigrés from those very countries) and could thus expect no refuge if they fled across the frontiers into Polish or Rumanian territory. It is reported that many of them had no other recourse but to take to the hills, where they are now being handled at leisure by the Hungarian "mopping up" patrols.

All this has been an experience which the Ukrainian nationalists will not be quick to forget. The result must undoubtedly be extensive disillusionment in the sincerity of German support and a certain degree of demoralization throughout the Ukrainian movement. There are no limits, of course, to the efficacy of a combination of propaganda and bribery in eastern Europe, and it is not impossible that in the course of time the Germans may, if they choose to, find new supporters among the Ukrainians to take the place of those whom they have disappointed. But for the immediate future, the discontented Ukrainians in Poland and the Soviet Union will have little choice but to come to terms as best they can with their present rulers.

In view of this fact, the plan fostered by certain German party circles for the breakup of Poland, Rumania, and the Soviet Union through political propaganda among the Ukrainian elements would seem to have received a pronounced setback, and it may be reasoned accordingly that if the Germans are going to expand further to the east in this area during the next few months such expansion will have to be carried out on a less subtle and more frankly militaristic basis than many Germans had hoped.

(Enclosure No. 1)

ÚŘADOVNA VLÁDY KARPATSKÉ UKRAJINY
V PRAZE

V. Praze, dne le 14 mars 1939

Č. j. 598

A SON EXCELLENCE L'HONORABLE
WILBUR JOHN CARR
LEGATION DES-ESTATES UNIS D'AMERIQUE

PRAGUE

Excellence,

En qualité de représentant plénipotentiaire de l'Ukrane Carpathique j'ai l'honneur de communiquer a votre Excellence ce qui suit:

Après la déclaration d'une indépendance complète de la Slovaquie, la République Tchecoslovaque s'est dissoute. C'est pourquoi l'Ukraine Carpathique s'est déclarée completement indépendante en se basant sur les principes de la décision de Munich relative au droit de l'autodisposition du peuple carpatho-ukrainien ainsi qu'en vertu de l'arbitrage de Vienne. Le peuple carpatho-ukrainien prie le Chef (Führer) de la Nation Allemande et le Gouvernement de l'Etat Allemand de ne pas refuser leur haute protection a l'Ukraine Carpathique indépendante.

Par ordre du Président des Ministres du Gouvernement de l'Ukraine Carpathique.

(signé) J. Revay, ministre

Pour l'Office du Gouvernement de l'Ukraine Carpathique à Prague:

(signature illegible)
Chancelier

(Enclosure No. 2)

ÚŘADOVNA VLÁDY KARPATSKÉ UKRAJINY
V PRAZE

V Praze, dne le 18 mars 1939

Č.j. 603/39

A SON EXCELLENCE L'HONORABLE
WILBUR JOHN CARR
LEGATION DES-ESTATS UNIS D'AMERIQUE

Prague

Excellence,

Nous nous permettons de porter à votre connaissance les faits suivants:

Une guerre sanglante sévit en Ukraine Carpathique sans aucune déclaration. Le gouvernement carpatho-ukrainien de Chust s'est adresse au gouvernement royal hongrois à Budapest en le demandant de suspendre les hostilités contre les Carpatho-Ukrainiens; malheureusement sans aucun succès. Une délégation ukrainienne fut envoyée à Budapest pour entamer des pourparlers avec les Hongrois. Néanmois l'armée hongroise continue à envahir le territoire carpatho-ukrainien.

L'affirmation qu'en Ukraine Carpathique des troubles auraient eu lieu, ne correspond pas à la réalité.

Il y a beaucoup de blessés et de tués. Les victimes innocents de l'invasion hongroise en Ukraine Carpathique s'adressent au monde civilisé en le demandant de prendre des mesures nécessaires afin que le carnage terrible dans leur pays soit cessé immédiatement.

Nous prions votre Excellence de vouloir bien communiquer ces faits au Gouvernement de votre pays ainsi que de présenter la demande du peuple et du gouvernement carpatho-ukrainien auprès de votre Gouvernement que tout carnage en Ukraine Carpathique soit suspendu et les différends entre le gouvernement carpatho-ukrainien et le gouvernment royal hongrois soient réglés par la voie paisible.

Pour le chancellerie du Gouvernement Carpatho-Ukrainien à Prague:

(signature illegible; not the same as
on the note dated March 14)

Chancelier

12. Report of March 29, 1939, on the new regime in Bohemia and Moravia

The purpose of this report is to outline the character of the new regime which is being established in the post-Munich remnants of Bohemia and Moravia. Special interest attaches not only from the point of view of their effect on the Czechs themselves but also from the point of view of precedent to the arrangements which are being made for the governing of this area. Since this is the first time that the National Socialist regime has absorbed an important and purely non-Germanic political unit, and since any further German expansion must now of necessity affect principally people other than Germans, the type of regime set up here may well give an indication of the form of domination which —if German hopes are successful—may later be applied to other parts of the continent.

To get a clear picture of the present situation, which is a rather complicated one, it is necessary to consider separately (a) the present temporary military regime, (b) the regime of the Protectorate which will be established when the Reichsprotektor arrives, and (c) the machinery of the autonomous Czech government which is to continue to function under the sovereignty and protection of the Reich.

a. The Temporary Military Regime

On March 16, the day following the occupation, it was announced in the Prague press that the entire executive power in the occupied areas had, by an order of the Reichschancellor, been assigned to the Commander in Chief of the German army, and that under the authority of the latter, General Blaskowitz, the Commander in Chief of the Heeres-

94

gruppe 3, and General List, Commander in Chief of the Heeresgruppe 5, would be entrusted with full executive power in Bohemia and Moravia, respectively. It was further announced that the two Gauleiters Henlein and Buerckel had been assigned to Generals Blaskowitz and List, respectively, in the capacity of deputies (Bearbeiter) for the civil administration. Finally, it was announced that a special official gazette would be published by the Commander in Chief of the Army, giving in the German and Czech languages all orders of a legislative nature issued for the occupied areas.

The publication of this announcement in the Prague press was accompanied by an order of General Blaskowitz assigning to Gauleiter Henlein authority over the entire public administration in the area occupied by Heeresgruppe 3 (namely, all the occupied territory in Bohemia).

It is on the basis of these measures that Bohemia and Moravia are at present being governed. The authority of the central Czech government in Prague is considered to be for the moment in abeyance. Certain functions of government, such as foreign affairs, customs administration, finance, etc., have already been taken over directly by Reichsgerman authorities other than the War Ministry. All remaining functions of government are under the control of the German military authorities. While this control is presumably being exercised directly by General Blaskowitz, orders of a legislative nature applicable to the occupied area continue to be issued by General von Brauchitsch, in his capacity as Commander in Chief of the Army.

One interesting point in connection with the present temporary regime is the apparent eclipse of Herr Henlein. Since General Blaskowitz's order placing him at the head of the public administration, nothing whatsoever has been heard from him, except for a brief press notice to the effect that "Gauleiter Konrad Henlein" was received by President Hacha. He has attended no public functions; his signature has appeared over no published documents; he has, as far as Bohemia is concerned, almost dropped out of existence. Nor is it evident that any other civilian has taken his place, although it has been rumored that both Herr Kundt, since Munich the leader of the Nazified Germans in Bohemia and Moravia, and Herr Frank, the Deputy Gauleiter of the Sudeten area, have been angling for this position.

The reasons for this procedure are anybody's guess. It is not difficult to see why Herr Henlein should have been removed. Nothing could have been better calculated to harden Czech hostility and suspicion than his presence at the head of public administration in Bohemia, and there have been numerous indications that what the Germans want most from the occupied areas is—for the moment—peace, quiet, and a minimum of bad feeling. But why then he should have been selected for this position in the first place is an open question, the answer to which would probably have to be sought in the obscure depths of internal Nazi party politics.

Strangely enough, Herr Buerckel seems also to have disappeared as chief of the public administration in Moravia, but in his case a replacement is in evidence in the person of Dr. Kurt von Burgsdorff. The latter is a prominent German administrative official, once Landespraesident in Leipzig, whose duties have heretofore confined him largely to Saxony and Austria but who now seems to have been chosen to play a prominent part in the Bohemian-Moravian protectorate.

b. The Protectorate

On March 16, a Reich law was issued incorporating Bohemia and Moravia into the Reich and establishing them as a Reich Protectorate. The law has subsequently been supplemented by an order of the Reichskanzler, dated March 22, making the Reichsprotektor directly responsible to the Reichskanzler and establishing the Ministry of the Interior as the channel for administrative control by the supreme German authorities over the affairs of the Protectorate.

The provisions of the Law of March 16 will, it is understood, go into effect formally only upon the arrival and entrance into office of the Reichsprotektor. Many of these provisions, however, have already been put into effect in practice. Local Germans have already, by decree of the military authorities, been placed under German jurisdiction. The foreign affairs of the former Czechoslovak state are, as far as they pertain to Bohemia, already being taken over by the Reich. (Herr Ritter, former German Ambassador to Brazil is in Prague supervising the liquidation of the Czechoslovak Foreign Office.) The transportation, postal, radio and telegraph-telephone systems are rapidly being taken into German hands.

As is commonly known, Baron von Neurath has been appointed as Reichsprotektor, and Karl Hermann Frank, the Deputy Gauleiter for the Sudeten area, as his first assistant, with the title of Secretary of State. Dr. Kurt von Burgsdorff, mentioned above, who is at present replacing Herr Buerckel as head of the public administration in Moravia, has also been attached to the Reichsprotektor in the capacity of Ministerial Director and will presumably serve as a sort of Chief of Chancery in the Reichsprotektor's office.

Dr. Stuckart, of the Reich Ministry of the Interior, has been placed in charge of the office in that Ministry through which all Reichsgerman action affecting the administration of the Protectorate will be coordinated. He will presumably have considerable influence over the affairs of the Protectorate, as far as the latter are directly under German control, whereas the functions of Baron von Neurath will be confined largely to the supervision of the acts of the Czech autonomous authorities who, according to the terms of the law establishing the Protectorate, still have a modest measure of control over their own people in certain restricted fields of public administration.

c. *The Autonomous Czech Government*

The Prague government is considered to be still in existence, but its functions are in abeyance and it has sunk in theory from the status of the sovereign government of Czechoslovakia to that of the autonomous regional government of those areas in Bohemia and Moravia which were not taken into the Reich last fall as a consequence of the Munich settlement.

President Hacha is remaining, reluctantly and out of a sense of duty, as the titular head of the Czech nation. He is entitled, according to the terms of the Protectorate, to the "protection and rights" of a head of state, and has been accorded the attendant honors by the German military authorities since the beginning of the occupation, although sometimes in circumstances which made them seem a mark rather of ridicule than of respect. As far as is known, he will continue to have his residence and office quarters in the Hradcany Palace and to receive all the honors to which he has been accustomed, together, apparently, with the additional honor of receiving Herr Hitler as an unannounced house guest whenever it suits the latter's convenience.

The Prague cabinet is likewise still in existence but has, pending the establishment of the Protectorate, nothing to do as a body. With the assumption of control by the Reich over foreign affairs and defense, these two portfolios are regarded as having ceased to exist, but the two incumbents, Chvalkovsky and Syrový, are still considered to be members of the government in the capacity of ministers without portfolio. General Syrový appears frequently at ceremonies in company with the German commanding officers.

There is no doubt whatsoever that the government will be reorganized as soon as the Reichsprotektor arrives. Not only will there presumably have to be a reclassification of portfolios but the personal composition of the body will probably have to be largely—if not entirely—changed. It is probable that most of the present ministers will be replaced with men heretofore little known to Czech political life.

As far as the political basis for the Czech autonomous

regime is concerned, things are in a state of complete flux. The moribund Czechoslovak Parliament was formally dissolved by President Hacha on March 21, an event which passed almost unnoticed after the developments of the last six months. There is no intention anywhere that another shall be elected. Interest now centers (and very little interest at that) on the efforts to create some channel for the "disciplined" expression of the political feelings of the Czech population.

The Czechs take to political parties like ducks to water, and the smaller the party, the greater their loyalty to its cause and the fiercer their jealousy of all others. For many years the Czech political parties have sat around the board and split any and all political spoils with the exactitude of small boys dividing a stolen melon. Their preoccupation with the relative size of their share, rather than with the extent of what was there to divide, has been one of the contributing factors in the catastrophe which has overcome the nation.

Throughout the period between Munich and the occupation, the Beran government made efforts to break up these old parties and to substitute a two-party system, in which the larger and more conservative party was to be called the Party of National Unity. Most of the Czech parties, after prolonged heart-searching, agreed to go into liquidation and to merge their following into the National Unity Party, but the old party clubs and cliques went on undisturbed and the merging of followers was in reality mostly on paper. Consequently, the rudiments of most of the old parties have remained and the natural tendency for Czech political sentiment would be to fall quietly back into the comfortable old channels. It is generally recognized, however, by intelligent people that such an outcome would bode no good for the unity and morale of the Czech people during the coming months or years of German domination, and consequently efforts have been made from several quarters to organize a

national unity movement for the furtherance of Czech culture
and the protection of Czech interests under German rule.

On the day of the occupation, General Gajda, the Czech
fascist leader, who evidently assumed that his day had come,
announced the establishment of a Czech national council,
with himself at the head. This council was supposed to be
the representative body of the Czech nation, and to have
its immediate roots in a single political party, to be called
the Fascist National Camp. The following day, Gajda and
a number of his followers were received by the commanding
German general in Prague, and the plan seemed to be well
on the way to realization.

At this point, however, President Hacha and Prime Minister Beran intervened in the situation. They agreed that there
should be established a single, national political organization,
headed by President Hacha himself, and that the National
Unity Party, insofar as it still existed, should be merged with
this new organization. This meant, of course, the elimination
of Gajda and his Council.

The Germans, interestingly enough, decided to support
Hacha and Beran. The result was that Gajda's Czech National Council was dissolved, and with it much of the influence of the Czech fascists over the current of events in
Bohemia.[1] In its place, President Hacha has now appointed
a new body, called the Committee for National Cooperation,
composed of fifty members, most of whom were heretofore
quite unknown in political life. They are in large part professional men: lawyers, teachers, engineers, etc., with a
strong minority of farmers and landowners. The chairman-
ship was assigned to Mr. Adolph Hruby, a Czech farmer who
was a deputy of the Agrarian Party in the Prague Parliament.

While the functions of the Committee for National Co-

---

[1] There are continued manifestations of the political activity of the
Czech fascists, and while Gajda himself denies all responsibility for
these manifestations, it is evident that he has by no means abandoned
his hopes of eventually playing the leading role in the Czech administration.

operation, as indeed of the Czech government itself, are still not clearly defined, it is evident that it will, for the present at least, confine itself principally to cultural matters and local administrative arrangements. A clue to its own conception of its duties can be obtained from the designations of the subcommittees which it has established. These are for economic matters, finance, social questions, agriculture, culture, public health, juvenile welfare, physical culture, etc. Some of these subcommittees have already gotten down to work, and the economic subcommittee has lost no time in recommending that the government take measures requiring the registration of all Jewish property before April 15.

The building and equipment of the dissolved Czechoslovak Parliament have been placed at the disposal of the Committee for National Cooperation, and it is evidently intended that it should become an organization of considerable outward importance and dignity. If the aims of its founders can be realized, it will play the leading part in preserving throughout the coming period of German domination the cultural and political integrity of the Czech people.

One interesting question which has been raised by the German occupation is that of the continued existence of the Sudetengau, as a separate administrative unit. Some of the responsible Czech leaders are beginning to wonder why, since all the Germans in post-Munich Bohemia and Moravia are now to enjoy Reichsgerman citizenship and be subject to the direct jurisdiction of the Reichsgerman authorities, the Czechs in the Sudeten areas should not be treated accordingly and be placed under the control and jurisdiction of the Czech autonomous government at Prague. Were something of this sort to be attempted, it would involve an interesting innovation in public administration, insofar as the territorial principle for the differentiation of administrative control would be dropped and the national principle substituted in its place. Thus there would no longer be a Sudetengau or a Czech portion of Bohemia in the territorial sense, but there would be two local governments functioning side by side in the same territory: one with control and jurisdiction over the Czechs, and the other with control and jurisdiction over the Germans. Questions such as communications, finance, etc., which could not be treated on this basis, are to be handled directly by the central authorities of the Reich in any case, so that no difficulties would arise on this score. Some solution along these lines would probably hold advantages for the Germans as well as for the Czechs, since the present Sudetengau is an unwieldy administrative unit, with no natural capital, and it is understood that its civil administration has not proved to be entirely satisfactory. The only place which is easily accessible to all the Germans of Bohemia and from which their affairs can be effectively administered is Prague.

13. Excerpts from a personal letter
of March 30, 1939

As to the situation here, I should like to say that I think the press has been a little inclined to exaggerate the horrors of these first two weeks of the German occupation. That there have been arrests, and that these arrests have run into the thousands, is doubtless true. A good proportion of the arrested persons, however, have been released after a few days' detention. The arrests, furthermore, seem to have been confined pretty well to Germans and Jews who have worked actively against German interests in recent years, or who have been conspicuous in communist and Social-Democratic activities. I have yet to learn of a single prominent Czech who has been molested. Many have lost their jobs but they all seem to be at liberty. There have been no scenes of Jew-baiting in the Prague streets, such as those which followed the Anschluss in Vienna. The German soldiers have maintained good discipline and a correct attitude. Their higher officers have done everything in their power, apparently, to placate Czech sensibilities, even to laying wreaths on the tomb of the unknown soldier.

All this I attribute not to any excess altruism on the part of the Germans but to a real desire that there should be—for the moment—the maximum of peace, quiet, and good feeling in Bohemia and Moravia. It now seems pretty evident that the occupation of these provinces was merely incidental to the achievement of more distant objectives. To the Germans, Bohemia and Moravia are now primarily lines of communication, and for this reason it is essential in the German view that they should not be centers of disorder. In the long run, to be sure, the provinces will probably feel the iron heel in many ways. The Jews, in particular, will doubtless meet essentially the same fate as those in the Reich proper, though attended, perhaps, with less brutality. But for the moment the Germans have been, in my view, surprisingly mild and conciliatory. In particular, those who have come down from Berlin have not seemed to identify themselves with the Sudeten Germans or with the Czech fascists, and I am encouraged to hope that their attitude toward the mass of the Czechs may turn out to be a more reasonable one than many had anticipated.

As far as the general situation in Central Europe is concerned, I have said above that this seems only to be a wayside stop for the Germans on the way toward the east. The schedule of this expansion is now the subject of lively comment and rumor here. I have heard several dates cited, allegedly from German military sources, for the main items on this schedule. They are conflicting, but they all indicate that the screws will be finally put on Hungary sometime in the end of April or May. But many other things can intervene and I can take no responsibility for the accuracy of these predictions.

That the Germans do try to stick to a schedule seems pretty evident. If there were no other proofs of this, I think it would be sufficient to cite an incident which occurred in Moravia, just after the occupation there. German soldiers went around in one of the towns putting up curfew announcements in two languages, as they did here in Prague. When it was pointed out to them that their posters were in German and Rumanian, instead of German and Czech, they hastily took them down and sent back to the supply department for the correct ones.

There is a widespread feeling here in well-informed circles that the German passivity in the face of the Slovak-Hungarian skirmishes along the old Ruthenian border reflects the same policy which Germany pursued with regard to Czech-Slovak differences during the last weeks before the occupation: namely, the policy of divide and rule, of encouraging conflict in order to have a pretext for intervention. Certainly, German military activities in Slovakia are being carried on with Hungary first and foremost in mind, and the speed with which they are being pushed shows that they are expected to be needed in the fairly near future.

14. Letter of April 3, 1939, from Consul General Linnell to the Chargé d'Affaires at Berlin concerning certain armed clashes that had occurred along the new Slovak-Hungarian border

The existing situation may be summed up as follows. About two weeks ago, just after the consolidation of their new position in Ruthenia proper, the Hungarian military forces began to advance in a westerly direction from the River Uh onto what the Slovaks regard as Slovak territory. (The Uh, called Ung in Hungarian, flows from the Polish frontier south through Užhorod into Hungary proper.) They were opposed only by weak formations of the Hlinka Guards (the Slovak defense organization) and units composed of Slovak soldiers who had been serving in the Czechoslovak army until the disintegration of the Republic and who had now been hastily reorganized into a "Slovak army." Infantry and artillery engagements took place and a number of casualties ensued. Since the Slovaks had a few planes from the military airports of the former Czechoslovak army, there was also a certain amount of aerial activity, which culminated in an attempt on the part of the Hungarians to bomb the military airport at Spisska Nova Ves (Neudorf on German maps), an important town on the main east-west railway line, some one hundred miles west of the Ruthenian frontier. This attack did little damage to the airport but caused the death of nearly a dozen civilians. Altogether the Hungarian troops penetrated a distance of some ten to twenty miles onto Slovak territory on the whole line from north to south, and have held their positions there up to the present time.

The Slovaks, of course, lost no time in taking diplomatic steps with a view to causing the Hungarians to withdraw. At the time the Hungarian advance began (which was apparently on March 22) the Slovak premier was concluding negotiations with the German government for the agreement placing Slovakia under the protection of the Reich. This agreement was apparently signed on March 23. It is quite probable that the Hungarian action was decided upon and undertaken on March 22 in the realization that the German guarantee of Slovakia's frontiers had not yet been signed and that the Germans would thus not be legally bound to demand that the Hungarians retire from whatever positions they might occupy during the following few hours.

The Slovaks at once protested to the Germans and demanded their intervention. While there is no record of the German reply, it is evident that the Germans refused to intervene and told the Slovaks to make up their differences through direct negotiations with Budapest.

As a result of the German attitude, a Slovak delegation went to Budapest. At first the conversations proceeded unfavorably. The Hungarians were apparently intransigent. Members of the Slovak delegation returned for instructions and even pleaded their case personally with higher German officials in Vienna or Bratislava, but to no avail. They were forced to return to Budapest and to announce that they would accept the Hungarian proposals as a basis for discussion. In view of this statement, it is thought likely that the line will finally be drawn approximately along the present position of the Hungarian troops, i.e., a line somewhere near the villages of Stakčin, Sobrance, and Pavlovce.

The position of the border between Slovakia and Ruthenia has been a subject of controversy for some time. According to the official Slovak press, this border was defined by the territorial commission of the Peace Conference at Paris in

1919 (First General Statute, Article II [a]; Confidential File No. 26.536/1919 of the Council of Ministers) as follows: ". . . the demarcation line between the Slovaks and the Ruthenians runs straight from the town of Čop to the northern part of the town of Užhorod in such a way that the railway remains in Slovakia and Užhorod in Subcarpathian Russia, and thence follows the River Uh to the Carpathians. All territory to the east of this line shall be considered as belonging to the autonomous Ruthenian territory."

It was evidently intended that some such delimitation should be adopted into the Czechoslovak constitution, for the Constitutional Charter of the Republic, introduced on February 29, 1920, provided (Art. 3, Par. 9) that "the law enacted by the Parliament defining the frontiers of Carpathian Russinia shall form part of the Constitutional Charter." Unfortunately, no such law ever was enacted, and the question, which after the founding of the Czechoslovak Republic became a purely internal one, was left without legal solution. For purposes of administration a line was adopted running in general somewhat west of the River Uh, in such a way as to include in Ruthenia most of the river valley itself. This line did not lie nearly as far west as the positions now occupied by the Hungarian troops. Moreover, the Slovaks contend that even the choice of this administrative boundary did not affect the question of the real boundary between the two provinces, and there is certainly a good deal of justice behind this contention. The Constitution had expressed the clear intention that the question of the true boundary was to be decided by act of Parliament, and the administrative authorities—who established the administrative boundary without parliamentary action—could scarcely have been competent to settle in this manner the permanent boundary between the two provinces. It is probably for this reason that the Czech military map makers continued throughout the duration of the Republic to show both lines:

the provincial boundary more or less as defined by the Peace Conference and the administrative boundary as determined for practical purposes by the Czech administrative authorities.

It has been stated several times in the foreign press that the Hungarian action was dictated by a desire to hold the railway line which follows the course of the River Uh and thus connects Hungary with Slovakia proper. This is probably true in a general sense, but the statement requires a little elucidation. The railway line follows the river bank very closely, running for the most part on the Slovak side but also in one section along the eastern shore. If the river were to constitute the boundary, the line would apparently be strategically indefensible for both parties. The advance of the Hungarian troops to points roughly fifteen miles west of the railway line is quite possibly dictated by the desire to command sufficient territory in that direction to eliminate the danger of the railway being covered by artillery fire from the heights along the western side of the river valley. While this is only one of three railway lines now connecting Hungary with Poland, its strategic importance is not to be minimized. All three lines are single-track and of small carrying capacity and all three would be urgently required for military operations in which the Poles and Hungarians were fighting as allies.

In view of this strategic importance which attaches to the Hungarian move, surprise has been expressed in many quarters over the passivity with which it has been witnessed by the Germans, whose frontiers are now the frontiers of Slovakia. No explanation of this phenomenon is available in Prague. It may be worth noting, however, that German military preparations in Slovakia have not revealed any particular interest in the territory affected by the recent Hungarian advance. The effect of the military clauses of the German-Slovak agreement was to make it possible for the

Reichswehr to control directly the important Žilina and Nemsova junctions and thus to command the five rail approaches to the Hungarian border on the south. No particular importance appears to have been attached to the maintenance of garrisons in the Prešov district, contiguous to the territory in which the Hungarians have now carried out their advance.

15. Letter of April 7, 1939, from Consul General Linnell to the Chargé d'Affaires at Berlin, concerning the arrival in Prague of the Reichsprotektor, Baron von Neurath

The efforts put forth by the Germans on April 5 to create an atmosphere of pomp and festivity as a setting for the arrival of the Reichsprotektor and the establishment of the new order were impressive. A program was drawn up which included a ceremonious greeting with a guard of honor at the station, a motorcar procession through the main streets, a formal welcome at the Palace by General von Brauchitsch, an exchange of visits between the Reichsprotektor and President Hacha (in which the latter paid the first call), a military parade on the Square of St. Wenceslas, a formal dinner, and a torchlight tattoo before the Palace in the evening. The day was declared a public holiday and the shops were required to close. House-owners were ordered to hang out flags: the swastika if they were Germans and the Czech national colors if they were Czechs.

Particular emphasis was placed on the reception of the Reichsprotektor at the station and his ride from the station to the Palace. The German colony were of course required to be on hand to the last man, and it seems that a few trainloads of people were even brought in from the Sudeten area for the occasion. The Czech school children were made to assemble in their school buildings (or, if the latter had been occupied by German troops, in the adjacent streets), whence they were marched to points along the route of the procession. Other Czech organizations, such as the Sokol, the fire department, the sharp-shooters association, and the Sea Scouts (for such, strange as it may seem, do exist in Bohemia) were also required to be represented by uniformed delegations. Even the members of the new Committee of the National Community,[1] which is now the nearest thing to a Czech parliament, were brought out in a body to greet the new potentate.

As far as the completion of the ceremonies depended on the efforts of the German military authorities, everything went off satisfactorily. It cannot be said, however, that the endeavor to enlist the participation of the Czech population in an exhibition of rejoicing was particularly successful. The measures of compulsion adopted by the authorities aroused real resentment. A number of houseowners elected to pay the six-hundred-crown fine rather than hang out their flags. The drafting of the school children was the cause of much bitter feeling, and many of the children were simply kept at home.

The ride of the Reichsprotektor from the station to the Palace made a particularly painful impression. The uniformed organizations sent only a handful of people apiece, and these appeared with an air which could scarcely have been grimmer were they being marched to their own slaughter. When the Reichsprotektor left the station there was a certain amount of cheering and waving of little swastika flags by the Germans who had been assembled in the immediate vicinity. By the time the motor cortege reached the top of the Square of St. Wenceslas, two blocks away, where the crowds were particularly thick, all was quiet except for a few feeble "heils" from some German schoolgirls. After that the cortege proceeded amid almost complete silence, save where the Czech members of the Committee of the National Community dutifully cried their "vlasti zdar." In many places, there were

[1] It has proved necessary to use this term, rather than "National Cooperation," as a translation of the name of President Hacha's new political party.

not even sufficient spectators to line the sidewalks along the route.

The same situation repeated itself later when the Reichsprotektor, still accompanied by his motorized guard of honor, proceeded to and from St. Wenceslas Square for the military parade. The sidewalks of the square were crowded throughout the parade, but no more than they are on any fine holiday morning; and a good half of the people preferred to stroll along in their wonted fashion rather than to join those who thronged the curb. The torchlight tattoo at night attracted no more than three or four hundred people, out of a city of a million, and most of those who attended were Germans.

The Germans presumably felt compelled to go through with this sort of program in order to maintain the fiction that Baron von Neurath was arriving in response to the spontaneous request of a Czech nation thirsty for order and protection after years of insecurity and misgovernment. The success which flags and drums and torchlights have had in stirring enthusiasm among their own people may even have misled them into the hope that the same effect could easily be achieved among the Czechs.

If so, their understanding of history is not as great as that which they would seem to claim through their countless public references to the days of the Holy Roman Empire. The differences between the Germans and the Czechs—although linguistic and psychological rather than racial—are too deep to be bridged by a few fanfares and a little bunting; and that the Germans, whether by misunderstanding or by design, should have chosen to flout this fact in so striking a manner is an omen of equal sadness for Czechs and Germans alike.

16. Letter of April 14, 1939, from Consul General Linnell to the Chargé d'Affaires at Berlin, commenting on the general situation in the Protectorate

For the moment, the processes of government here are obscure. Formally, the military authorities turned the civil power over to the Czech government upon the arrival of the Reichsprotektor, over a week ago. The Czech government has not been reorganized, however, and the Reichsprotektor, who left Prague immediately after his ceremonious entrance, has not yet returned and assumed his duties. Until the Czech government is reorganized and until Baron von Neurath is on hand to "supervise" it, the machinery of the Protectorate, as established by the Law of March 16, will not really begin to function. Meanwhile, administrative authority seems still to be exercised by the "chiefs of the civil administration" whom the military authorities had appointed for Bohemia and Moravia, respectively.

All this, however, is the merest detail. Whatever the machinery of government, German domination is complete, and that, for the average citizen of Bohemia or Moravia, is the main thing. The outward signs of Nazism are now almost all represented in the Prague scene, from infinite varieties of uniforms to the "Aryan shop" placards on the stores. Perhaps the only phenomenon of Nazi life which Prague has happily been spared is the sight of brutality against Jews in public places.

The Czech press, in particular, has been "gleichgeschaltet" in no uncertain way. Its columns, aside from the sports and business sections, are nine-tenths filled with material on foreign affairs provided by the Reich Propaganda Ministry. The few items which deal with the life of Bohemia and Moravia already have a depressingly familiar aspect to anyone who has ever browsed through the press of Europe's prewar empires in their most reactionary moments. The suburban travel at Easter time, changes in the Prague zoo, traffic accidents, anecdotes, and death notices: these are the stuff that local news is now composed of. The process has been so complete that a delegation of Czech journalists who came to see President Hacha felt themselves compelled to ask whether the President knew of any reason why their papers should continue to appear. They were told, however, that there were such reasons: that to close the papers down would annoy the Germans, and that Czech journalism would be needed to maintain the power of Czech culture during a period when such maintenance would require all possible support. Thus they returned to their jobs, to make attractive arrangements of the copious news copy received constantly from the busy minions of Dr. Goebbels, and to search daily for new editorial subjects sufficiently remote from politics to spare German feelings.

In the former task, they have thus far shown more good will than discrimination, and some of the editions of the Nazified Czech papers have been the cause of considerable amusement locally. One boulevard sheet appeared, some days after the occupation, with a front-page story (lifted from a Berlin paper) in which there were listed "fourteen lies of the democratic press." Lie No. 11 was that German troops would occupy Memel in a few days. This whole story was run immediately under the front-page leader, which announced, to the accompaniment of screaming headlines, that Memel had been occupied by the Germans. More recently, a local German paper which devoted four pages to abuse of the British for becoming alarmed over the fate of Poland, followed it up with a fifth-page story entitled: "Surprise Is Half the Victory. General Franco adopts the well-tried German methods of battle."

The favorite subject of conversation in Prague during these last two or three weeks has been the effect which firsthand contact with local conditions has produced on German troops who had been filled up before their arrival with tales of disorder and misery in Czechoslovakia. The obvious enjoyment and astonishment with which the German officers and men set about to consume Bohemian food and to purchase Bohemian goods has created a deep impression on everyone who has witnessed it. With the mark made legal tender at a conversation rate of ten crowns to one mark, Prague shops and restaurants have done a thriving business. Clothing stores have had to keep their doors closed for all except one or two hours a day, in order to cope with the demand; and people vie in the repetition of tales of the gargantuan exploits of German officers and men in the local restaurants and beer halls.

All this, however, has only been the outward—and more humorous—aspect of a much more serious development. The fact is that the Germans have been plundering the Protectorate behind the scenes in no uncertain way. Heavy orders have been placed by the Germans with many Czech industries, and no questions asked about price. Germany has over two million crowns mopped up from the population of the Sudeten area, and the fact that the placing of these crowns into circulation in the reduced territory of the Protectorate might be supposed to have an inflationary effect is not going to be much of a deterrent for persons accustomed to defying the laws of orthodox economics in the manipulation of the Reichsmark. There seems, furthermore, to be little doubt that considerable quantities of foodstuffs and other supplies have been removed directly from Prague warehouses and simply trucked off to the Reich. The first signs of food shortage have already made their appearance in a scarcity of eggs and certain kinds of meat on the Prague market.

A special piquancy has been given to this situation through

the activities in Prague of the so-called "Bayrischer Hilfszug." No sooner was the occupation completed than the Germans ostentatiously rushed to Prague a caravan of trucks, apparently supplied by the Bavarian section of the Winterhilfe organization. The aim of this outfit was apparently to demonstrate German concern for the well-being of the Czechs by feeding the starving elements of the population until the new order could provide work and bread for everyone. Its staff proceeded to establish distribution points at various places in the city and announced that free meals would be issued at a fixed hour. The Czech welfare authorities, who had been feeding a certain number of refugees from the Sudeten areas, philosophically sent their charges over to the Bayrischer Hilfszug and sold to the latter, according to local reports, the supplies which they themselves would otherwise have given to the refugees. Photographers from the Reich went out daily to record for their papers the generosity of the German authorities. A marked lack of children in the bread lines was easily remedied by the photographers, who took to asking Czech children to demonstrate how they said their prayers, and then sent off photographs showing the little tots down on their knees with uplifted arms, begging their deliverers for bread. After a week or so, however, the contrast between the activities of the Bayrischer Hilfszug and the sight of German troops stuffing themselves in the Prague restaurants became the subject of too much comment locally, and the Hilfszug retired to Bavaria with all the self-satisfaction of the fly in the Russian fable who rode on the oxen's nose all day and greeted the villagers in the evening with the announcement: "We've been ploughing."

The Czechs themselves are rapidly reverting in the face of German domination to the psychological attitude with which they countered Austrian rule for so many years. Toward their rulers they show—like the "brave soldier Švejk" of Czech literary fame—a baffling willingness to comply with any and all demands and an equally baffling ability to execute them in such a way that the effect is quite different from that contemplated by those who did the commanding. Among themselves and with their friends, they treat the whole situation with that dry, ironic humor to which their language so easily lends itself. But at heart they are very bitter indeed and the effects of this bitterness are often evident. A news shot of Prime Minister Beran greeting the Reichsprotektor was jeered and hissed in the local cinemas. The military commander of the Moravska-Ostrava (Mährisch-Ostrau) district found it necessary to forbid the "increasing" wearing of badges bearing the inscriptions "We will not surrender" and "Beneš is not asleep." There can be no doubt of the existence of clandestine political groups, both on the right and on the left.

This bitterness will have little effect for the time being. No one dreams of offering any serious challenge to German political control at the moment. But just as the Czechs waited for the World War to wrest their freedom from the Austrian Empire, so now they place their hopes again on war, as the development which will bring the restoration of their political freedom. There is probably no country in Europe where war—and war at the earliest possible date—is so universally desired as in the Protectorate of Bohemia and Moravia. One hears this sentiment expressed daily on every hand. In the event of an unsuccessful war at any time during the next few years, the Germans will probably find that the Czech spirit of independence, despite the subjection of the people to all the propaganda methods of the modern totalitarian state, has shown surprising powers of endurance.

17. Excerpts from two memoranda of April 14, 1939, for the Consul General, summing up certain aspects of the constitutional and juridical situation prevailing in the Historic Provinces and Slovakia

The Protectorate was supposed, according to the press, to go into effect on April 5 upon the arrival in Prague of the Reichsprotektor, Baron von Neurath. Actually, Baron von Neurath left town again immediately after his official welcome without having taken over the executive power from the military officials. The executive power is consequently still being exercised by the commanding generals in Bohemia and Moravia, respectively, acting on the authority of the Commander in Chief of the Reichswehr. These two generals have each appointed "chiefs of the civil administration" to act in their behalf on civil matters, but the Chief of the Civil Administration in Prague (still theoretically Herr Henlein) is very little in evidence.

Decrees are now being issued in some instances by the military authorities themselves, in others by the chiefs of the civil administration, and in still others by the Czech government. In the latter case, it is stated in the decrees that they are issued by the government "with the consent of the holders of the executive power."

The Department will recall that under the terms of the Protectorate, the administration was to be in the hands of the

Czech government, acting under the supervision of the Reichsprotektor. It is presumed, consequently, that the officials will be mostly Czechs.

The position of Slovakia is based on three documents: (1) Law number 1 of March 16 of the Slovak government, proclaiming Slovakia an independent state, (2) Chancellor Hitler's telegram of March 16 to the Slovak President, Mgr. Tiso, assuming the protection of the Slovak state, and (3) the treaty concluded at Berlin on March 23 between Slovakia and the Reich regulating the questions which arose through the placing of Slovakia under the protection of the Reich.

The main difference between the status of Slovakia and that of Bohemia and Moravia is that in Slovakia no Reichsprotektor's office has been established and the Slovak government is, in the German view, still sovereign within the limits prescribed by treaty. It has now been recognized as an independent state by Germany, Poland, Hungary, Italy, and the Vatican. Nevertheless, the servitudes which the Slovak government has accepted in the treaty with the Reich are as far-reaching as those usually imposed upon an outright Protectorate. It is a question, consequently, of how far a state may go in the acceptance of servitudes in favor of a neighboring state and still retain its claim to an independent status.

The delay in the putting into force of the machinery of the Protectorate is causing considerable speculation and has led to suspicion that changes in German plans with regard to Bohemia and Moravia may be under consideration. It is stated in the local German press that von Neurath, who left town immediately after his official welcome, will return sometime during the next few days "for a protracted stay" and that Hitler's birthday will mark the conversion of the present provisional conditions into a permanent status.

It may be not without significance in this respect that Czech fascist circles are still active and that a new fascist party has sprung up which—in contrast to the Gajda group

—is rumored to command considerable confidence in German circles.

The Beran cabinet is meeting today, presumably for the last time. A new government is expected to be formed within the next three or four days, composed mostly of persons hitherto little known in Czech politics.

18. Letter of April 17, 1939, from Consul General Linnell to the Chargé d'Affaires at Berlin, concerning the problem of a Slovak currency

One of the first and most urgent problems to confront the Slovak government after the breakup of the Republic was that of the currency to be used by the new state. There was at first an obvious tendency among the Slovak leaders (based no doubt on considerations of prestige) to establish an entirely new unit of currency. A number of names for this unit were even publicly suggested and discussed. In the end, however, more practical considerations seem to have prevailed, and the Slovak government has now decided on a course which is equivalent in effect to the retention of the existing crown.

Whereas there was in the past a single Czechoslovak crown, there will now be, for the immediate future at any rate, a Czech crown and a Slovak crown, with a parity of one to one. The old bank notes are simply to be stamped over in order to obtain validity as Slovak currency. The coin will remain in circulation, with the exception of one small unit (the 25 heller piece) which will be withdrawn.

The Slovak government, however, has come to the conclusion that the amount of coin in circulation is too small, and intends to add an additional 200,000,000 to the existing 300,-000,000 crowns of circulating coin. Since the total currency circulation in Slovakia has hitherto been only about 1,500,-000,000 crowns, and probably corresponded pretty closely to the normal requirements of a primitive peasant population, the additional issuance of 200,000,000 crowns of small change may be expected to have a certain inflationary effect. The minting of coin for the Czechoslovak Republic has heretofore been carried out in Slovakia, whereas bank notes were printed in Prague. It is not difficult to see, consequently, why the Slovak government should have chosen the minting of small change as the most convenient means of boosting revenues.

A Slovak national bank has now been established which will serve as a bank of issue. Its capitalization is being taken care of by a highly ingenious arrangement, whereby the bank is to have a capital of 100,000,000 crowns, in the form of shares (presumably held by the government) bearing an interest rate of not more than six percent, but will be obliged to make loans without interest to the government up to a total amount of 100,000,000 crowns. It looks, consequently, as though the bank's capital would be mostly on paper. As security for the bank notes which it issued, the bank is to hold only certain amounts of foreign currencies which can be freely exchanged for gold. There has—perhaps wisely—been no attempt to establish any fixed percentage of coverage, nor to explain where the Slovak national bank intends to acquire such foreign exchange holdings.

The bank has a governor, a vice-governor, and a board of directors with eight members. The number of Slovaks who have any knowledge of foreign banking and of currency issuance is very small and the rumored activities of the higher officials of the Slovak national bank have occasioned considerable amusement in Prague business circles.

It might be added that the issuance of the added 200,000,-000 crowns of small change should be a considerable help in balancing the regular Slovak budget for the current year. The deficit on the regular provincial Slovak budget, before the breakup of the Republic, was estimated at roughly 300,-

000,000 crowns. The deficits on the special budgets for public works and for enterprises of the state were, to be sure, far higher. An added 200,000,000 crowns, however, ought to take care of the regular administrative expenses of the state for several months, and this, after all, is the most urgent requirement.

19. Letter of April 18, 1939, from Consul General Linnell to the Chargé d'Affaires at Berlin, concerning conditions in Slovakia

Conditions in Slovakia seem now to have quieted down considerably. The Hungarian border question has been settled for the immediate present. The civil administration, after being purged of many Czech officials, is functioning after a fashion with the assistance of the Hlinka Guards. The country is under German military occupation, and German influence over the policies and actions of the Slovak government—an influence less direct but little less effective than in Bohemia and Moravia—has already become routine.

A great many problems, however, will now have to be faced before the position of Slovakia can attain anything resembling stability. A number of these problems are the direct result of the breakup of the Czechoslovak Republic and have international connotations. What proportion of the liabilities of the Czechoslovak Republic are to be assumed by Slovakia? To what portion of the property of the Czechoslovak state has Slovakia a claim? Who is to make up the huge budget deficit of the Slovak government, which was formerly taken care of by the central budget of the Republic? How are the currency and trade systems of Slovakia to be tallied with those of surrounding countries, particularly those of Germany and of the Protectorate of Bohemia and Moravia?

With the exception of the question of the Slovak currency, which has already been settled in principle and which was the subject of a separate letter which went forward yesterday, all these questions are being discussed at present in Berlin or Vienna, in mixed German-Slovak commissions.

Prague is excluded from the conversations entirely, the interests of Bohemia and Moravia being "protected"—whatever that may mean in the given instance—by the government of the Reich. Actually, the Slovak representatives in these commissions are present rather in the capacity of experts than of bargaining partners, for the final decision rests in most cases with the Germans themselves.

With regard to internal policies, the Slovak leaders are being permitted to struggle along for the moment without much direct tutelage from the German side. Their views of life are, after all, copied so extensively from those of the German National Socialists, that the latter can safely afford to give them a long leash—at the outset, in any case—in the consolidation of their rule.

It is expected that around the end of this month the Slovak Parliament will again be assembled and its approval solicited for a number of measures. One of these may well be a constitutional nature. The constitutional basis of the present government is very slim, consisting only of a brief measure of the Slovak Parliament declaring the country's independence; and the government leaders, who would scarcely command the support of a majority of the population in a free election, seem to feel the need of something which would bolster the system they have established.

Another law may well affect the reorganization of the Hlinka People's Party into an exclusive, state party. This, to be sure, it already is, in a rough sort of way, but many details remain to be worked out and the leaders desire that the party's position should become firmly anchored in the framework of the state by appropriate legislation.

A third subject for the consideration of the Slovak Parliament may well be that of land reform. Very few of the actual or potential supporters of the present Slovak regime are large landowners. The Slovak leaders would consequently stand little to lose and possibly something to gain by expropriating real estate from the larger landowners—many of whom, whatever passports they hold, are Czechs or other "foreigners" in the Slovak view—and distributing it to small proprietors who have supported them in the past or might be inclined to do so in return for a share of the loot.

Finally, the Slovak Parliament will be faced again with the necessity of passing some sort of legislation on the status of Jews in Slovakia. This question has been bothering the Slovak leaders ever since their seizure of local power last fall, after the Munich Agreement. A rousing anti-Semitism has always been one of the leading planks in their party platform and has proved its worth as a means of enlisting the support of certain elements in the population. It has, however, placed the regime in the position of being forced to produce, sooner or later, something in the nature of a Slovak Nuremberg law, and this task has proved more diffi-cult than the leaders had supposed. During the fall and the winter the Czechs, who had a certain control through the pursestrings, stood in the way. Now the Czechs are elimi-nated, but other difficulties still exist. The Roman Catholic Church, the influence of which in Slovakia is second only to that of the Germans, feels compelled to insist on the ob-servance of a certain restraint on the part of the government with respect to the Church's numerous recent converts from Judaism. And too savage an attack on the economic life of the Jewish community may well have unfavorable repercus-sions on the general economic life of the country, which is al-ready none too thriving a plant. Thus the government's plans for this anti-Semitic legislation, which will presumably be submitted to Parliament at the end of this month, are already taking on a form which is probably not one hundred percent satisfactory to Germany.

The bill in its present stage envisages the relegation of Jews, together with thieves, criminals, swindlers, insane people, and alcoholics, to a so-called "second-category" of citizenship, the members of which will be called "subjects" rather than "citizens" and will not be permitted to serve in the army, to take any part in public life, or to be members of the state political party or of social or cultural societies. It also contains provisions for the aryanization of Jewish enterprises. In discussing the bill, however, the Slovak propaganda chief, Mr. Mach, recently made the surprising statement that there were some decent Jews among the lot and that these would not have to fear for their bread and their freedom in the Slovak state. He also stated that the government would place no obstacle in the path of Jews who wished to leave the country.

On one question of internal policy a fairly sharp conflict has arisen between the Slovaks and the Germans. This is the question of the German minority in Slovakia. Not only has the Slovak government shown a tendency to give all available jobs to Slovaks rather than Germans, but the Slovak leaders have also taken the position that both the Hungarian and German minority organizations must be subordinated to the single Slovak national party which is to be established. Mr. Mach, whose faults do not include a lack of courage, has stated that the German minority leaders must in any case take orders from the highest Slovak party authorities if not from the local Slovak party leaders. The official German press in Bratislava has let it be known that the Germans consider this demand as quite intolerable and in violation of the assurance given by Tiso with respect to the treatment of the German minority.

While it is not to be expected that this quarrel will get much farther, its very existence is indicative of the extent to which the Slovaks have been encouraged to think that they are going to be permitted to run their own show, internally. This impression, combined with a certain unpredictableness of Slovak character, may cause the Germans more than one surprise in the coming months.

20. Letter of April 21, 1939, from Consul General Linnell to the Chargé d'Affaires at Berlin, concerning the celebration of Hitler's birthday in Prague

I should like to report that the celebration of Herr Hitler's birthday passed off in Prague quietly and without incidents, but also, as in the case of the arrival of the Reichsprotektor, with a notable lack of enthusiasm on the part of the Czech population.

It seems that there was a certain amount of hesitation on the German part as to whether the Czech population should be asked to participate at all in the festivities. It was finally decided, probably as a result of the experience of April 5 (the day of the Reichsprotektor's arrival) that while the day would be a legal holiday and all official buildings would be closed and decorated with both German and Czech flags, the participation of the Czech population in the festivities should be made largely voluntary.

The result was that the atmosphere differed very little from that of any normal Sunday or holiday. The houses in the main streets were almost all flagged, apparently as a result of particular efforts on the part of the police. Off the main streets, however, there was very little attempt at decorations; except for the government buildings not one house in ten showed a flag. A military parade was held in the Masaryk Stadium at 11 o'clock. No motorized equipment was shown. Approximately 5,000 troops, who were formed on the field prior to the beginning of the ceremony, marched past the reviewing officers, General von Schwedler, Commander of the Fourth

Division in Prague, and General Friderici, representative of the Wehrmacht in the Protectorate. Of these troops roughly 4,000 belonged to the Reichswehr and the remaining 1,000 men comprised the S.S. Standarte Germania, which has been assigned as guard of honor for the Reichsprotektor. Some fifty planes were flown across, of which about one-half were two-motor bombers and the remainder fast-pursuit planes. The local German residents were present in force and their numbers were probably supplemented by thousands of others who have congregated here in the last weeks. A sprinkling of Czechs was interspersed in the crowd. Altogether, however, the attendance was not enough to fill the tribune along one side of the Masaryk Stadium and the other three sides were empty.

21. Report, written about April 26-27, 1939, on conditions in the Moravska-Ostrava district

Things seem to be very quiet just at present around Moravska-Ostrava. Nearly all the German troops have left. They have apparently returned to Silesia. I suspect that the remaining garrison consists mostly of an air-force detachment which will doubtless be kept there indefinitely to operate the local airport. The commanding general of that district has been absent from his post most of the time during the last two weeks (apparently shooting in Silesia) and the parade in honor of Hitler's birthday was taken by a lieutenant of the air force, who seemed to be the ranking officer in town on that day.

The same quiet prevails on the Polish side. Only the normal garrisons are being maintained there. According to local inhabitants, no attempt has been made to fortify the Teschen district. It is my impression that the Poles do not intend to attempt any serious defense of this district in the event of war with Germany, but will probably fall back on the positions which they held and presumably fortified before Munich, when the Teschen district was still part of Czechoslovakia.

Thus there were no signs on either side of any preparations for early hostilities.

As far as I could ascertain, there have been no frontier incidents in the usual sense along that border, since the German occupation of Moravska-Ostrava. But one bit of shooting did—I am told—take place there and it is probably this which accounts for the wounded German soldiers whose presence in Olomouc and Prague hospitals was so often reported. It seems that the Germans asked for permission to move two trainloads of troops through Oderberg (Bohumin) across the Teschen district to Čadca, on the Polish-Slovak frontier, i.e., across the section of railway on Polish territory which the Germans themselves covet. The Poles granted permission after obtaining assurances from the Germans that the trains would not halt on the way and that there would be no debarkation of German troops on Polish territory. They placed no great confidence, however, in the sincerity of these assurances, and took measures of precaution to prevent these troops from establishing themselves along the route. When the movement took place, the Germans did attempt to unload their troops (this was probably right at the railway junction of Oderberg) and the Poles, who were ready for them, apparently opened fire and forced them to move on in a hurry.

There can be no doubt, incidentally, of the German desire to get hold of this bit of railway. It is a section of the main connection between Berlin and Budapest, and the only section which is not really in German or Hungarian hands. It is the most convenient connection between Silesia and the German fortified zone in Slovakia. The railway station at Oderberg, only three or four miles from the German frontier, is one of the most important junctions in the vicinity, handling not only the Berlin-Budapest and Berlin-Istanbul trains but also trains between Warsaw on the one hand and Budapest, Prague, and Vienna, on the other. The Poles take the position that by building some twenty miles of new line in the Javorina mountains, the Germans could easily provide a substitute route, but I am afraid that this suggestion is a little overoptimistic from both the technical and the political standpoint.

It is interesting to note that Moravska-Ostrava, despite

the relative scarcity of German troops, makes much more the impression of a Nazi city than do Prague and the other cities of the interior of Bohemia. The official German attitude toward the border towns with a sizeable percentage of Germans (in Moravska-Ostrava it is scarcely more than 20 percent, but that seems to be enough) is apparently different from the attitude toward the purely Czech communities. In the latter there is no tendency at present to try to Germanize the Czechs. In the border communities, however, where nationality lines are vague and can be determined if at all only by language, the Germans seem to want to give the whole community a German National Socialist imprint. This was true of the communities in the Sudeten area. It is also true at present of Brno, Plzen, Olomouc, etc. Czechs in these communities, in contrast to the people in Prague, feel that if they are to please the authorities they must profess themselves to German culture and to the Nazi ideology.

The result is that in Moravska-Ostrava the fascist greeting and the ubiquitous "Heil Hitler" are used even by the Czech waiters in the hotels. Pictures of the Führer hang in the public places. Inhabitants are not encouraged to fly Czech flags. Whatever its racial composition may really be, the city is expected to behave like a German community.

This is particularly evident in the attitude toward the Jews. Expropriation of Jewish property has gone very far. The Gestapo is housed in the villa of the wealthiest Jewish merchant. Jews are hounded out of all public places. One doctor, I am told, has attended thirty-three Jewish suicides since the occupation.

It should be added, however, that this complete Nazification of Moravska-Ostrava is not solely the product of the recent occupation. There are many indications that the district was pretty well sold out to the Germans long before March 14. This is not surprising. It is an extremely drab industrial district with a dispirited and poverty-stricken proletariat, among whom the lines of nationality are unusually vague, even for Central Europe. There are many people who really cannot tell what their nationality is. Venality is almost universal, and there is little that cannot be obtained by a combination of bribery and intimidation. Many of the wealthier industrialists are Germans, and they were exerting pressure on their workmen in the direction of Germanization long before the occupation.

As a result of all this, a great deal of hedging in behalf of Germany took place during the months which followed Munich. The local branch of the Czech secret police was actually subordinated to the Gestapo as early as January. Conversions to German nationality and to Nazi ideology were thick and fast. It became difficult to tell where Czech left off and German began. When the German troops finally entered the city (which was in the early evening of March 14, before President Hacha had even arrived in Berlin), no one was much surprised. The real occupation had begun long before. The troops were just a finishing touch.

22. Report, written about May 1, 1939, on conditions in Slovakia

The situation which prevailed in Slovakia during the winter was outlined in a report which went forward on January 14, 1939.[1]

Despite the sensational character of subsequent events, few words are needed to bring this report up to date. What has happened is simply that the Germans, by exploiting the violently anti-Czech sentiments of the radical wing of the Hlinka People's Party, have now broken up the Czechoslovak Republic, made Slovakia a nominally independent state under German protection, and eliminated the last vestiges of Prague's influence in the province. Character and policies of the Slovak leaders have remained unchanged. German influence continues to be paramount.

Personally, I see little that is obscure about the present position of Slovakia. It is just one more instance of that time-honored and convenient instrument of imperialism: the puppet state. In many ways its position vis-à-vis Germany is parallel to that of Outer Mongolia vis-à-vis the Soviet Union. It is garrisoned in certain districts by German troops, but is allowed to maintain a local militia in the form of the Slovak remnants of the Czechoslovak army. Its foreign policy is subordinated by open agreement to that of the Reich. In internal matters, it has exactly the same independence as a dog on a leash. As long as the dog trots quietly and cheerfully at his master's side—and in the same direction—he is quite free; if he starts out on any tangents of his own, he feels the pull at once. The Slovak leaders, to be sure, cannot resist an occasional tangent, and there will doubtless have to be frequent short tugs of the leash. But in general they

[1] See document No. 4, above.

are filled with an honest intention of proceeding in the same direction as the master and of remaining fairly close to his heels. And as long as this condition prevails, it may be expected that the association will remain reasonably successful.

The immediate future of Slovakia depends not on what happens within the province itself but on the development of high politics in Europe.

If there is a general war, or an immediate prospect of one, the chances are that the Slovak regime will prove too inefficient and undependable to be of use to the Germans and will have to give way to a more direct form of German control.

It seems to be the consensus of well-informed opinion in Bratislava that barring the eventuality of war the present arrangement will be maintained at least until German differences with Poland have been settled (for the immediate future) to Germany's satisfaction and until Germany feels that her control of Hungary is entirely secure. In the event that these conditions should be fulfilled, Germany would probably be willing to hand over the portion of the province east of the River Vah to Hungary. A Hungarian government which had been forced to accept an open and complete German domination would doubtless need something to bolster its prestige with its own population. If its capitulation before Germany even involved the abandonment of long-standing territorial claims against other neighbors, its need for some sort of political compensation would be particularly great. In these circumstances it would only be the natural thing to reward Hungary with a province which was once under the crown of St. Stephen and which, in the long run, can be only a political and financial burden to Germany. This thought is in everybody's mind, in Bratislava, and there are even some who feel that Hungary made a mistake in not taking the entire province, up to the River Vah, immediately after March 13.

In case Slovakia were to be given to Hungary, the Germans would probably incorporate either into the Reich proper or into the Protectorate of Bohemia and Moravia the narrow strip of territory west of the Vah in which, according to the terms of the German-Slovak Treaty of March 23, they have the right to maintain garrisons and to build fortifications. Since the translation of this Treaty which appeared in the *New York Times* was inaccurate and highly misleading, . . . I am attaching . . . a translation of the document as it was published in the local press, together with . . . a small outline map on which there is marked out in blue pencil the zone described in Article 2, where the Germans may have garrisons and fortifications.[2] As far as I have been able to learn, the Germans have no garrisons outside this zone at the present time. Žilina and Malacky seem to be the chief centers of their military activity, and I think it probable that military establishments in those two districts are subordinated to different commands: those in Žilina to the higher military authorities in Silesia and those in Malacky to the authorities in Vienna.

For the time being, the Germans are keeping both Slovakia and Hungary in the traces by playing them off against each other without mercy. There is little doubt that the Hungarian invasion of eastern Slovakia took place with the acquiescence —if not the encouragement—of the Germans. The German and Hungarian minorities in Slovakia often work hand in hand against the Slovak government. On the other hand, Slovak revisionist propaganda continues, obviously with German approval. Observers in Bratislava point out that the German and Slovak minorities in Hungary, numbering at least a million people, are now both in German hands and can both be used as weapons against Hungary.

Part of this duality of German policy may be attributed to divergences of opinion and authority within the Reich. People

[2] The translation of the Treaty is included here. The map, which may be found in the National Archives, is omitted.

in Bratislava are convinced that there is a cleavage of policy and a certain amount of jealousy between the party authorities in Berlin and in Vienna. The Vienna leaders, conscious that pan-Germanism was originally an Austrian and Sudeten-German movement, are said to have a proprietary attitude with regard to plans for German expansion in Central Europe, to feel that they are the heirs to Austrian tradition and experience in handling the non-Germanic races, to look with contempt on the attempts of the Prussians to map out policy in the southeastern area, and to be inclined to take an independent line wherever possible. Hence, according to this explanation, the spectacular role played by Vienna in the final breakup of Czechoslovakia.

It is agreed, however, that if such divergences do indeed exist, Herr Hitler and his highest advisors have shown a marked ability for turning them to good account. Local Nazi leaders—it is felt in Bratislava—are given a long rope. If they are unsuccessful, they hang themselves on it; if they succeed, the Reich takes the credit. Thus there are those who fear that even if certain contradictions of German policy toward Slovakia are the result of inner-German differences, it will be Slovakia and Hungary rather than the Germans themselves who will suffer for it in the end.

While the internal policies of the present Slovak leaders—policies which have thus far been manifested more in words than in deeds—probably command the approval of most of the population, I believe that the majority of the Slovak people have misgivings about their present international position. Few of them, except the Protestants, are pro-Czech, but there is a general dim realization that their leaders have burned too many bridges behind them and that they themselves are not apt to fare as well for many years to come as they did before the breakup of the Republic. This realization has doubtless also begun to dawn in the minds of some of the leaders as well. But the latter have gone too far to turn back. They stand committed to what they have done and they have no other course but to keep up their courage and play the game with the Germans.

The misgivings of the population have naturally strengthened the opposition which the Slovak leaders have to face among their own people. This opposition falls into three groups.

There are in the first place the Protestants. Many of these belong to the Czechoslovak Church, an organization which severed connections with Rome, which has endeavored to contribute to Czechoslovak unity through its religious work, and which is hated on both counts by the Slovak Catholics. Most of the Protestants have felt themselves discriminated against in Slovakia and well-treated by the Czechs. They were consequently loyal to the Republic and always opposed the Hlinka autonomy movement which is the foundation of the present Slovak government.

A second opposition group, which is only now arising, is made up of those nationalist Slovaks who are followers of Hlinka and fought for autonomy but who feel that the present government has sold out too far to the Germans. This group will probably center around the popular young Slovak leader, Sidor, who tried to act as a brake on the independence movement in March, incurred German ire, and has now been eliminated from the government. Sidor—despite his reputation for being bought up by the Poles—is apparently a very patriotic Slovak at heart and has a devoted following in the Hlinka People's Party. There has recently been extensive purging of the officers of the Hlinka Guard, and many of the purged or dissatisfied guardsmen will probably flock to his standard. His opposition, however, will be more in the nature of an inner-party faction than a movement designed to overthrow the regime.

The widespread communist sentiment in eastern Slovakia is a bird of a different color. In former circumstances, it would have had little chances for success. Eastern Slovakia is not an industrialized region and normally offers barren soil for Marxism. The events of the last year, however, have had some strange effects, and one of them has been an upsurge of communist sentiment among many people—not only in eastern Slovakia but throughout the former territory of the Republic—who have no interest in communist theory but feel that communism with its Russian backing is the only possible weapon against Germany. The faith of these people in Russia is only strengthened by their ignorance; and there is no one to explain to them that they are looking to one form of Bolshevism to rescue them from another. Their strength lies in their capable leadership and in the guidance and financial support which Moscow is able to give them at any time. Of all the groups they will probably present the most difficult problem for the Gestapo.

As long as the Germans sit tight in the saddle, none of these opposition groups is apt to start any trouble. But if there are ever any signs that German support of the present Slovak regime is weakening, they might all forthwith become forces to be reckoned with.

ANNEX TO NO. 22

SOURCE: PRAGER TAGBLATT, March 24, 1939 (DNB report from Berlin)

(Translation)

In compliance with the request of the Slovak government to the Führer that he undertake the protection of the Slovak State, the following treaty was concluded at the Foreign Office in Berlin on March 23, 1939:

Having placed the Slovak state under the protection of the German Reich, the German government and the Slovak government have agreed to regulate the questions arising therefrom through a treaty. To this end the undersigned plenipotentiary representatives of the two governments have agreed upon the following points:

ARTICLE 1

The German Reich undertakes the protection of the political independence of the Slovak state and the integrity of its territory.

ARTICLE 2

In order to make effective the protection undertaken by the Reich, the German armed force shall be authorized at all times to erect military facilities within a zone bordered on the west by the frontier of the Slovak state and on the east by the general line of the eastern slopes of the Little Carpathians, the White Carpathians, and the Javornik Mountains, and to keep them garrisoned at whatever strength may be deemed necessary. The Slovak government will see to it that the land necessary for these facilities is placed at the disposal of the German armed force. Furthermore, the Slovak government will give its consent to such arrangements as are necessary to assure the duty-free provisioning of the German troops and the duty-free delivery of the facilities from the Reich.

The military rights of sovereignty within the zone outlined in Article 1 shall be exercised by the German armed force.

German citizens who, on the basis of private contracts, may be engaged in the erection of facilities within the mentioned zone shall be subject to German jurisdiction.

ARTICLE 3

The Slovak government will organize its own military forces in close collaboration with the German armed force.

ARTICLE 4

In accordance with the protection relationship agreed upon, the Slovak government will always conduct its foreign policy in close agreement with the German government.

ARTICLE 5

The present treaty shall become operative immediately and shall remain in force for a period of 25 years. The two governments will inform each other in good time before the end of this period concerning an extension of the validity of the treaty.

In witness whereof, the respective plenipotentiary representatives have signed this treaty in duplicate.

Vienna, this 18th day of March 1939
Berlin, this 23rd day of March 1939

For the German government: VON RIBBENTROP
For the Slovak government: TISO
TUKA
DURČANSKY

23. Letter of May 4, 1939, from Consul General Linnell to the Chargé d'Affaires at Berlin, concerning the appointment of the new government of the Protectorate of Bohemia and Moravia

I am enclosing herewith a sheet setting forth the composition of the new government of the Protectorate of Bohemia and Moravia which was appointed by President Hacha on April 27, 1939.

This is in reality the Protectorate's first government. The last government actually resigned on March 13, although this fact was kept secret at the time. President Hacha accepted the resignation but requested the members of the government to continue to act in an interim capacity until a new government might be formed. Under the terms of the Law of March 16, 1939, appointments to position on the cabinet of the Protectorate require the confirmation of the Reichsprotektor. Since the machinery of the Protectorate, however, did not go into effect until April 16, no progress could be made toward the appointment of a new government before that date.

The outstanding characteristic of the new government is that it is merely an expurgated edition of the last one. It does not contain a single man who was not likewise a member of the last Beran government. Beran himself has been eliminated and his place taken by General Eliáš, heretofore Minister of Communications. The latter Ministry has been taken over by Dr. Havelka, who was minister without portfolio in the last government. Dr. Havelka, whose activities in the government prior to March 15 were somewhat nebulous, seems to have been distinctly persona grata to the Germans who came to Prague after the occupation. This may account for his having been given a portfolio which—even in the government of the Protectorate—has considerable importance in German eyes. The two portfolios of Defense and of Foreign Affairs have been abolished altogether, since the government of the Protectorate is not to concern itself with these matters at all. General Syrový has simply retired. Dr. Chvalkovsky is going as Czech Minister to Berlin, where his position will presumably be roughly analogous to that of the ministers whom the constituent German states, such as Bavaria, formerly maintained in Berlin. In addition to these changes, Dr. Fischer, former Minister of the Interior, has now also been eliminated and that Ministry placed for the time being directly under the new Prime Minister. Otherwise the last Beran government has simply been retained.

In gauging the significance of this decision, it must be borne in mind that for some time prior to the appointment of this government strenuous efforts were being made by President Hacha and people connected with him to form a new and comprehensive political party. This party, to be called the "National Community," was to be organized along the lines of the National Socialist Worker's Party of Germany. This was apparently being done at German insistence, and the Germans had given their support to the National Community movement against the Czech fascists, who were its only serious competitors. One of the aims which was being pursued in this work of political organization had been the elimination of the old party groups and differences and consequently of persons who had been prominently identified with Czech politics in the past. A national committee, set up to head the new movement, was selected almost exclusively from persons hitherto unknown in Czech politics. It was assumed that the same principle would be observed in the appointment of a new government, and that the new cabinet ministers would be drawn at least in part from persons active in the National Community movement.

Least of all did anyone suspect that any number of the former cabinet members would be retained. The resignations of some of them were reported to be demanded by the Germans long before the occupation. Šadek and Čipera, in particular, were generally considered to be in ill-repute with the Germans, on account of their alleged membership in Masonic lodges and for other reasons as well. Čipera is a high official of the Bat'a concern, for which the Germans have no liking, and it has been reported through private channels that his apartment in Zlin was recently subjected to a search at the hands of the Gestapo.

For these reasons, it will be understood that the news of the composition of the new government, as reported in my telegram of April 28, was received with astonishment by the public of the Protectorate, and that few can believe that this government is intended to last for any length of time. But the question at once presents itself: why should a temporary government have been appointed rather than a body which could be expected to serve for a long term and which could thus give to conditions in the Protectorate that stability which is so conspicuously lacking and which the Germans have more reason than anyone else to wish to see introduced without delay?

The answer to this question is guesswork. But the hypothesis which unfortunately has the most to commend it is that Berlin intends at an early date to abandon or modify the system of the Protectorate, as outlined in the Law of March 16, in favor of some more direct method of governing the Czech people. The character of the new government is not the only evidence in this direction. Rumors to this effect, purporting to have originated with high-placed persons, have not been lacking. The office of the Reichsprotektor, furthermore, has been rapidly growing into dimensions far exceeding those indicated by the functions assigned to it through the terms of the Protectorate. It already bears a suspicious resemblance to something designed as the seat of all public administration in the Historic Provinces. A cryptic press notice concerning a reorganization of the administrative apparatus in Moravia entirely ignored the autonomous government at Prague, to which the administrative apparatus was presumably to be immediately subjected, and spoke only of the direct responsibility of the administrative authorities to the office of the Reichsprotektor. Despite the nominal entrance into effect of the Protectorate, there has been noted no tendency to do away with the special German commissars who have been wielding all the real power in the Czech offices since the occupation. Finally, one can again discern in the official German pronouncements certain veiled threats ominously similar to those which were being made in February and March to the effect that the tempo of the "reorganization" of Czech life must be accelerated, and that the future of the Czech people will depend on the speed and tact with which they accept the conciliatory hand of Germany, that the time at their disposal to effect this adjustment is not unlimited, etc., etc. In introducing his government to the Reichsprotektor, General Eliáš acknowledged that: "My government is confronted with unusually responsible tasks. The successful completion of these tasks is a matter of life and death for the Czech people." Baron von Neurath's answer was singularly noncommittal.

There could be several reasons for a waning of German enthusiasm for the Protectorate idea. It is understood that there is considerable pressure from the Goering side to expedite the coordination of Czech industry into the German Four-Year Plan system. The mere existence of a Czech government as a channel for legislation might—however servile its members—complicate and delay this task. The Protectorate, furthermore, was devised at a time when many of the Germans, according to all indications, expected to be able to extend their hegemony peacefully at an early date to

Hungary and other central European countries. Thus the terms of the Czech Protectorate would have had importance as a precedent, and particularly as an encouragement to other countries to feel that absorption into the German orbit would not necessarily mean the termination of their national existence. But these plans, if they existed, must have been fairly well shattered by subsequent developments: by the British guarantees and the attitude of Poland. If any further German expansion in central and eastern Europe (with the possible exception of Hungary) is going to have to take place on a frankly military basis, there will be no room for even the nominal observance of local autonomy and similar amenities. If this is the case, why should the Germans in Bohemia and Moravia continue to wear a mask, in the form of the Protectorate system, which only handicaps their movements?

Should the Protectorate system be extensively modified or abandoned, it is probable that there would then be another revision of administrative boundaries. Such towns as Plzen, Olomouc, Brno, and Moravska-Ostrava would probably be transferred to the Sudetengau or other purely German *gaus*, leaving merely the cores of Bohemia and Moravia subject to some direct but special form of German administration. Otherwise it cannot be said that the change would make much difference to the Czech people. Its effect would be greatest in those countries farther east and south where the treatment of Germany's first alien conquest is being scrutinized with more than academic interest.

GOVERNMENT

of the
Protectorate of Bohemia and Moravia
appointed by President Hacha
April 27, 1939

PRIME MINISTER AND
MINISTER OF THE INTERIOR   General Alois Eliáš

New Government of the Protectorate

FINANCE	Dr. Josef Kalfus
EDUCATION	Prof. Jan Kapras
JUSTICE	Dr. Jaroslav Krejci
INDUSTRY, COMMERCE, AND TRADE	Dr. Vlastimil Šadek
COMMUNICATIONS	Dr. Jiri Havelka
PUBLIC WORKS	Dominik Čipera
AGRICULTURE	Dr. Ladislav Feierabend
SOCIAL WELFARE AND PUBLIC HEALTH	Dr. Vladislav Klumpar

24. Despatch of May 10, 1939, from Consul General Linnell to the Department of State, on the new law limiting the rights and activities of Jews in Slovakia

I have the honor to report that on April 20, 1939, the Slovak government finally published in its Collection of Laws the text of a decree defining what shall constitute a Jew in Slovakia and restricting the participation of Jews in certain free professions.

A copy of the decree in question is enclosed in translation.

This Slovak Jewish law is the product of long and difficult deliberations on the part of the Slovak leaders—deliberations which began many months before the declaration of Slovak independence and which have been complicated by the conflicting attitudes of the Hlinka People's Party, the Catholic Church, and the business interests.

As far as the definition of what constitutes a Jew is concerned, the Slovak law is in some respects harsher and in others more liberal than the Nuremberg Laws (see Article 5 of the "Erste Verordnung zum Reichsbürgergesetz vom 15. September 1935"). In Slovakia religion rather than blood has been taken as the basis for legislation. Anyone who is—or who was as late as October 30, 1918—a member of the Israelitic confession is a Jew. Of those who left the Israelitic church before 1918, the ones who became baptized in another church (here the Slovak legislators were thinking mostly of the Roman Catholic Church) are considered Aryans even though they may be full-fledged Jews by blood, whereas those who remained without confession are considered full-fledged Jews, even though two of their grandparents may have been Aryans. The status of children and spouses follows closely that of the parents or the marriage partner, respectively. On the other hand, there are no intermediate categories. In Slovakia a person is either a Jew or he is not.

The remainder of the law deals with the restriction of Jewish participation in the free professions. A *numerus clausus* of 4 percent is established for the legal profession and Aryans may not, in normal circumstances, be represented at court by Jewish lawyers. Jews are excluded entirely from being notaries public. They may serve as editors only of Jewish periodicals. No mention is made of the medical profession. The law likewise contains no provisions affecting the status of the Jews in commerce: an omission which is particularly interesting for the reason that this was so frequently mentioned as one of the problems which the law would have to regulate.

In general, the purpose of the Slovak legislation may be said to have been to segregate out of the body of the population all those Jews who have not long since become Catholics, to stamp these people definitely as Jews, and to limit their participation in the free professions. This is, of course, only a portion of the anti-Semitic program of the Slovak leaders. The problems connected with the role of the Jews in the medical profession, with Jewish predominance in business and finance and with Jewish ownership of land, still remain for future legislative treatment. There is, furthermore, a very wide field in the treatment of the Jews which must of necessity be left to local administrative authorities and to irresponsible elements of the population. There is little doubt that in Slovakia these elements will keep pace with the legislative authorities in the general endeavor to reduce the wealth and influence of the Jewish population.

ANNEX TO DOCUMENT NO. 24

> SOURCE: Slovak Collection of Laws,
> Issue No. 14
> April 20, 1939
> (Item No. 63)

(TRANSLATION)

GOVERNMENT DECREE OF APRIL 18, 1939 CONCERNING THE DEFINITION OF THE TERM "JEW" AND THE RESTRICTION OF THE NUMBER OF JEWS IN CERTAIN FREE PROFESSIONS

The Government of the Slovak state, acting on the authority of Paragraph 4 of the Law of March 14, 1939, published in Issue No. 1 of the Slovak Collection of Laws concerning the independent Slovak state, decrees the following:

PART I
The Definition of the Term "Jew"

PARAGRAPH 1

(1) The following persons, regardless of sex and citizenship, shall be considered Jews:

1. Persons who are or have been of Israelitic confession, even if in the latter case the person concerned has changed to a Christian confession after October 30, 1918;

2. Persons who are or have been without a confession and have or have had at least one parent of Israelitic confession;

3. Descendants of persons mentioned above, excepting such descendants as have themselves changed to a Christian confession prior to October 30, 1918;

4. Persons who, subsequent to the date of promulgation of this government decree, enter into marriage with a person mentioned above, and in this case for the period of validity of such a marriage;

151

5. Persons who, after the promulgation of this government decree, live with a Jewish person in an illegitimate relationship, as well as children who issue therefrom.

(2) In cases deserving of special consideration the government may make exceptions.

PARAGRAPH 2

(1) In doubtful cases concerning persons held to be Jews according to the terms of this decree, the matter shall be decided by the district administrative office in the district of which the person concerned has his domicile or is living.

(2) An application for such a decision may be submitted by the person concerning whom the doubt has arisen or by any other person (physical or in law) who has himself a legal interest in whether the person in question is or is not held to be a Jew. A decision may also be rendered at the instance of an administrative office or a court.

(3) Appeals may be made against the decisions of the district office within 15 days after the date of the decision (Par. 72 [2] of the Government Decree of January 13, 1928, Issue No. 8/28 of the Collection of Laws and Orders, concerning judicial procedure) to the Ministry of the Interior. Appeals must be filed with the district administrative office which rendered the decision in question. No complaint to the Supreme Administrative Court will be permitted.

PART II

The Restriction of the Number of Jews in Certain Free Professions

Section 1

In the Legal Profession

PARAGRAPH 3

The number of Jewish lawyers (or lawyer's assistants)

shall be fixed at four percent of the total number of registered members of the respective bar association.

PARAGRAPH 4

(1) A number of Jewish lawyers (or lawyer's assistants) shall be excluded from the lists of the respective bar associations.

(2) In particular, there shall be excluded those who:

- (a) have not settled their due taxes, contributions, fees, or other public obligations;
- (b) in view of their personal fortune or in view of their earnings in another position, are not dependent on this profession;
- (c) are not conducting any active practice;
- (d) do not have an appropriate command of the state language;
- (e) are undesirable in this profession for any other important public reason.

PARAGRAPH 5

(1) On grounds of urgent necessity or for other reasons warranting special consideration the Ministry of Justice may, as long as these reasons prevail, permit Jewish lawyers in excess of the number provided in Paragraph 3 to continue in their profession.

(2) The number of those thus permitted to continue shall in no case exceed ten percent of the total membership of the respective bar association.

PARAGRAPH 6

(1) Exclusions in the sense of Paragraph 4 shall be effected by the board of the respective bar association.

(2) Appeals against exclusion may be taken within 15 days to the Ministry of Justice. An appeal has no delaying effect. The Minister of Justice shall decide such appeals in the last instance.

PARAGRAPH 7

(1) A Jewish lawyer may represent only Jews, except

in cases where there is no other lawyer except a Jew, in the court district where the latter resides, who could take over the representation. [sic].

(2) These provisions apply equally to substitute representatives, and among lawyers as well as lawyer's assistants.

(3) Associations, as well as business and economic societies and other persons in law, excepting such as promote the interests of the Jewish faith and Jewish culture, may not be represented by Jewish lawyers.

(4) A violation of these provisions shall have the same legal effect as though the party had had no legal representation at all. Responsibility for these consequences in the property as well as the disciplinary sense shall be borne by the Jewish lawyer who accepts the representation, and insofar as responsibility in the property sense is concerned, the lawyer shall be responsible to the person entrusting him with the representation and to this person's heirs as well.

PARAGRAPH 8

The Minister of Justice may permit a notary public to represent a party before a district court in a district where there is only one lawyer or in a district where there are several lawyers but where none is willing to represent the interests of the respective client. The Minister of Justice may retract this permission at any time at the instance of the respective bar association.

Section 2
In the Public Notarial Profession

PARAGRAPH 9

A Jew may not be a notary public.

Section 3
In the Editorial Profession

PARAGRAPH 10

A Jew may be an editor only of a Jewish periodical, that is, of a periodical which is expressly designated as such and which promotes the interest of the Jewish faith and of Jewish culture.

Section 4
PARAGRAPH 11
General Provisions

As far as the dismissal from civil service (or private employment) in consequence of this government decree is concerned, the provisions of the government decree of April 18, 1939 (No. 65 of Collection of Slovak Laws) concerning the shortening of the period of notice in civil service jobs subject to the Code of Civil Law and concerning the final settlement in cases of dismissal, shall be applied.

PARAGRAPH 12

The following persons shall be considered to have committed an offense and to be liable to punishment at the hands of the competent district court with imprisonment accompanied by forced labor not exceeding three months and with a fine from 1,000 to 5,000 crowns:

a) whoever, although excluded according to this government decree from the exercise of his profession, continues in this profession;

b) whoever employs or makes possible the employment in a profession of a person excluded from that profession;

c) whoever in any way directly or indirectly enables a person excluded according to this decree from a given profession to continue to work in that profession;

d) whoever violates the provisions of Paragraph 7.

(2) A member of a bar or notarial association who violates the provisions of points (a) to (d) also shall lose his right to practice and be excluded from membership in the respective association.

(3) No postponement of the execution of the punishments fixed by this paragraph shall be permitted.

PART III

Concluding Provisions

PARAGRAPH 13

This government decree shall become effective on the date of promulgation and shall be executed by the Minister of Justice in collaboration with the other ministers concerned.

Dr. TISO

Dr. Tuka	Dr. Fritz
Dr. Durčansky	Medrický
Dr. Pružinsky	Čatloš
Sivák	and for Minister Stano

25. Letter of May 11, 1939, from Consul General Linnell to the Chargé d'Affaires at Berlin, concerning the political situation in Bohemia

The last fortnight has seen a conspicuous increase in the self-confidence and the national spirit of the Czech population and has been marked by a number of pointed demonstrations of Czech national feeling.

In the first place there was the remarkable outcome of President Hacha's effort to enlist the adult male population of the country in a new and united political organization called the National Community. Although this action had been undertaken at the instance of the Germans and in imitation of German political methods, it was interpreted by the rank and file of the Czechs as an opportunity to demonstrate their numerical strength and their enthusiasm in the face of the German domination. The result was that of those considered eligible, a total of 97.4 percent registered in the ranks of the new party, a result better than those usually achieved by the genuinely totalitarian states in similar instances. In a number of communities, particularly those with a sizeable percentage of German inhabitants, the registration ran well over 100 percent of the eligible Czechs supposed to be on hand, a phenomenon which has been officially explained by the fact that many Czechs recently returned from Slovakia or Ruthenia and others recently dismissed from the police or military services had never been included in the voting lists. It is doubtful, however, whether even this would explain the large numbers in excess of 100 percent (in Brno it is said to have been 120 percent) who went to sign up for membership in the Czech National Community. Either there was some sort of faking of the registers or a number of persons who had been commonly regarded as belonging to other nationalities must have taken this opportunity of identifying themselves with the Czech cause. In any case the vote caused considerable perplexity and misgivings to the Germans, who still do not quite know what to make of the results. They had expected to teach the Czechs a few lessons in the control of popular opinion and instead of doing so they received one themselves. The result has been that since that time they have been saying to the Czech authorities: "You people seem to have excellent means of propaganda and a surprising control of public opinion in your country. We suggest that it would be useful if all this were to be applied toward increasing the love for Germany among the Czechs rather than achieving quite implausible demonstrations of national solidarity."

German suspicions have been increased by a number of other ingeniously conceived demonstrations of national feeling on the part of the Czechs. For the most part these have taken the form of a mass deposit of small bouquets of flowers on certain monuments in the city. At first this was done only on the tomb of the unknown soldier. Then on the eve of Hitler's birthday hundreds of people began suddenly to lay flowers on the base of the Hus monument in the Old Town Square. On May 5 the same thing was done at the Wilson monument before the Wilson station. There is no doubt that these last two incidents were very carefully arranged by certain elements who remained behind the scenes; but since the persons who came with flowers did not come in groups but simply appeared individually among the passers-by on the sidewalk, it was difficult to treat them as organized demonstrators.

A further occurrence of this sort took place last Sunday when the remains of the first great modern Czech poet (of the early nineteenth century), Macha, were brought to Prague from the Sudeten area where they had been buried up to this time and, after lying in state in the Pantheon, were reinterred in the Vysehrad cemetery beside those of many other famous Czechs. This occasion was utilized by the Prague Czechs—no one knows whether by a preconceived plan or by spontaneous action—as another pretext for showing their sense of national pride and solidarity. Many more Czech flags were in evidence in the streets than on either of the German holidays when the people had been asked to hang out their national colors. The ceremonies were attended by crowds far greater than any which had assembled for the German ceremonies.

Finally, there was the recent scene at the National Theater where the Prague Orchestra's rendition of Smetana's patriotic suite, "Ma Vlast" (My Country), was followed by a wild ovation which lasted for a full quarter of an hour and which ended with the conductor kissing the score and holding it up before the audience.

Incidents of this sort obviously represent the form which the Czechs have found for manifesting their disapproval of what has happened, their solidarity in the face of the German invasion, and their determination to retain their national spirit and unity for a better day. President Hacha and some of the other members of the government have begun to experience a little alarm lest these manifestations become a serious annoyance to the Germans and bring about retaliatory action. Thus far the Germans have been more or less baffled as to how to deal with them. It is difficult to stop a person from laying a bouquet of flowers on a public monument or from applauding a symphony concert. But that these events have proved irritating to some of the German officials is certain and the fears of the Czech leaders for their possible consequences may be only too well justified.

26. Despatch of May 15, 1939, from Consul General Linnell to the Department of State, on conditions in Slovakia

I have the honor to report that according to such information as is received here little progress is being made toward overcoming the difficulties which surround the existence of a nominally independent Slovakia.

The utter penury of the government continues to represent one of the most serious problems. The popular loan floated during the spring with well-tried totalitarian methods netted only some 60,000,000 crowns, or roughly one-fifth of the expected amount. The hopes of raising revenue by minting more coin (the mint for the Czechoslovak Republic happened to be in Slovakia and thus fell into the hands of the present Slovak government) are understood to have received a setback through the high cost of nickel and the difficulty of obtaining it. At best, more than 200,000,000 crowns could hardly be raised in this way—and these only at the price of further inflation. Probably the largest single item of revenue which the Slovak government has yet received was a sum of 90,000,000 crowns, belonging in reality to the national bank in Prague, which fell into Slovak hands more or less by accident at the time of the declaration of independence. But all these items of revenue, supplemented by cash on hand in the autonomous Slovak government on March 13 and by subsequent current revenues, could not have yielded up to this time more than 400,000,000 crowns. This would be enough to pay the regular expenditures of administration (to say nothing of the public works budget) for less than four months in normal times, and these have been no normal times. Thus the government is already urgently short of cash—with a partially inflated currency, with an exhausted internal capital market, with no credit whatsoever beyond its own borders, with a population whose taxable capacity is already inadequate to bear the costs of public administration and is declining rapidly. In many instances, the ministries have not even been able to pay their employees the full salaries.

During the two months that have now elapsed since the Slovak political crisis and the declaration of Slovak independence, trade between Slovakia and the outside world has, except for some of the most necessary items, been almost at a standstill. The movement of merchandise between the Protectorate and Slovakia has been made possible through a clearing agreement arrived at in the middle of April, whereby goods can be exchanged whenever currency balances are available. As far as other countries are concerned, the Slovak authorities have tried to maintain some basis for a continuance of foreign trade by announcing that they would regard all Czechoslovak trade treaties as still in force for the territory of Slovakia, until such time as they might be replaced by new agreements negotiated directly with the Slovak government. This policy, however, has not proved very successful. In a number of cases the other countries concerned have not shown a willingness to recognize such an arrangement. And even where there has been such a willingness, the disorganization and lack of confidence engendered by the political changes have had a crippling effect on foreign trade operations.

The only new commercial arrangements arrived at by the Slovak government have been with Poland. Early in May, after negotiations with a Polish delegation at Bratislava, a most-favored-nation agreement, a clearing agreement, and a tourist traffic agreement were concluded. Negotiations looking toward the conclusion of a quota agreement are still continuing. The importance of these agreements, however, is lessened by the fact that the two countries are both primarily agricultural and have not a great deal to offer each other in the commercial field.

Negotiations with a German delegation have been proceeding in Bratislava simultaneously with the Slovak-Polish negotiations, but have not yet led to any concrete results. The chief difficulties seem to lie in the question of payment for foreign trade transactions.

It had been planned to open negotiations with Hungary in the beginning of May. These conversations have now been postponed. Meanwhile trade between the two countries, which is of considerable importance to Slovakia, is languishing. France has blocked all balances in French banks which might be used by Slovak interests. It is reported that the French will not even free the balances which have arisen since the establishment of the independent Slovak state. With Rumania, nothing has yet been done to reestablish trade connections. The attitude of our own government needs no mention.

Practically all branches of Slovak industry are beginning to feel the effects of this decline in foreign trade. The glass industry has been adversely affected by the increased American duties and is working at half capacity. The cellulose industry although not so hard-hit as the glass factories, is also reported to be having difficulties in retaining its American market. Lack of raw materials is becoming general. The paper industry has been particularly handicapped by the stoppage of coal imports from Hungary. One paper mill, in Slovošovce, has been forced to close altogether. A number of enterprises, particularly in the metal-working, paper, and chemical branches, are suffering from the absence of the price-fixing arrangements of the Czechoslovak cartels, which were broken up by the collapse of the Republic. The only branch of Slovak industry which is doing a thriving business is mining. The metallurgical industries in the district of Teschen and Moravska-Ostrava are working at full tilt on both the German and the Polish sides, and there has been a lively demand for Slovak iron ore, in particular. Otherwise, Slovak industry is facing increasing difficulties.

Meanwhile the belief continues to spread that it will not be long before Slovakia is ripe for partition. It was related in the report accompanying my despatch of May 2, 1939, that a partition of the country, through which all territory west of the River Vah would go to Germany and the remainder to Hungary, would probably be forthcoming whenever German-Polish difficulties might be composed. It now appears possible that the Germans may not wait for the settlement of their differences with Poland, but may endeavor to carry out the partition in such a manner as to make it a weapon directed against the Poles. In this case, not only the territory west of the Vah (and including its valley) but the entire Žilina district and the High Tatras as far east as Proprad would probably be taken by Germany and combined with a Moravia which will be at that time quite possibly an integral part of the Reich. The remainder of Slovakia would go to Hungary in return for Hungarian promises to permit the present Slovak leaders to carry on as an autonomous regime. In addition to this, the Hungarians would be expected to agree to restore Father Vološin and his "Ukrainian" friends to a form of autonomous power in Ruthenia. While the latter suggestion may seem somewhat fantastic, it is privately reported that Vološin, who has recently been living in Bratislava together with a few helpless survivors of the Sich, has just returned from a visit to Berlin and has professed himself highly satisfied with the results of his trip. Through the reestablishment of such a regime in Ruthenia, the Germans would doubtless hope to revive something of the separatist feeling among the Polish Ukrainians.

These possibilities are mentioned not as definite plans of the Germans, scheduled for completion at any given date. Conditions are extremely fluid in this area and strategy changes day by day. But there is evidence that these are the lines along which many German minds are working at this moment.

It might be added that the reference to Slovakia in Hitler's speech failed to carry much reassurance to the Slovaks. It will be recalled that the Reichskanzler listed, as one of the concessions which Germany was prepared to make, the following: "To guarantee the independence of the Slovak state by Germany, Poland, and Hungary jointly —which means in practice the renunciation of any unilateral German hegemony in this territory." Now in the first place, Germany had already guaranteed the independence of the Slovak state in the German-Slovak Treaty of March 23, 1939, Article I of which reads: "The German Reich undertakes the protection of the political independence of the Slovak state. . . ." Thus what the Reichskanzler was offering the Poles as a concession from Germany was something he had already done. Furthermore, the statement that a *joint* guarantee of Slovak independence would mean "the renunciation of any unilateral German hegemony in this territory" is faint comfort to the Slovaks. They can only assume that in the absence of such a joint guarantee, no renunciation of German hegemony can be expected; otherwise the offer would have no sense at all. Thus the only effect of the Reichskanzler's words has been to increase confusion and doubt concerning Slovakia's future and to lend strength to the assumption that the country's nominal independence will not endure for long.

27. Memorandum,
of May 15, 1939,
on the trend of developments
in Bohemia and Moravia

I should like to submit below certain considerations concerning the trend of developments in this country which I believe to be of significance not only from the standpoint of the Czech people but also for their bearing on the future of German expansion in Central Europe.

A fact which cannot fail to strike the foreign observer in Prague is the universal sense of impending disaster. He will scarcely meet a single well-informed and intelligent Czech who foresees any possibility of a consolidation of conditions under the present German rule or who anticipates any immediate future for his own country other than the breakdown and disintegration of all public life. And these forebodings apply not only to the eventuality of war; they are felt no less strongly by those who envisage a situation in which Germany would have every possibility to cope in peace and at leisure with the responsibilities which she has undertaken in this area.

What accounts for this feeling? Why this lack of confidence in the ability of the Germans to organize and govern successfully a highly developed, fruitful province, situated in the midst of their own territories—a province where every possibility of armed resistance has been forfeited and where German rule has been established beyond a shadow of a dispute?

If this question were to be put to the average well-informed Czech, the chances are that he would reply by pointing to several or all of the following considerations:

Developments in Bohemia and Moravia

1. The relatively sound economy of the country, built up by twenty years of industry, frugality, and business sense, is at present being undermined with terrifying rapidity. A concealed inflation already exists; complete inflation seems inevitable within a few months. The Germans have already put into circulation in the reduced territory of the Protectorate at least half of the 3,000,000,000 odd crowns which they acquired through the occupation of the Sudeten areas. Eight hundred million are said to have been given to the German-controlled Bohemian Union Bank for the acquisition of real and industrial property in Bohemia and Moravia in behalf of German interests. Another 500,000,000 are said to have been paid for deliveries of armaments from Czech factories. More have doubtless been used for other purposes. German troops, for example, are no longer permitted to use marks directly for their local purchases but are required to use crowns, which they obtain from the German authorities. As to the source of these crowns, few doubts exist. (In addition to this, it must be borne in mind that the Germans have simply expropriated and carted off to Germany, with no compensation at all, Czech government property to the value of many hundreds of millions of crowns.)

The Czech authorities even suspect that when the supplies of Sudeten crowns are exhausted (and this cannot be far off) the Germans will not hesitate to print Czech crowns in order to continue the plundering of the Historic Provinces without any real cost to themselves. There is reason to believe that the Czech authorities, in order to forestall this move, are now themselves printing hundred-crown notes without restraint and with utter disregard of all financial principles. Believing inflation to be inevitable, they are doing their best to get their share of the rake-off, and are experiencing a certain malicious satisfaction at the thought that it is the Germans who, in the end, will have to find some way to clean up the mess. As one Czech put it: "The ship has been taken by pirates, and the crew are quietly opening the pet-cocks."

The government is putting up a great show of determination to prevent the rise of prices. An elaborate authority is being established, armed with formidable powers, for the regulation of prices and wages. But this is all window-dressing. At best, its result will be the typical phenomena of concealed inflation in its more advanced stages: two-price system, a goods shortage, and a bootlegging of commodities. To a certain extent, this process has already set in. Commodities are disappearing one by one from the market. A Prague department store with a normal display of nearly 4,000 articles has already withdrawn over 800 of these from its counters, either because they are not available or because they cannot profitably be sold at the fixed prices. On the other hand, eggs, which can no longer always be had in the shops in the desired quantities, are readily available in the country—at higher prices.

Intimately connected with these problems is the question of foreign trade and raw material supply. No one knows what the exports from the Protectorate have been since the occupation, but it is obvious that they could have amounted to only a fraction of what they were before March 15. The result has been a shortage of foreign exchange and inability to import the needed quantities of raw materials. The foreign exchange holdings of the National Bank are now reported to amount to no more than $2,000,000. The textile factories have on an average only about three weeks' supply of raw materials on hand. Other Czech industries are in a similar situation. What is to happen when these reserves are at an end? Can one hope that Germany, herself seriously deficient of both of these items, will be able to give adequate assistance to the Czechs?

2. The political arrangements which have been established in Bohemia and Moravia show little more stability than the economic life of the provinces. It is doubtful whether the Protectorate system, with its fiction of an autonomous Czech government, is satisfying the hopes of its

authors. It has not lured much foreign exchange into the Reich; nor has it inspired other central European statesmen to follow in the footsteps of President Hacha. The suspicion is growing, in consequence, that the Germans are seeking a pretext which will permit them at any convenient time to establish a more direct form of domination over these provinces.

For inscrutable reasons, the Germans have reappointed a Prague government in which they obviously have little confidence. Having long encouraged the Czechs to do away with their party quarrels and to establish a single, authoritative political party, they are now annoyed with them for having obeyed these instructions too implicitly and are openly attacking President Hacha's "National Community" for having embraced practically the entire eligible Czech population in its membership. The German official press in Prague has explained that it was one thing for Henlein to demand the one hundred percent support of the Sudeten Germans, because he had a militant cause to pursue, but that for the Czechs, being under the protection of the Führer, "there will never again be a militant cause," and that there was therefore no need to arouse the Czech population to such a sensational demonstration of unity. One might almost suspect that there was a certain regret in German minds that the result of the enlistments for the new party left no sizeable minority among the Czechs which could be provoked and incited against the majority if a pretext were ever to be required for a further drastic German action in the Protectorate.

In view of the united front put up by the Czech population, Moravia seems to have been selected this time as the weak point to which the pressure must be applied. The large admixture of Germans in its cities and the numerous German "language islands" in its countryside render it a favorable field for international jealousies—another Sudeten area, if you will, with a Czech rather than a German majority. In contrast to Bohemia, the province is being subjected to steady pressure in the direction of Germanization—pressure

which is bound to arouse and embitter the Czech population. Nationalistic feeling among the Germans, already at
white heat, is given an occasional fanning to keep relations
between Czechs and Germans at a proper state of tension.
Quite recently relations between the Czech and the German
officials in Brünn have deteriorated seriously. Even the
Czech fascists throughout Moravia—a tiny but vociferous
group—are being given hopeful encouragement by the Germans. If conditions in Moravia, as a result of these artificial
stimulants, were to prove too unsettled, and if the Germans
were to find "themselves forced" to take it under a more
direct control, would there be any point in retaining the Protectorate system for the remainder of Bohemia proper—
for this tiny Slav enclave in the midst of Greater Germany?

Many people ask: what would it matter if the Protectorate
were to be abolished? German hegemony is complete in
either case. But the moral effect of the Protectorate should not
be dismissed too lightly. However great the suspicion with
which it may be regarded, it means that the rank and file of
the administration are Czech. It is equivalent, furthermore, to
a promissory note from the Germans for the preservation of
Czech culture and national pride, a symbol of at least the
professed intention of the Germans to treat the Czech nation
with respect. It is an arrangement which the Czechs would
have been overjoyed to receive—even on paper—during the
last years of Austrian rule. If it goes, the rift between Czechs
and Germans, already tragically wide, becomes irreparable.

3. Were all this taking place under a German administration firm in its purpose, conscious of its responsibilities,
integrated in its activities, and incorruptible in the performance of its duties, there would be less cause for misgivings.
Granted such an administration on the part of the Germans,
Bohemia and Moravia could look forward even to complete
incorporation in the Reich and to the substitution of the
mark for the crown with some hopes for at least a tolerable
economic future. But the impression made by the German

officials who have come to the Czech communities since the occupation has been anything but that described above. There is a great deal of indecision, unclarity, internal rivalry, and working at cross-purposes among them. Many of the civilians, notably the officials of the Gestapo, appear to be cynical in their attitude toward their own functions and frequently outrightly corrupt. Reports are common of the lukewarm attitude of German army officers toward their own political leadership. It is quite probable that the bad effect of service in Czech communities on the morale of the troops was the reason for the early withdrawal of so many of the units which took part in the occupation and for the subsequent frequent changing of the garrisons. Altogether the German administration makes upon the Czechs the impression of a regime in an advanced stage of moral disintegration rather than of the youthful, fanatical political movement which it would like to be considered. . . .

The Czechs feel that conditions are bad in Germany proper, worse in Austria, serious in the Sudeten area, and that Bohemia will be the final breaking point. This impression is not one to win their respect or cooperation. The result is that the Czechs are entering with complete abandon into the spirit of what they consider to be a desperate situation. Even Czech officials who have heretofore been relatively honest now take bribes with complete unconcern, and their superiors look on with approval, feeling that the greater the disintegration of the integrity of the administration, the more difficult things will be for the Germans. Sloppiness, irresponsibility, passive resistance are becoming universal. The result is an atmosphere of outward submission and inner demoralization which defies description and the inevitable consequences of which are not pleasant to contemplate.

If these considerations are sound—and I would hazard the assumption that they are not far from the truth—one can predict no successful future for the German attempt to rule the Historic Provinces. Inflation, impoverishment, economic disruption, bitterness, lack of confidence, and the moral disintegration of public administration can reap no good harvest either for victors or vanquished. For these who may have hoped that German domination would at least create economic stability and orderly conditions where shortsighted particularism and national rivalries have reigned before, this situation can bring only disappointment. The fate of this area is no longer a question of Czechs and Germans. It has become an internal German problem. The responsibility lies with Berlin, and until the German people develop greater spiritual power and greater political maturity they will stand little chance of success as heirs to the responsibilities which were borne for many centuries—and at times not uncreditably—by the Catholic Church and the Hapsburg Empire.

28. Despatch of May 23, 1939, from Consul General Linnell to the Department of State, concerning the situation in Bohemia and Moravia[1]

I have the honor to report that the past week has shown a still further deterioration in the relations between Czechs and Germans, and that the resulting tension is approaching a point where the Czech leaders themselves may find it impossible to continue their cooperation in the maintenance of the fiction of a Czech autonomous regime.

That Czech "autonomy" has proved a fiction is no longer open to doubt. Despite continued German assurances to the contrary, the Protectorate system, as guaranteed to the Czechs by the Reichskanzler in his decree of March 16, has never been seriously put into effect. Such steps as were originally taken towards even the formal observance of its provisions are now being steadily retracted in practice if not theory.

The civil administration, which was supposed to have been restored to the Czech authorities upon the relinquishment of executive authority by the Reichswehr in April, has actually remained in German hands. There has been no move to withdraw the numerous commissars, many of them Sudeten Germans with various personal axes to grind, who were appointed to all the central ministries and to many municipal offices and state enterprises in March. The same is true of the German "Landrats" who were set up throughout the countryside during the period of the exercise of civil authority by the Reichswehr. Each of these officials has assigned to him a given field of competence comprising several of the

[1] *Foreign Relations of the United States*, 1939, Vol. I, pp. 63-68.

existing Czech administrative districts (comparable to our counties). In these territories they continue to exercise real administrative authority with no legal basis whatsoever. The Czech district officials often report to them and take orders from them rather than from their own dormant Ministry of the Interior. Cases are known where failure to do this, or at least to obey the Landrat's instructions, has been followed by prompt arrest. The Landrats themselves are subordinated through the Reichsprotektor's office to the Reich Ministry of the Interior. Last week they were all summoned to Prague to confer directly with Herr von Stuckart, who handles Protectorate affairs in that Ministry and who came to Prague expressly for this purpose.

In many instances, the Czech authorities are being simply displaced by those of the Reich. This has been the case, for example, with the customs officials on the Polish and Slovak borders. It is characteristic that the Czech central authorities no longer even know precisely where these borders lie. There are indications—although the Slovaks deny this—that the Germans have been altering the Slovak-Moravian border at will, during the last few weeks, with no consultation of the Czech authorities. Quite probably, the same thing has been happening on the other frontiers as well.

In their administrative activities the German authorities are actively assisted by the various German police units— Schutzpolizei, S.S., and Gestapo—which are present in all sizeable Czech communities despite the fact that the Law of March 16 provides as little justification for their presence as for that of the Landrats and the Commissars. Quite recently, these police units have developed intense activity. As nearly as can be ascertained in the absence of official information, the number of arrests has been increasing daily. The existing prisons are overcrowded and old ones, long in disuse under the Czech regime, are again being put into operation. Tales of brutality, of physical and mental torture, seem unfortunately to be only too well authenticated. All in all, it would scarcely be an exaggeration to say that "terror," in the accepted totalitarian sense, had now begun, and that the Czech authorities are quite powerless to oppose it.

It is obvious that in these circumstances, the position of the Czech government is anything but enviable. As far as I am aware, it has had nothing of any importance to do during the last month but to draft two laws at German behest and submit them to the Reichsprotektor for consideration. Meanwhile personal relations between some of its members and leaders of the Reichsprotektor's office have become strained. As was anticipated, Baron von Neurath seems to be playing a much less conspicuous role in Prague than certain of his subordinates. Herr Frank (formerly deputy Gauleiter in the Sudeten district) and Dr. Sebekovsky (formerly Regierungspräsident in Karlsbad) are now said to be the most active members of his staff. Both are Sudeten Germans and neither is in any sense persona grata to the Czechs. In general, it may be said that if the Germans ever had any intention of appeasing the Czechs, the widespread admission of Sudeten Germans to positions of influence in the Protectorate has been the worst mistake they could have made. During the past century, if we may believe the historians, it was largely the Sudetens who ruined relations between the Czechs and Vienna. They are now in a fair way to repeating this performance with respect to the relations between the Czechs and Berlin.

But Czech anxiety is not confined to the future of the Czech administration, which they regard as a lost cause in any case. It is the German attitude with respect to President Hacha's new Czech political movement, the so-called "National Community," which is arousing the greatest apprehension in influential Czech circles. For it is on this movement that they are depending for the preservation of their own unity and discipline pending the day when it may again become possible for them to assert themselves actively in opposition to the German rule.

It has been related in previous communications from this office that the organization of the National Community was a conspicuous success and that its leaders even succeeded in gaining the adherence of over 97 percent of those eligible for membership. While the movement first seemed to find favor in German eyes as a gesture towards totalitarianism, its success aroused definite irritation in German circles. The Czechs, it seems, were expected to make the effort but they were not expected to succeed. The Germans had evidently hoped that a large proportion of the Czechs would remain outside the movement and would thus constitute an element which could always be played off against the remainder of the Czech population for the advancement of German aims. Since this hope did not materialize, the Germans have now adopted a definitely hostile tone toward the movement and are using the only remaining available element, namely the Czech fascists, as a lever for the creation of dissension among the Czech population.

It will be recalled that the Czech fascists, under the leadership of General Gajda, endeavored to gain control of Czech political life immediately after the occupation but were pushed out with German connivance in favor of President Hacha and his friends. For some time after that the fascists wavered. They were torn between admiration for National-Socialist methods, which drew them toward the Germans, and nationalistic tendencies, which drew them toward the overwhelming anti-German majority of the Czech population. Their indecision was aggravated by the personality of their leader, who commanded little confidence among the Germans and who was himself never marked by any great clarity or firmness of decision. Dissension soon developed between the Moravian and the Bohemian sections. More recently, the Moravian section began to receive extensive support, financially and otherwise, from the Gestapo. At the beginning of May, Gajda, finally disillusioned with German motives, tried to lead his followers into a dissolution of the whole movement, to be followed by a merging with the National Community. Had this step succeeded, the Czech nation would have been truly united in the face of German occupation. But the Moravian wing, acting doubtless on Gestapo inspiration, revolted, carrying with it a portion of the Bohemian party as well, and has now set itself up in opposition not only to Gajda but also to President Hacha and the "National Community." The result has been retaliation on the part of the President through the removal of the recalcitrant fascist members of the Committee of National Community. The break is now complete, and is fraught with danger for the preservation of Czech unity. For while the fascists have thus far been numerically insignificant, German support is nothing to be sneezed at. Money is always a powerful weapon, and the fascist press claims that membership is now increasing rapidly, 10,000 members having been added within the last week.

In the face of this situation the Czech leaders are now wondering whether the disadvantages of nominal cooperation with the Germans are not beginning to outweigh the advantages. They see clearly what the Germans are trying to do to them. They are afraid that their continued participation—however devoid of content—in the Protectorate Government will only compromise them in the eyes of their own people without accomplishing anything tangible for their followers. They are coming to the conclusion that they would have better chances of preserving Czech unity as frank opponents of the German rule rather than as nominal participants in it.

For these reasons, I am reliably informed, they are contemplating some sort of voluntary step on their own part which would put an end to their participation in the government and to their cooperation with the Germans in general and would leave them in a position to come out openly in opposition to the Germans, as wholehearted protagonists and leaders of Czech separatism. They would prefer this course, which might well turn out to be a form of martyrdom, to the continuance of a cooperation which has proved so one-sided.

They are waiting at the present moment only for the favorable outcome of the Anglo-Russian conversations before taking this step. Despite the various disillusionments of the past year, they still have great hopes for the eventual efficacy of support from England and the United States, and they feel that if Germany were to be backed to the wall diplomatically there might be some possibility for at least a partial retraction of the action which the Germans have taken in the Czech lands. How long they can continue to wait, however, is problematical. The situation is becoming daily more difficult for them, and they have always to bear in mind the possibility that the Germans may anticipate them by abolishing or changing the Protectorate before they get around to making their own move.

If President Hacha and the National Community should back out on the Germans in this fashion, it is difficult to predict what would follow. The fascists are already pressing for seats on the Protectorate Government, and there might be an attempt to set up another government composed exclusively of Czech fascists. But the moral authority of such a body—which represents its chief value to the Germans—would be minimal, and its popularity no greater than those of the puppet regimes established by the Japanese in China. The job of finding a new president would present a problem of particular difficulty.

Whether such a regime could serve as an effective instrument of German control is doubtful. I consider it more probable that the Germans will find themselves forced in the end to sweep away the last figments of Czech autonomy, to place their reliance solely on their bayonets, and to attempt to crush by sheer force the powerful Czech nationalism which they have hitherto tried to exploit. In this case, it is outright war: an undeclared war in which imprisonments, shootings, deportations, intimidation, and bribery on the one side would be pitted against passive resistance, sabotage, espionage, and conspiracy on the other. If it comes to this, the Germans will probably hold the upper hand without undue difficulty as long as the broad basis of National Socialist power remains intact. But they will have no happy time of it, and if the tide ever turns, Czech retaliation will be fearful to contemplate.

29. Despatch of June 6, 1939, from Consul General Linnell to the Department of State, concerning the situation in Bohemia and Moravia

With reference to my despatch . . . May 23, 1939,[1] concerning the mounting tension between Czechs and Germans, I have the honor to report that the fortnight which has elapsed since this despatch was written has seen no essential alterations but only a clarification of the situation as outlined at that time. In particular, the relations between the Czechs and the German authorities have shown no signs of improvement. The same doubt prevails as to how long it will prove possible to maintain the nominal cooperation of the Czechs with the German administration.

The outstanding event of the end of last week as far as the Protectorate is concerned has been Baron von Neurath's visit to the Reichskanzler. Official Czech circles here are satisfied that Baron von Neurath's purpose in making this visit was to protest not only against his own relatively powerless position but also against the policies which Herr Frank has been pursuing with relation to the Czechs. The members of the Czech government have not yet been informed of the outcome of this conversation but they have little hope that it will be favorable. They point out that Baron von Neurath is not the type of man whose advice would be apt to sway the Führer at the present moment. It will be easy, they feel, for Herr Frank to convince the Reichskanzler that Baron von Neurath's views are only the products of an old-fashioned

[1] See above, document No. 28.

179

liberalism as little in keeping with the principles of National Socialism as with the stern necessities of the moment.

These forebodings received a certain confirmation in the words used by Herr Frank in a speech which he delivered Sunday before a convention of German Nazi officials held in the South-Bohemian town of Budějovice (Budweis in German). This speech, which constituted the high point of the proceedings, was made up of what Karl Radek used to refer to as "the combination of the candy and the whip." Its mixture of promises and warnings brought to mind the old German saying:

> Willst Du nicht mein Bruder sein,
> Schlag ich Dir den Schädel ein.

It contained a sharp warning to the Czechs not to place any hopes in an early end of German rule. The German Reich, Herr Frank reminded his hearers, was not Austria-Hungary. The history of 1918 would not repeat itself. The Germans knew very well who their enemies were within the country and "when we clamp down, neither Mr. Prchala[2] nor Mr. Osusky will save them." The speech closed with a reminder to the Czech government that its responsibility to the Germans was only increased by the almost unanimous support which Dr. Hacha had found in the Czech population, that it would be held to account for any continuation of the underground opposition activities, and that it would be expected to use its prestige in order to further the popularity of the Germans among the Czech people. In this, as in other German statements, no indication was given of the exact nature of the action which the Germans intend to take if the Czechs fail to show a greater appreciation for the advantages brought to them by the inclusion in the Greater Reich.

This Budějovice convention was itself an interesting com-

---

[2] General Prchala, former commander of the Czechoslovak troops in Slovakia and Minister in the late Ruthenian Regional Government, is now in Poland, where he is said to be organizing a Czech legion which would assist the Poles in the event of hostilities against Germany.

mentary on the relations between Czechs and Germans. Budějovice has, in the firm opinion of its Czech citizens, a Czech
majority of roughly 80 percent. Conceding that this figure
may be exaggerated, it can safely be said (and even the
Germans do not attempt to dispute the fact) that the majority
of the inhabitants are Czech. The spot was nevertheless
chosen for a district conference of some 40,000 officials of
the National Socialist Party together with delegations from
numerous other German organizations. A good proportion of
the guests came from nearby portions of the Reich proper.
The local Nazi leader felt it necessary to reassure the Czech
population in advance that this event did not have for its
purpose an occupation of the town or its inclusion in the
Reich. The Czech National Community was induced to put
out a similar proclamation advising the Czechs that the
visitors from the Reich were coming merely to become
acquainted with their new comrades and to see the beauties
of the city, that they were to be welcomed hospitably, and
that the Czechs should not run away to the countryside but
should remain and participate in the festivities. In particular,
the Czechs were advised that on this occasion it would be
well to hang flags, and that the showing of any flag other
than the swastika would not be tactful. Reassuring as these
proclamations may have been, the Czech inhabitants of the
city must have received something of a shock to hear Herr
Frank say that Budweis was once a German town, that
despite all manipulations and all census figures the city had
retained its German character and that in the future it would
become a German town again.

There has been no relaxation in the activities of the German police. I am told that an average of between 20 and
40 arrests are being made daily of Czechs who were concerned with the administration of the Sudeten districts at one
time or another during the last few years. Another sensational series of arrests has been connected with the government land office, the institution which was charged with the

breaking-up of the large estates in Czechoslovakia and the redistribution of the land to small farmers. Not only have practically all of the leading officials of this office been imprisoned, but other high officials in the Ministry of Agriculture and in the general forestry administration have met with the same fate. The official charges against these men mention corruption. While no one seems to doubt the possibility —or even the probability—that corruption was practiced in these institutions, very few believe that this was the real reason for the German action. In the administration of the land reform legislation there is reason to suppose that the Czech officials showed particular zeal in breaking up German estates and distributing the land to Czech farmers. The Germans who were thus deprived of their holdings are now doubtless taking their revenge.

Another incident, less serious in its implications but more striking to the imagination, has been the object of lively discussion during the last few days. A local high-school class, consisting of some 63 students of both sexes in the ages of 15-16, went off during the Whitsuntide holidays for a visit to the Bat'a works at Zlin. While there the young people, according to the story which has reached the Consulate General, attended a movie. Here they demonstrated sentiments which were not pleasing to the German authorities. The result was that the lights were immediately turned on and that two or three of the ringleaders were arrested by the German police. They were taken outside and as they were being marched through a park one of them attempted to run away and was shot twice through the arm. The remainder were shepherded back to their railway carriage and packed off to Prague. On the stretch where the train goes through Reich-German territory to the north of Moravia, some of the students replied to "Heil Hitler" greetings by shouting "Heil Moskau." The result was that the entire class including sixteen young girls was promptly arrested and detained first in the railway car and subsequently in the prison at Sumperk.

There are allegations that they have been brutally treated and in particular that they were made to walk a gauntlet between Sudeten-German children. The German officials in the Protectorate plead lack of competence to effect the release of the party and the Czech authorities have not been able to make any headway with the Sudeten administration at Troppau. Meanwhile anxious parents are besieging the Council of Ministers and indignation in Czech circles is running very high.

In these circumstances the members of the Czech government are remaining firm in their intention to terminate their cooperation with the Germans whenever the moment comes when they can feel that this would have any useful effect. They are definitely reluctant to proceed with this plan until they are sure that the Western powers are also going to take a strong stand against Germany. As a pledge for the attitude of the Western powers they are now inclined to look not only to a conclusion of the agreement with Russia but also to the retirement of Chamberlain. They feel that the latter can never be relied on to maintain a firm attitude toward Germany for any length of time. Until he has left and been replaced by someone in whom they have more confidence they do not feel inclined to take a step which, unless supported elsewhere, might have fateful results for the Czech nation.

From the German side the merits of the present system depend in large measure on the contribution which it can make to the solution of Germany's present economic difficulties. At the present moment it is still too early to say what this contribution will be. The following observations, however, may be worthy of note.

Probably the greatest economic asset which the Germans have thus far obtained through their occupation of the Czech lands is the enormous stores of war materials and military equipment which they have trundled off to the Reich. Some idea of the extent of these German acquisitions will be obtained from the figures given in the Reichskanzler's recent speech. Certainly the stores were worth hundreds of millions of dollars and must have relieved the industrial requirements of the German army to an important degree and thus freed certain branches of German industry from some of the pressure to which they have heretofore been subjected.

The Germans have been steadily acquiring industrial property in the Protectorate, partly through normal purchase operations involving the use of crowns obtained in the Sudeten areas, and partly, I suspect, through the complicated processes of "Aryanization." Their control of Czech industry should soon be complete. It is anticipated that they will use their power to eliminate a number of the light-industry enterprises which might compete with similar establishments in Germany and will retain the great metallurgical plants, such as the Škoda and the Vitkovice, as well as the strictly military enterprises such as the poison gas establishment near Olomouc, the Brno machine-gun plant, etc.

However, the problem presented to the Germans by Czech industry is not solved by its passage to German ownership and German control. There remains the question of how raw materials are to be obtained. The supply of these plants with raw materials was made possible before the occupation only through the receipts of the highly developed Czechoslovak export trade. One of the things which the Germans undoubtedly had in mind in establishing the Protectorate was the desirability of seeing this export trade continue as nearly as possible without disturbance, something which would have been quite out of the question had the Czech lands been incorporated entirely into the Reich.

It is still impossible to say how much foreign exchange the Protectorate can be made to yield. Foreign trade figures which have been published for the period from March 15 to May 1 present a very rosy picture, exports being at a level considerably higher than that prevailing before the occupation and imports remaining more or less the same.

These figures, however, do not reveal the real situation in respect to foreign exchange. In the first place they include deliveries made on orders placed before and at the time of the occupation. Many foreign firms placed extra orders just at that time in the hopes that they could "get under the fence" before Czechoslovakia should become completely included in the German trade system. Furthermore these figures include all the trade with Germany proper and the Sudeten areas, which trade can of course not be considered as a source of foreign exchange from the German standpoint. It is understood that exports to the United States and to other "free currency" countries have declined heavily. The receipts of the Czech National Bank in free foreign exchange must consequently have declined accordingly, although the requirements of Czech industry in the way of raw materials are presumably as great as ever.

Strenuous efforts have been made in Berlin to work out new clearing agreements for the Protectorate with those countries which do not care to recognize the Protectorate as the heir to their former trade agreements with Czechoslovakia. It is still too early, however, to say how successful these efforts will be and local opinion is, in general, pessimistic on this subject.

The Czech National Bank continues to publish its statements and to show nearly $30,000,000 worth of foreign currency assets. This, however, includes all those assets which are blocked abroad and a large part of these apparently consist of credits opened up for the former Czechoslovak government as a result of the British post-Munich loans. Actually the amount of foreign exchange at the free disposal of the Czech National Bank is now thought to be less than $2,000,000. While the Czech officials are fatalistic and would witness the dissipation of this remaining fund with equanimity if not with a certain "Schadenfreude," the Germans are guarding it with the greatest care and no expenditures may be made from it without their permission.

The position of the internal Czech finances is said to be quite favorable, due partly to the cessation of military expenditures and partly to the high yield recently shown by certain government-owned enterprises. There is a feeling, however, in Czech circles, that the Germans are endeavoring to exploit the favorable rate they have established for the crown (ten crowns to one Reichsmark) in order to impress certain sections of the Czech population with their benevolence and with the economic advantages of "cooperation." This rate makes it possible for the tens of thousands of Czech workers who have already found employment in the Reich to send home very sizeable sums in crowns. The Germans also hope that when harvest time comes they will be able to buy the favor of the Czech farmers by paying handsome prices in crowns for agricultural products. There is a divergence of opinion within the Czech government as to how this situation should be met. The inflationary process has already been given a good start by German action in replacing the Sudeten crowns in circulation, by the virtual loss of the gold reserve, and the heavy flight from the crown. One group, headed by the present Finance Minister, believes that the government should be guided by the rules of orthodox economics and should attempt to avoid further inflation. Other ministers feel that such a course would only help the Germans, that extensive inflation is inevitable anyway in the long run and that the Czech government may as well utilize the process to its own purposes. This group believes that an inflationary financial policy would permit the Czech leaders rather than the Germans to take credit for certain momentary and illusory social improvements and thus prevent workmen and peasants from being bought over to a pro-German attitude. Higher domestic prices within the Protectorate would also nullify the effect of the relatively higher wages and prices which the Reich is prepared to pay.

The elaborate price control organization set up by the Czechs at German suggestion is functioning in a halfhearted manner. I believe that it is being applied most rigorously against Jewish enterprises. Aryan Czech businessmen seem to find ways of eluding its vigilance and a continued rise in prices can be observed.

In general it is obvious that matters have not yet progressed to a point where even the Germans can judge what the ultimate economic effect of the present system will be. It may be presumed, therefore, that unless their political irritation with the Czechs becomes too great and makes them feel that they have no choice but to establish a more direct form of control, the tendency of the Germans will be to maintain the present system intact, insofar as it involves the preservation of the Protectorate as a semi-independent economic unit, for a further period of at least several months.

30. Despatch of July 3, 1939, from Consul General Linnell to the Department of State, on general conditions in Bohemia and Moravia

The outstanding developments in the Czech lands during the month of June have been the following:

1. The inroads of the Germans on the authority which the autonomous Czech government was supposed—according to the terms of the Protectorate—to enjoy have progressed to a point where the Protectorate system must be considered as already abandoned in everything but name.

2. The Germans have become increasingly dissatisfied with those Czech officials who now bear public responsibility and the latter increasingly discouraged over their own chances for usefulness in the present setup; thus it is hardly probable that these men can remain much longer in office.

3. There has been no decline in the number of unpleasant clashes and incidents between Czechs and Germans; feeling continues to run high and the nerves of both parties are becoming markedly frayed.

With regard to the first of these points, it will be recalled that the Reichskanzler, in framing his decree of March 16 which established the Protectorate, quite evidently envisaged the role of the Reichsprotektor as that of advisor and comptroller over an autonomous Czech government. Legislative and executive authority were normally to be exercised by the Czech officials. The Reichsprotektor was authorized "to inform himself about all measures taken by the government of the Protectorate and to give advice." He could, to be sure, "object to measures calculated to injure the Reich" and "when delay seems dangerous" could himself take measures necessary in the common interest. There was nothing to indicate that he was to exercise any administrative or legislative functions in normal circumstances.

Nevertheless, on June 20 and 21 the Reichsprotektor issued two highly important legislative acts over his own signature, with no participation of the Czech authorities. The first of these was the Jewish law. . . . This law, which gives the Reichsprotektor dictatorial power over the transfer of at least half a billion dollars worth of Jewish property, is of the utmost importance to the Czechs, who are interested in seeing that all this booty is not turned over to German interests. In this instance, however, the Reichsprotektor did not even bother to inform the Czech authorities in advance of his intention to issue the law on his own authority, so that its appearance (it was officially published not in the Collection of Laws of the Protectorate but in the local German newspaper) came as a complete surprise to them. It should be explained that this act of the Reichsprotektor was preceded by long wrangling between German and Czech authorities over the text of the law. The Czechs were thus aware that the measure was in course of preparation but presumed that their agreement and signature would be enlisted before it was published. The second of these legislative acts was a decree assigning to the Reich authorities all the rights formerly accruing to the Czechoslovak government by virtue of the law for the Defense of the State of May 13, 1936. The importance to the Czechs of the questions involved in this decision was no less than that of the questions connected with the Jewish law. Among other things, the Law of May 13, 1936, authorized the government in time of mobilization to enlist for compulsory labor service all persons unfit for actual military service. Thus one of the major questions concerning the position of the Czech population in the event of a war in which Germany was involved has now been partially decided in advance with no consultation of the Czech authorities. These decrees were followed in a few days time by another decree authorizing the Reichsprotektor to alter existing Czech law at will and to declare invalid any existing laws which he finds to be in contradiction with the spirit of the protection undertaken by the Reich. While this latter power was reserved to the Germans by the terms of the Protectorate in the first instance, its specific assignment to the Reichsprotektor—taken together with his issuance of the other important decrees—shows only too clearly that his office has been converted from that of an adviser and comptroller to that of a provincial governor armed with dictatorial powers—both administrative and legislative—in all matters not specifically reserved to the direct competence of the central Reich authorities. At the present moment, legislative and administrative authority in the Protectorate is simply divided between the Reichsprotektor and the central authorities. In neither field do the Czech authorities play any serious part. Thus the extensive modification of the Protectorate system, as generally foreseen by local observers through the past spring, may now be considered as having already taken place.

The question of whether the present Czech leaders, including President Hacha, the members of the government, and the leaders of the National Community, are to remain in office or not, has an importance far exceeding that of the functions which they fulfill. They are still the symbol of Czech nationhood. They are the only remaining link between the past and the present political systems. They are the only group which could pretend to speak for the nation as a whole and which is permitted—however futilely—to do so. As long as they remain, the Czechs feel that they have some sort of open national leadership and are recognized as a nation rather than a mere minority or—as one Czech put it—a picturesque costume group. If they go, much of the whole theory of voluntary cooperation of Czechs with Germans goes with them.

President Hacha himself is reported to have been endeavoring to resign for the last six weeks. All reports indicate that he is thoroughly fed up personally with his position and has remained in it this long only because he feels that it has been for the good of the Czech people. I understand that he is now seeking another personal interview with Herr Hitler, for the purpose of laying before the Reichskanzler the many grievances of the Czechs against the German administration. He doubts that the complaints made here to the Reichsprotektor's office or direct to the German government through the Czech Minister in Berlin have ever reached the Reichskanzler's ears, and he sees this as the last hope for better treatment. If this attempt fails, he will probably resign. I am even told that he has mentioned suicide as a last gesture, in case everything else fails; and such a threat might well be more than mere heroics, inasmuch as he is an old man with few family ties, who has borne much of the tragedy of his people on his own shoulders during the last six months, is thoroughly tired and discouraged, and has relatively little to look forward to in the best of circumstances.

The members of the government continue to toy with the idea of resigning voluntarily, as a gesture. They expect to be arrested the day after doing so. But whether their resignations will be voluntary seems increasingly doubtful. Being Czechs, they have a remarkable capacity of delay, and in all probability they will keep on putting things off until they find themselves thrown out by the Germans. They want their resignations to be a gesture and to have some effect. For this reason they want a more favorable international political constellation and they want an issue. They almost—but not quite—decided to make an issue out of the imposition of the Jewish law in the middle of June. They are now inclined to think that a suitable occasion will be the issuance of the

191

anticipated German decree providing for the mobilization of approximately 1,000,000 Czech men from the former army lists, in the time of war, as a military labor force.

Meanwhile, however, the Germans are getting more and more displeased with them and suspicious of them, and are casting about energetically for some group which could take their place. Dr. Hans Blaschek, Director of the National Political Section of the Reichsprotektor's office, recently wrote for the official German paper in Prague a front-page Sunday leading article which contained the following characteristic passage: "In case certain people think that perhaps whispering propaganda, chain letters, or the assumption of a double face are the marks of great statesmanship, I may say that we have little understanding for such a policy. But we are also firmly convinced that the majority of the Czech people wish to follow the path of honest cooperation, and that the men will be found who will lead them. . . . We will not mind if these have to be entirely new men." The hint could not be clearer.

The Germans now seem to have given up the hope of using the Moravian fascists as successors to the present government. This group, financed by the Gestapo, is made up in large part of criminal elements, and led by a man who until a month or two ago kept a hotel of ill repute in Brno. Altogether, it seems to be too unsavory an organization to be of use for much of anything beyond the beating up of Jews in the Moravian cafés.

A more likely group to succeed the present members of the government is the Vlajka group, a small band of people, not entirely devoid of sincerity, who have wavered around for the last few months between the Czech fascists, the Germans, and the Czech National Community. More recently the Vlayka leaders seem to have found much in common with the Germans. Of particular interest is the fact that the Committee of the National Community has recently appointed a committee to study the activities of the Freemasons in Bohemia and Moravia and has asked the cooperation of the Vlayka people, who have particularly strong views on this subject. To this attempt at appeasement the Vlayka leaders have replied by saying that they will cooperate only if all the leading officials in the government and the National Community (this applies especially to members of the Cabinet) will sign declarations to the effect that they are not and never were members of Masonic lodges. Since several members of the government are believed to be Freemasons, this may well be the opening for their removal and their replacement with Vlayka people.

Unless President Hacha remains, a government composed of members of the Vlajka group would carry very little weight with the mass of the Czech people and would probably be regarded by most Czechs as a body of out-and-out traitors.

Meanwhile, the National Community leaders are making complete preparations for going "underground" and carrying the whole organization with them. An extensive underground organization already exists and will soon be ready to take over the political leadership of the people whenever the present public leaders retire. This organization is a loose one but widespread. It penetrates into almost every Czech office, particularly into the police and gendarmerie organizations. (For this reason, the latter may well be replaced entirely by Germans before long, particularly if there is another international crisis.) Through the cooperation of the police, it has been possible to preserve and conceal a certain amount of arms and ammunition.

Compared, for example, with illegal communist organization in other countries, the Czech underground movement seems lax and amateurish. But the Gestapo apparently finds it hard to cope with it. The unanimous dislike of Germans among the Czech population and the intricacies of the Czech tongue are worth years of conspiratorial experience to the underground leaders. It is not easy to find stool pigeons, even among the Sudeten Germans, who speak the language well enough to pass off with impunity as genuine Czechs, and very few real Czechs could be found who would be willing—or could be trusted—to do this work.

With regard to the general atmosphere, it can only be said that feeling among the Czechs could scarcely be more bitter than it is at the present without giving rise to real disorder. The Department is familiar with the circumstances of the Kladno and Náchod incidents. Although there can no longer be any doubt that the German policeman in Kladno was shot by another German, not all of the punitive measures against the community have been withdrawn, nor has any retribution been made for the sufferings inflicted on the officials and inhabitants. The fact that the Germans have now tacitly recognized the innocence of the Czech authorities is little consolation to the family of the Mayor, who is understood to have jumped to his death from the upper floor of the building in which he was confined, and whose body is said to have been found in a wretched condition which could not have resulted exclusively from the fall. It is incidents like this which put the iron into the hostility of the Czech population.

The greater this hostility becomes, the greater becomes the nervousness of those Sudeten Germans and Gestapo leaders who have taken responsibility for handling the Czech population and fitting it into the life of the Greater Reich, and the more these Germans tend to rely on the bayonet in their dealings with the newly acquired provinces. Repression breeds bitterness, and bitterness breeds more repression. In this way, a vicious circle is created from which, at the moment, there seems to be no escape.

For any remedy of this situation, good will on both sides would be required. There are no signs of this anywhere. The Germans are absorbed with plans for a new and drastic language law which will touch the Czechs on their most sensitive spot and carry the whole problem right back to the days of the Austro-Hungarian Empire, and for a measure which will make it possible to mobilize Czech manpower for compulsory labor in time of war. The Czechs have no hope or desire for a successful association with their German masters and are concentrating chiefly on an illegal organization which will permit them to retain an effective unity of their people, to make trouble for the Germans, and to take advantage of the first sign of German weakness with a view to regaining their independence. What the results will be, it is difficult to say, but they can hardly be pleasant.

31. Despatch of July 12, 1939, from Consul General Linnell to the Department of State, concerning appointment of a new Interior Minister in the Protectorate Government

I have the honor to report that President Hacha, acting with the approval of the Reichsprotektor, has relieved General Eliáš of the position of Minister of the Interior, which he has heretofore held together with the premiership, and has assigned the Interior portfolio to Gendarmerie General Joseph Ježek. The exact date of these changes has not been published, but it is believed to have been June 30.

General Ježek has heretofore been in command of the state gendarmerie throughout the province of Bohemia. He was born in 1884 in Žamberk (Senftenberg), a town which lies in eastern Bohemia not far from the language border between the German- and Czech-speaking districts. He entered the Austrian military service as a cadet in the Vienna Landwehr Military Academy and later served as an officer in the Landwehr and the Austrian gendarmerie and as an official in the Imperial Ministry of Defense. It was only after the war that he returned to Bohemia and entered the service of the new Czech gendarmerie. Thus his entire early background was that of an official of the Austro-Hungarian Empire.

While no reason has been given for his appointment, it is not difficult to see that it holds certain advantages for the Germans. The Czech Ministry of the Interior is very nearly dormant at the present time. The only branch of its apparatus which continues to play an active and important part in the life of the country is the gendarmerie, and the Germans have a particular interest in this service because they are dependent on it for the maintenance of their police power throughout the country districts. Lack of qualified personnel as well as considerations of personal safety have heretofore made it inadvisable for the Germans to maintain their own officials in the villages and smaller communities. The German police authorities in the towns have therefore been compelled to rely on the Czech gendarmes to carry their power into the countryside.

In order to deal with the central headquarters of the Czech gendarmerie, the Germans have heretofore had—at least formally—to go through General Eliáš, the Prime Minister, who was simultaneously Minister of the Interior. General Eliáš does not speak German and does not particularly like Germans. The Germans doubtless found it more satisfactory to deal directly with General Ježek, whose long experience as an Austrian official had doubtless given him not only a perfect command of German but also that ease of manner for which the officials of the old Empire were noted. General Ježek, furthermore, is known to have long had certain fascist sympathies, and while he is considered to be a loyal Czech, it will surely be easier for him to adapt himself to the German point of view than it is for those Czechs whose attitude toward the present Germany is influenced by ideological as well as national differences. Since the Interior portfolio was really going begging, nothing could have been easier than to simplify German control of the Czech gendarmerie by making the relatively acceptable gendarmerie commander Minister of the Interior.

32. Report of July 13, 1939, on conditions in Slovakia

I have just returned from a brief visit to Slovakia, which consisted of a twenty-four-hour motor trip through the north-western and central sections of the country and a twenty-four-hour stop in Bratislava.

On the basis of what I was able to see and hear on this occasion and of the available published information, I am inclined to feel that there has been a certain temporary consolidation of conditions there since I last visited the country in April, but that formidable difficulties remain to be overcome before the new state can be considered as on anything like a sound permanent basis.

The following observations on several angles of the situation may be of interest in this report:

1. Internal Finance

An analysis of the internal financial position of the Slovak government can be made at the present time only on the basis of the following sets of statistics: (a) the 1939 budget of the regional Slovak government, which was approved in February of this year and formed part of the general Czecho-slovak budget; (b) the revised Slovak state budget, approved May 26, which adapted the former regional budget to the new situation created by the establishment of a nominally independent Slovak government; (c) the figures for actual state expenditure for the first six months of the year; and (d) the figures for actual state receipts during the first five months of this year. All of these figures are available and could be submitted if desirable. I presume, however, that the following table, compiled after considerable study and analysis of all this material, will be sufficient:

SLOVAK GOVERNMENT FINANCES
FOR THE YEAR 1939

			crowns
1.	Probable regular budget expenditures, based on figures for first 6 months		974,392,300
2.	Probable receipts from taxes and fees, based on figures for first 5 months		−845,555,000
3.	Probable regular budget deficit		128,837,300
4.	Estimated loss on state enterprises		+ 81,349,200
5.	Planned expenditures on public works		+480,738,300
6.	A non-recurring expenditure made to cover a deficiency from last year's provincial budget		+ 62,308,200
	Total deficit		753,233,000
	Special non-budgetary receipts:		
7.	Cash from Bratislava branch of Czechoslovak state bank	90,000,000	
8.	Estimate receipts from reconstruction loan	60,000,000	
		150,000,000	−150,000,000
	Total uncovered deficit		603,233,000

With regard to item No. 1, it may be explained that this estimate is based on the statement of M. Pružinsky, the Slovak Finance Minister, to the effect that actual expenditures of administration for the first six months had been only 487,-296,166 crowns, as compared with 722,307,751 crowns envisaged in the budget. We are not told whether this saving is due to a real decline in the cost of administration over that estimated at the time the budget was prepared or whether the expenditures for the last six months will simply have to be so much greater to make up the difference. In the above estimates, the benefit of this doubt has been given to the Slovak government, it being assumed that the costs of administration have declined generally and that the last half year will show a similar saving. Should this not be the case, the uncovered deficit might turn out to be greater by some hundreds of millions of crowns.

The question now presents itself as to how this deficit is to be met. The Slovak Finance Minister has intimated that a good portion of it is to be met from the receipts of the Reconstruction Loan and from the emission of new coin. The receipts of the Reconstruction Loan to date, namely, 56,-070,000 crowns, have already been reckoned with in the above table in Item No. 8, together with a small amount which might still be collected under this heading. I cannot believe that much more than 60,000,000 crowns in all could be collected, since contributions have now practically ceased and it is generally assumed that the available capital market is substantially exhausted. As far as the emission of new coin is concerned, this is technically possible, inasmuch as the mint of the former Czechoslovak Republic is situated in the territory of the present Slovak state. It is understood, however, that it is the intention of the government to mint such coin only in an amount which would bring the circulation of coin in the country up to about 200 crowns per head. This would mean a total circulation of roughly 540,000,000 crowns, as contrasted with some 300,000,000 crowns now in circulation—or an increase of some 240,000,000 crowns. Any greater emission of currency could hardly fail to have a definitely inflationary effect, since the total currency in circulation in the country is estimated at only 1,500,000 crowns. Even assuming that the necessary raw materials are available (the import of nickel is a problem for a regime whose foreign currency reserves are very low) and that these 240,000,000 crowns can be minted, there still remains an uncovered deficit of over 350,000,000 crowns.

In what has become "normal" government finance, such a deficit would be met by an increase in the national debt. In Slovakia this does not seem possible, because there is no further capital market on which to draw. There is always the possibility of enriching the government through the obscure processes of "aryanization" and this possibility is doubtless receiving most careful and sympathetic consideration on the part of the Slovak leaders. But even this could scarcely be expected to yield any great quantities of cash without inflicting palpable damage on the economic life of the country.

Presumably, therefore, there would be no other alternative for the Slovak authorities but to curtail expenditures. Here the obvious item would be the millions of crowns spent quite gratuitously for public works. But it is right at this point that Slovak economic difficulties present a problem to the Germans. The projects now under development are in large measure ones in which the Germans may be presumed to have an active interest. There can be no doubt as to the value which German military circles attach to the highway construction northwest of Žilina, which is designed to give the Germans a new and easy approach from Silesia across the Javornik mountains to their fortified zone in Slovakia, in place of the approach cut off by the Poles through their seizure of the Teschen district. It also seems doubtful whether the Germans would wish to see work curtailed, for example, on the new railway line from Diviaky to Banska Bystrica; for when this costly mountain job is completed it should give a new rail approach to the Polish border from Austria.

Will the Germans permit the Slovaks to go broke trying to maintain public works projects of this sort? Interested observers in Bratislava, who have every reason to wish for an affirmative answer to this question, say no. Their opinion is that somehow or other the Germans will keep the present Slovak regime alive as long as they have an interest in its existence. But any German attempt to do this involves questions of transfer and balance of payments, and these must receive separate treatment.

2. The German-Slovak Transfer Problem

The facts concerning the foreign trade and the balance of payments of the new Slovak state remain shrouded in a veil of official secrecy. This veil is particularly thick over everything connected with Slovak-German economic relations, a fact which, as I was forced to point out to a Slovak official, does little to support the demand that Slovakia be considered as an independent state.

The foreigner who inquires in Bratislava concerning the foreign trade statistics for Slovakia during the first four months of its independent existence, will be told that they are not yet compiled, that it takes time to establish a statistical office, etc., etc. He will not find it easy to make his own estimate, because the foreign trade of Slovakia was never separately shown in the old Czechoslovak customs statistics and the economy of the province was formerly so closely interwoven with that of Bohemia and Moravia that it was quite impossible to tell where Slovak foreign trade began and where it left off.

It is known that Slovak exports to free currency countries have been just about negligible and the same, aside from certain oil and raw material purchases, must be true of imports from these countries. Most of Slovak foreign trade, including the trade with Germany, is on a clearing basis. It is claimed in Bratislava, and I know of no reason to doubt the assertion, that with all the major clearing countries except Poland, Slovak foreign trade has shown an active balance. The passive balance in the case of Poland is the result of coal imports from the Teschen district. It had been hoped to balance these imports, as they had been balanced when all these districts belonged to the Czechoslovak Republic, by shipments of Slovak iron ore to the Teschen metallurgical plants, but this was vetoed, I am told, by the Germans, who wanted the iron ore for themselves.

In any case, it is important to note that the Slovak balance with Germany is active. This means that a balance of marks has already accumulated to Slovak credit in Berlin. This balance must be constantly augmented through wage payments to Slovak workers in Germany. It is understood that there are already as many as 35,000 Slovaks employed in Germany, and the Germans have announced their intention to increase this number to 60,000 before the end of the year.

Taking into consideration the wages paid to these people, the clearing rate between marks and Slovak crowns, and the percentage of the wages which the workers can be expected to want to send home to their families, it can be calculated that some 25,000,000 marks (215,000,000 crowns) will be submitted for transfer this year by Slovak workers. To this must be added the costs of the maintenance of the German military forces and of German military construction in Slovakia. All this together is going to pile up a formidable balance in marks in favor partly of the Slovak government and partly of individuals in Slovakia.

Since in Slovakia marks are not legal tender, as they are in the Protectorate, it is difficult to understand how these sums can be transferred, unless it be through greatly increased Slovak purchases. But so far Slovak purchases have not been sufficient to cover the visible, much less the invisible, exports to Germany. The Germans hope that they can soon be increased, but it will take some time before they could be expected to wipe out the active balance in marks. Slovak merchants find German goods high in price and poor in quality in comparison with those which they have been accustomed to receive from Bohemia and Moravia.

Now if the Germans were really going to try to lend or give to the Slovak government 300,000,000-400,000,000 million crowns in order to solve the Slovak budget difficulties, just how could they approach the problem technically? They presumably have no appreciable balance of crowns in Slovakia which they could turn over to the government. They have nothing with which to purchase such crowns except German goods, which they cannot export to Slovakia in sufficient quantities, or German marks, of which the Slovaks already have far too many.

The only answer I can see to this problem is inflation, and it is apparently in this direction that the Germans are urging the Slovaks to proceed. On June 6, a Berlin report to the official Prague German paper, *Der Neue Tag*, quoted *Der*

Deutsche Volkswirt as saying the following: "The assumption that Slovak businessmen lack the cash for further purchases (of German goods) has proved erroneous. It is true that in many cases liquid balances are lacking, but the bank note circulation is still capable of expansion and the President of the National Bank takes the sound position that bank notes should be issued only when there is commercial paper to back them up." This is a pretty clear hint to the Slovak government to help itself—and incidentally Germany—by resorting to the printing presses, and since the Germans own 49 percent of the stock of the Slovak National Bank, this advice is not apt to go unheeded.

Such advice to the Slovaks on Germany's part—coming at a time when the Slovaks are already carrying out at least a 15 percent inflation of their currency through the issuance of coin—bears witness to a desire on the German part to see things tided over at any cost for the next few months. It does not reveal any particular German concern for the permanent prosperity of Slovakia as an independent state. But while it bears out the thesis that German interest in an independent Slovakia will not be of long duration, it also shows that the Germans will not be lacking in devices to keep the show going, if need be, for the next few months.

3. *The General Balance of Payments*

It is not possible to learn the amount of foreign currency holdings of the Slovak National Bank. It is known that the bank started almost from scratch in this respect. The Germans are now said to have turned over to it certain small amounts recovered from gold and foreign currency assets of the former Czechoslovak Republic, and in general it is believed that the holdings of the bank are increasing. They should be augmented by about $500,000 worth of gold normally mined annually within the country.

While the assets of the new Slovak state in free currencies will probably remain small, this should not be taken too tragically or made the basis for predictions of the "break-down" of Slovakia. Most of Slovak foreign trade is with clearing countries, particularly Germany, the Protectorate and Hungary (no clearing agreement with Hungary exists at present but it is hoped to negotiate one this summer). As long as this trade remains generally active there is no reason to fear that Slovakia will not be able to satisfy her most urgent needs for imports. It must not be forgotten that in a small and largely agricultural province of this sort, these needs are extremely elastic. There may have to be adjustments in the standard of living, but these adjustments are much easier than they would be in a highly urbanized and industrialized territory, and there is no reason to suppose that they cannot be made without undue difficulty.

4. *Opposition Activities*

Anti-German sentiment is still widespread throughout the country. In many cases it is accompanied by a more friendly attitude toward the Czechs, which has led to the *bon mot* that it took the Germans to make the Slovaks like the Czechs. Friction between Germans and Slovaks occurs from time to time, particularly where, as in Žilina, German and Slovak troops are quartered in intimate proximity. Nevertheless, there is general agreement that with the despatch of M. Sidor, the former Minister of the Interior, as first Slovak envoy to the Vatican, the anti-German opposition lost its focal point and no longer presents at the moment any immediate danger to the regime.

5. *Fears of Partition*

While Slovak leaders still profess the utmost confidence in the Führer's guarantee of Slovak independence (a guarantee which, incidentally, seems to have slipped Herr Hitler's mind when he made his famous speech in April) no one else in Bratislava seems to feel that the Germans will keep this regime in power one day longer than they consider it to their own advantage to do so. It is obvious that at the present moment, with a German-Polish crisis ripening and with Russo-British talks still unconcluded, no further major decisions respecting the Slovak area can be made; nor would the Germans, at such a moment, have any reason to consider the sacrifice of a Slovak regime which, whatever its economic problems, is completely subservient to German wishes and can hold the territory conveniently at Germany's disposal until it becomes possible to make plans of a more long-term nature. But the general expectation continues to be that the Germans will someday offer a good part of the province to Hungary. There is no doubt in anyone's mind that when that day comes, the price demanded will be a high one—quite possibly Hungarian cooperation in a campaign against Rumania and the admission of German troops to Hungarian territory. If this turns out to be the case, much will depend on the position and attitude of the Hungarian government at the moment in question.

33. Despatch of July 17, 1939, from Consul General Linnell to the Department of State, on the situation in the Protectorate

Relations between the Czech and German authorities have now developed into a curious duel over what might be called the fascist fringes of Czech political life, and in this duel Czech leaders—to their own pleasure and surprise— find themselves holding the upper hand. As fast as the Germans find factions which might split the Czechs, the Czechs reply by splitting the factions. A Czech official recently pointed out to a member of my staff that all three of the groups through which the Germans have hitherto tried to break up Czech unity—namely, the Gajda fascists, the Moravian fascists, and the Vlajka group—are themselves just at present torn by internal dissension to such a point that they are of very little use to the Germans. "This," he added with simple pride, "is entirely our work."

The Germans are now having a new try with a fourth group. Gestapo agents are busy in an attempt to found a new Czech National Socialist party and they are seeking adherents—characteristically enough—in one of Prague's most communistic suburbs. But this last undertaking has caused more relief than alarm among well-informed Czechs, for they regard it as proof that German angling in Czech political waters has thus far produced no results and that the Germans have been reduced to extreme and rather laughable expedients.

It is probably this failure to find suitable successors which has prevented the Germans from removing from office the present members of the autonomous Czech government. The latter are well aware of the fact and are making the most of it. It accounts for the firmer tone which they have recently taken with the Germans. One of them recently told Herr Frank: "You can remove us if you like; but it won't do you much good. We are the last decent Czechs you will have to deal with. After us come the criminals."

The strength and popularity of President Hacha and the Czech ministers have received a considerable boost during the last few weeks through the action of the Germans in issuing decrees on important matters without the cooperation of the Czech authorities. In the first instance, that of the Jewish law, the Czechs were given no opportunity to refuse to sign. The issuance of the decree was simply sprung on them. But they were not slow to sense the political value of this situation and they flatly declined to have anything to do with the order placing certain Czech cities under the dictatorial authority of German commissars. Thus they have been able to saddle the Germans with the entire onus of the acts in question and have disarmed many of the charges to the effect that they were playing the Germans' game. The Germans are quite exercised over this new policy of passivity and are losing no opportunity to stress the thesis that German-Czech cooperation can be effective only if the Czechs contribute to it through their own initiative. As far as can now be seen, they retained these men in office after the occupation in the hopes of discrediting them with their own people. If this goal is to be attained, it is essential that they should play a prominent part in the most unpopular policies.

Altogether the Czech leaders have been somewhat heartened of late by their success in preserving their own prestige and with it the unity of Czech people. If the Germans continue to help them by making mistakes at the same rate as heretofore and if they get no more encouragement with regard to the international situation than they have had up to this moment, their resignations may not be forthcoming for a considerable time.

Outside of the official circles, the constant friction between Germans and Czechs continues unabated. The examples range from the tragic to the ridiculous. The telephone wires of the Reichswehr authorities are frequently cut by mysterious hands. People in the motion-picture theatres make wisecracks, under cover of the darkness, over the German newsreels. Czech waiters in the cafés infuriate their German patrons by always handing them the *Voelkischer Beobachter* face down. Germans sometimes find their parked cars decorated with the hammer and sickle, and the old CSR license tags (Czechoslovak Republic) changed to read USSR.

To all this the Germans react with a lack of psychological insight which at times seems scarcely credible. Many examples could be cited but I think the following two will suffice.

In a Prague beer garden, one warm summer evening, a group of Czech students who had had too much beer to take their troubles seriously gave vent to their feelings by shouting, "We want colonies," "Colonies for the Czechs," etc. The humor appealed to the other good burghers, who took up the cry with enthusiasm, and for a while the whole garden rang with Czech demands for Lebensraum. Two Germans who were sitting at a table by themselves became quite excited over this demonstration. They thought they had discovered the real sympathy of the Czech people for German foreign policies. They ran off and reported the event to the editor of the official German news service, who got out a very serious and "significant" article on the subject of the Czechs and colonies, citing the incident in all earnestness as proof of Czech appreciation of the benefits which they would receive from Germany's recovery of a colonial empire.

The second example is of a more serious nature. The town of Jihlava (Iglau), which—whatever the actual percentage —certainly has a Czech majority, has been probably as hard hit by Germanization as any town in the Protectorate. The Czech national monuments have been defiled and dragged away. Street signs have been rewritten in German. Aryanization has proceeded apace.

Recently a celebration was held on the town square—where the Masaryk monument used to stand—in honor of a returning resident. The returning resident was "Retired Gauleiter and Oberführer of the S.S. Professor, Engineer Rudolf Jung," and the whole proceeding had an air of "local boy makes good." Jung, who is a native of the Sudeten area, was one of the few pre-Hitler Nazis, having founded in 1913 the German National Socialist Workers Party, the so-called DNSAP, from which the present NSDAP was in part derived. He lived for a long time in Jihlava in his youth. After the war he became . . . the head of the regular Nazi Party in Czechoslovakia, which was finally dissolved by the Czech government and the place of which was taken by the Henlein Sudeten-German Party. Jung himself was imprisoned for several months for his activities but was later released and went to Germany. He may be considered as in every respect the perfect example of the type of man who, if German-Czech cooperation were ever to be more than a name, would have to be rigidly excluded from the picture.

In his speech, Jung gloated at length over the fall of the Czech state. "It was not even twenty years old," he said, with mock pathos. "It left us in the flower of its years. It was struck with consumption just as it was about to put on its best clothes. And justly so." "Had this state," he continued, "been sensible, it might have continued to exist. But, God be thanked, the Czechs have never been sensible. They always were Hussites and Hussites they remain." Jung then reverted to a conversation which he had had some years before with a Czech politician, Stříbny. "We Czechs," the Czech had said, "are an unbridled people. We have experienced one Lipany, and I fear we shall experience another." (By Lipany, he was referring to the instance in which Czechs fought against Czechs in the fifteenth century in the wake of the Hussite movement.) "Stříbny," Jung added, "feared a second Lipany but I hoped for it, and that was the difference between us. And now they have suffered their second Lipany."

A few days later the Brno *Deutsche Volkszeitung*, in which the account of this speech had been published, referred to it as one of the conciliatory speeches recently given by high German officials, and again warned the Czechs not to ignore these German efforts to "wipe out the past."

I cite this incident simply because it seems to me to illustrate clearly the frame of mind of a certain type of German leader in the Protectorate. While not all Germans think this way, men of this background and this mentality now occupy the majority of the important administrative positions in the historic provinces. Quite possibly some of them sincerely believe that they are being models of patience, generosity, and conciliation. In that case, however, they certainly do not understand the Czechs or the effect which their words and acts must have on Czech minds. In these circumstances, there is little to be added to the remarks made in previous despatches on the relations between the two peoples. They are simply going different roads, and nothing serious is being done to bring them together.

34. Despatch of July 24, 1939, from Consul General Linnell to the Department of State, on the new Slovak constitution

On July 23 the Slovak Parliament unanimously passed a fundamental law designed to serve as the Constitution of the new Slovak state.

As the first constitution drawn up quite definitely under German influence, this document holds an interest for the outside world greater than that of its mere effect on the methods of government in Slovakia. In the eyes of the Germans themselves it provides, according to the leader of the German minority in Slovakia, "a new form of the living-together and the working-together of the peoples, which will be able to serve as a model for all of Europe."

According to this new constitution, the country is described as a "republic." The main units in the machinery of government are the President, the Cabinet, the State Council, the Parliament, the national minorities, and the corporations. The President is to be elected by the Parliament, for a period of seven years. He may serve only two terms. He appoints the members of the Cabinet, who have executive authority, but the latter are also responsible in a sense to the Parliament.

Legislative power is to be exercised in general by the Parliament, which is to consist of eighty members. While the deputies are to be elected by the people, the list of candidates is to be drawn up by the State Council from the single parties which will be permitted to represent each nationality group, including the Slovaks. The State Council will consist of some thirty members, chosen in such a way as to make it completely an organ of the Slovak Hlinka People's Party.

Thus the party will in reality select the parliamentary candidates from among its own faithful servants and whether the electors choose this one or another can remain a matter of indifference to the party leaders.

Freedom of confession, of speech, and of scientific and artistic activity are guaranteed as long as they do not conflict with legislation, with the public order, or with Christian customs; in other words, they are not guaranteed at all.

It is provided that the present Parliament may remain in office, if it is so desired, until December 31, 1943, and as long as it remains, its present number—63—shall be regarded as normal. Since the present Parliament is largely a creation of the governing group, there would seem to be no necessity for any new elections in the near future. President Tiso, however, will have to stand for reelection within ninety days after the constitution goes into effect. Whether this will lead to a renewal of personal rivalry for the leading position remains to be seen.

Dr. Voitech Tuka, one of the most active figures in post-Munich Slovakia, describes the new constitution as "neither democratic, authoritarian, cooperative nor social." It is true that it is not authoritarian in the sense of providing for the exercise of great power by a single individual. The powers of the President are notably restricted. In this point, the document faithfully reflects the present political situation in Slovakia, where the death of Father Hlinka has left only a number of minor prophets, each jealous of the others and none with quite the stature of a Slovak Duce.

On the other hand, there is little in the constitution which would limit the collective authority of these same men, gathered together as the bosses of the Slovak Hlinka People's Party. A constitution providing for a one-party system means, as can be clearly seen in the Russian example, no constitution at all, insofar as the most vital processes of political life—those concerned with the delegation of power—are concerned. For the one-party system relegates all these processes to the sphere of inner-party politics, where they are free from constitutional restriction and from public scrutiny and where—if we are to credit the experiences of other authoritative regimes—they generally become the vortex of the foulest sorts of deceit, sycophancy, and intrigue.

Some of the most interesting of the clauses of the constitution are those which deal with the treatment of national minorities. These clauses were practically drafted by the leaders of the German minority in Slovakia and it is not surprising that they should have been so phrased as to accord to the German government that extraterritorial power and jurisdiction over persons of German blood which has become one of the most common demands of the Reich on all of its neighbors except Italy. The word "minority" was carefully avoided, the term "national group" being employed in its stead: "The national groups which have their homes on the territory of Slovakia shall have the right to organize culturally and politically under their own leadership. The national groups and their members may establish and cultivate cultural contacts with their mother-peoples. The national groups shall have the right to use their own language in public life and in the schools, on which subject a special law shall be issued."

This liberal doctrine is modified, however, by a proviso which, conveniently enough, could apply to every other national group in Slovakia but not to the Germans. According to this proviso, the rights of the national groups specified in the constitution apply only insofar as the Slovak minority on the territory of the mother state of the national group concerned actually enjoys the same rights. This proviso—which makes it a part of the fundamental law of the state that certain categories of citizens shall serve as hostages for the behavior of foreign governments—is an eloquent testimonial to the decline in respect for individual dignity in Central Europe. It applies particularly to the Hungarian minority and was passed over the opposition of Count Esterhazy, the leader of that minority group.

Another interesting feature of the constitution, equally characteristic of the direction in which political winds have blown during the last few years, is the provision that parliamentary deputies shall enjoy immunity for all offenses except acts committed in the capacity of editors of publications. This is a naïvely frank admission that in the conception of the Slovak leaders there is no crime, no injustice, and no brutality so heinous as criticism of themselves. Aside from this reservation, the granting of immunity to the deputies, whose function is at best a formal one, is just another of the numerous concessions made by the Slovaks to Western parliamentary institutions, with which they did not have the courage to break altogether.

One of the chief aims of the Slovak leaders in the promulgation of this new constitutional act was to lend solidity to their new state structure in the midst of a dizzily rocking continent. But in this they probably overrated the benevolence of their German protectors. It has now become a custom for the Germans to greet every new arrangement in Central Europe with solemn warnings that nothing is settled thereby —that the proof of the pudding will be in the eating. Thus the German Bratislava *Grenzbote*, which—rather than the *Slovak*—is the real official organ in Slovakia, reverts to this theme in welcoming the new constitution, and points out that the document will remain a scrap of paper if the proper spirit is not behind it. Referring to occasional manifestations of anti-German content, the paper adds the following: "These are phenomena which will have to be removed, and the more rapidly and energetically this happens, the better it will be for the future of this country. Thus we see in the constitution not a final point but a test as to whether the peoples of this Lebensraum are mature enough to give it a new physiognomy. This will determine whether we can make a contribution to the new order, to a new order built on principles established by the Führer."

To the uninitiated such warnings, coming from the representatives of a ruler who has undertaken unreservedly to protect the political independence of the Slovak state and the integrity of its territory for twenty-five years to come, may sound strange. But to the Czechs, who have learned to take warnings more seriously than promises, the tone is already only too familiar, and the Slovaks will also doubtless accustom themselves to it in the course of time.

35. *Despatch of August 19, 1939, from Consul General Linnell to the Department of State, on the general trend of developments in Bohemia and Moravia*

Another summer is now drawing to an end—the unhappiest which this area has known since the days of the World War. It has been a strange summer, characterized by frequent and destructive electrical storms which damaged crops to the extent of hundreds of millions of crowns and seemed grimly symbolic of the rapidly alternating hopes and fears in the minds of the people. Work has gone on as usual. Even now the peasants are struggling—encouraged by the Germans and deterred by the frequent showers—to get in the harvest before the newest crisis reaches its culminating point. And the industries are busy enough trying to still the insatiable appetite of the Reich for their products. But all other manifestations of human activity seem afflicted by a strange lethargy, almost a paralysis. Everything is in suspense. No one takes initiative; no one plans for the future. Cultural life and amusements continue in a half-hearted, mechanical spirit. Theatres and public amusements attract only scanty and indifferent crowds. People prefer to sit through the summer evenings in the beer gardens or the little parks along the rivers, to bandy the innumerable rumors in which they themselves scarcely believe, and to wait with involuntary patience for the approach of something which none of them could quite describe but which they are all convinced must come and must affect all their lives profoundly. The near future should show whether this waiting attitude is the result of a sound instinct or whether it merely expresses the natural reluctance of a people which has just awakened from a twenty-year dream of independence to accept again the status of a nation of servants.

The German camp continues to reflect all the current manifestations of National Socialism. Herr Frank, the real leader, sits at his desk in the Czernin Palace, the perfect image of the German "Halbgebildeter" whom National Socialism has raised to power. It is difficult to tell whether his ruthless zeal is the result of political ambition or of a self-righteous belief in the innate sinfulness of the Czechs. Behind him stand his forces: the dignified but inactive Baron von Neurath, the careerist intellectuals of the party, the underworld figures of the Gestapo, the correct and impassive officers of the Reichswehr.

Outwardly, the responsible Germans profess a calm optimism which is in striking contrast to the frank despair of the Czechs. They point out that Czechs and Germans got along well enough for centuries until the rise of the romantic Czech nationalism of the nineteenth century, and this despite the fact that the Germans usually held the upper hand. They are confident, they say, that this state of affairs can soon be restored. But beneath this optimistic exterior there is a marked nervousness among many of them, and there are even those who are already hedging and trying quietly to cultivate Czech favor.

The truth of the matter is, of course, that these are not the same type of Germans as those who formerly ruled the Czech lands with reasonable success. In vision, in sense of responsibility, in cultural background they can scarcely be compared with many of their predecessors. In their dealings with the Czechs they have made the mistake that Machiavelli warned against when he wrote that "men must be either caressed or annihilated," that "they will revenge themselves for small injuries but cannot do so for great ones" and that "the injury we do a man must be so great that we need not fear his vengeance." They have antagonized the Czechs without annihilating them and they are now divided among themselves as to the best way of remedying the situation—some advocating more caresses and the others complete annihilation.

The high Czech officials continue to spend their time in the resplendent offices inherited from the former regime, even though they have little with which to occupy themselves. They are fully alive to the awkwardness of their position and most unhappy about it. They would like nothing more than to abandon their positions, but the chances of their doing so in the near future are slight. The Germans seem as far as ever from the discovery of suitable successors to them. And the circumstances are increasingly unfavorable for their voluntary retirement. The international situation has given them no encouragement. Their success in uniting and retaining the discipline of their own people has created a situation in which they feel that it would be dangerous to allow other and less scrupulous men to hold even the nominal attributes of power. Finally, they have now developed their contacts with the new Czech emigration. They have been able to explain their position to the émigré leaders and to reach an understanding whereby the latter, far from continuing to reproach them for their cooperation with the Germans, actually approve this course of action. So they continue to sit in their uneasy seats, to do their best to preserve unity and calm among their people, and to prevent the rise of futile demonstrations and provocations which could bring only further misfortune to the nation as a whole without doing any substantial damage to the Germans.

German complaints of Czech passivity continue. But they no longer carry the force they did a month ago. In this respect the Czechs may be said to have won a skirmish; for the Germans seem to entertain few hopes at present of realizing any appreciable part of their program through the cooperation of the Czech authorities. The only two important measures on which they are seriously trying to make the Czechs share responsibility are those dealing with the language question and with the conscription of labor. These two bones of contention continue to be tossed back and forth between the two camps.

On the language question,[1] the Germans have receded somewhat from their original position, which was to demand that German should be the authentic language for all official communication, even between Czech offices. They are now prepared to recognize something like an equal status for the two tongues. But even this seems unnecessarily harsh to the Czechs, who see no necessity for adopting the use of German at all, except in communication with German officials or individuals.

With respect to compulsory labor service, the Czech authorities have no objection in principle. Indeed, the Prime Minister, General Eliáš, is inclined to favor the idea as a useful educational, disciplinary, and democratizing force among the youth. But the Czechs insist that such labor as their young people may be called upon to perform must be carried out within the confines of the Protectorate. They fear an arrangement which might make it possible for the Germans to use young Czechs as a sort of cheap peon labor force in the Reich or—even worse—as cannon fodder to carry out dangerous work near the front lines in the event of a war.

On most of the remaining points of their program, the Germans now seem willing to proceed independently, with the ample administrative and legislative powers at their disposal. Instead of fighting, for example, with the central Czech

---

[1] Since the typing of this despatch was begun, the language law has been enacted and published. It provides for the use of German in all communication with German offices, enterprises, and individuals and for the use of both languages in instructions of Czech offices to subordinates. Otherwise the Czech administration is apparently free to continue the use of Czech alone.

authorities over further anti-Semitic measures, they have simply ordered the German-controlled municipal administrations in the large cities to issue local regulations calling for the labelling of Jewish shops and cafés, the banning of Jews from restaurants, hotels, public parks, public bathing establishments, hospitals, etc., and all the other discriminations required by the code of German anti-Semitism. It is true that they have unleashed against the Czech government the lunatic fringe of Czech fascism, banded together in an organization called the Czech Aryan Cultural Society. Prime Minister Eliáš has been compelled to receive these people and to listen to their demands for radio time, for an anti-Semitic teachers' college, for a racial protection law, for the assignment to themselves of the state subsidy heretofore granted to the Jewish Cultural Community, and to the other proposals in which confused minds see the salvation of a people. On some of these points the Czech authorities may have to take further action; but in general the Jewish question is no longer the acute source of conflict between Germans and Czechs which it was some weeks ago.

A more important field in which the German authorities are proceeding quite independently is that of Germanization. It was explained in previous despatches that immediately after the occupation the line was taken by the Germans that they, being outstanding proponents of national pride and racial purity, had the fullest respect for the national feeling of the Czechs, that the Czechs would be encouraged to foster their own national institutions and would not be forced to fly the swastika, give the Nazi salute, use the Nazi greeting, or profess devotion to the Führer. It has also been related how this theory began to break down, first among the Czechs of the Sudeten areas and then in the big provincial cities of the Protectorate, all of which lie within a very short distance of the Protectorate frontiers and all of which have sufficiently sizeable German minorities to raise the question in German minds whether they should not be treated as German cities pure and simple.

There are now indications that this distinction is beginning to break down altogether and that the Germans are starting out on a campaign of indiscriminate Germanization wherever they see possibilities of progress in this direction. This campaign is particularly intensive in Moravia, and has aroused the greatest resentment in that province. German officials have received instructions calling upon them to create a completely German corridor all the way through from Moravska Ostrava (Mährisch-Ostrau) to Brno (Brünn), thus cutting off the main body of Czechs from the Slavs to the east and rendering them in the literal sense an ethnological enclave in Greater Germany. But the efforts toward Germanization have not been restricted to Moravia. Even in Prague, Czech shopkeepers are being forced to acquire pictures of the Führer to place in their windows on special occasions. The Germans, furthermore, have been simply expropriating estates in various parts of the country which belonged in some way or other to the former Czechoslovak government and are preparing to settle German farmers on them. There is good reason to expect that provision will be made in this manner for some of the farmers expelled from the Southern Tyrol. Efforts are being made by the German Landrats to induce Czech farmers to exchange their farms in the Protectorate for ones elsewhere in the Reich, the object being to bring in German farmers—presumably Tyrolese—to take their places. The scions of the great Czech noble families, who rank among the oldest and most distinguished of Europe's aristocracy, are being called upon to profess themselves Germans and to join the National Socialist Party. It is darkly hinted that the alternative may be the loss of their lands and family seats. To men who have prided themselves on their Czech nationality and have brought up their children to consider themselves Czechs and yet who feel a deep responsibility for the preservation of estates which have been in the families for centuries, this is a cruel choice; and it is at best ironic that it should be forced upon them by a regime dedicated to the principles of pride in nationality. But the Germans are not abashed by irony. Their theories are nothing if not pliable; and they will tell the curious inquirer that the racial doctrines enunciated in *Mein Kampf* are only the "Old Testament," that the New Testament is now coming into existence through the practical necessities of the situation, and that there is no reason why the line between Czechs and Germans—already vague enough in many instances—should not be entirely obliterated to German advantage.

Perhaps the main reason for German willingness to let the Czech "autonomous" authorities vegetate in peace is the increasing preoccupation with the preparation of Bohemia and Moravia as a military hinterland for the event of war. During the last few days the reports have mounted of arrangements looking toward an early outbreak of hostilities. Road improvement work has been wound up and the roads cleared of obstacles so as to permit the passage of troops. The railway authorities have been required to work out and to hold in readiness a wartime schedule to replace that now in effect. Textile mills are under orders to wind up their work on civilian orders and to place themselves at the disposal of the military authorities. Hospital and garage space is being set aside for military use. The Prague municipal authorities claim to have received instructions to prepare for the passage through the city of great bodies of troops at an early date. Altogether, the Czech authorities have the impression that the Germans are preparing for hostilities in a very thorough way.

Bohemia and Moravia remain among the few places in the world where a war is earnestly desired. The Czechs see war as the only hope for the recovery of their independence, and the German-inspired warnings of their leaders have changed nothing in this respect. If there is to be no war, they will be faced with the task of adjusting themselves to the domination of a regime intent on their disappearance as a nation. If war comes, they can continue to hope for a recovery in some measure of their lost self-government, if not for a restoration of the Czechoslovak Republic.

But it should be carefully borne in mind that whether there is war or not, the Bohemia and Moravia of the future will never be quite the same as those which were left by President Beneš and his advisors last autumn. Time does not stand still and the turbulent events of the last year have not been without their modifying effect on Czech character. It is true that if the pendulum ever starts to swing in the other direction, there may be terrible anti-German excesses. It is likewise true that German clumsiness has given to Beneš's name a superficial boulevard popularity which his personality on its own merits was never able to command. But that the Czechs will ever restore in full their past institutions and their past leaders is doubtful. Misfortune has left many marks; and among them is a deep sense of the necessity for unity and discipline in a small people so unhappily situated as themselves. Few will wish for the return of the many squabbling political parties, the petty-bourgeois timidity, and the shallow materialism which seems to have characterized at least the lower organs of public administration under the former regime. Czech nationalism will flourish indeed, but with it there will be a demand for greater personal responsibility and greater spiritual authority among those who pretend to lead. One of the most interesting features of the post-Munich era in the history of the Czech lands has been the religious revival which has brought people in swarms to the churches and to the pilgrimage places and has restored something of the influence of the pulpit on public opinion. If last September it was the Hussite sentiment which was stimulated by the prevailing mood of bitterness and defiance, it is now the Roman Catholic faith, with its mysticism, its ceremony, and its greater tolerance of human imperfection, to which people are drawn. The leadership which the Church failed to seize of its own initiative is now being forced upon it by the Germans, and its influence can hardly fail to increase proportionately.

It is difficult to predict the exact course which this influence—and the sentiment which has given rise to it—will take. Much will depend on the attitude of the young people who are now coming into maturity under difficult conditions and who are going to demand their share of any national life which may be restored to their country. No one knows what slogans and what people they will demand, but one thing seems certain: it will not be the slogans nor the people that prevailed before the catastrophe.

36. Report, written October 1940, on "A Year and a Half of the Protectorate of Bohemia and Moravia"

The morning of March 15, 1939, when the German motorized divisions pushed their way through blinding snowstorms into the cities of Bohemia and Moravia, marked a turning point in the history of these provinces no less revolutionary than the Battle of the White Mountain in 1620 or the establishment of the Czechoslovak state in the fall of 1918. The events leading up to this overturn were the center of world attention and were described in detail by a horde of foreign observers. The events which followed have been observed by few outsiders and understood by less. The experiences of these unhappy provinces have been increasingly overshadowed by the more momentous developments into which they were merged. The Protectorate, however, has become one of Germany's most important internal problems, and an attempt to evaluate the changes wrought here by a year and a half of German rule finds its justification in the importance of German internal problems for the world at large.

The outward changes in the Protectorate are neither great nor important. German signs have appeared on the streets. Bookstore windows and newspaper stands show the marks of German influence. The usual phenomena of the war are in evidence. Motor traffic has declined. People are more plainly dressed. Shop windows are less attractive. But the ravages of direct hostilities, as the Czechs are unceasingly being reminded by their German mentors, have been avoided. Bohemia has retained its muddy villages, its geese, its beer, its earthy fertility. And the city of Prague, to which Italian

226

and Austrian architects long ago gave a grace and harmony unrivalled in central or northern Europe, has not lost its charm. It wields its power over Czechs and Germans alike, and life within its walls still has a flavor and subtlety compared to which the life of the great German cities to the north seems flat in the extreme.

Under the surface, on the other hand, the changes have been profound. Economically, the outstanding development has been the shift of national substance from Czech to German; the passage of immovable property into German ownership or German control, the transfer of movable property out of the Protectorate into the Reich proper.

Statistics on these points are inadequate. A great deal of immovable property has simply been bought up by the Germans, partly with crowns which they happened to have at their disposal, partly with marks, partly on credit. A great deal has passed into German control—if not direct German ownership—through the aryanization proceedings. The property thus affected runs into at least several billion crowns. In many of the large non-Jewish concerns, the Germans have managed to acquire the controlling interest. It is understood, for example, that the Vitkovice concern, valued at some 5,-000,000,000 crowns, was entirely taken over. In Škoda the Germans are said now to have a direct 40 percent control, and it is safe to assume that their influence over the remaining shares is decisive. The Bat'a shoe works are still in Czech possession, but under German control. The Sigmund pump works, one of the world's greatest manufacturers of anything to do with poison gas, is believed to have been taken over by the Germans on the basis of aryanization. Certainly no Czech now has any decisive voice in the conduct of its affairs. The Bohemian Union Bank now belongs to the Deutsche Bank. The Escompte Bank belongs to the Dresdener Bank. Only one or two Czech banks, like the Živnostenska and the Anglo banks, the shares of which were held by large numbers of small Czech investors, have been retained in Czech hands. But the banking interests now held or controlled by the Germans are enough to give them a dominant place in the financial sphere. And the picture becomes complete if it be taken into consideration that practically every large concern which has not been bought up has assigned to it a German commissar to see that its activities are conducted in accordance with the policies of the Reich.

Well-informed Czechs estimate the value of movable property—Czech or Jewish—taken over by the Germans during the first year of the Protectorate, i.e., up to March 1940, at 22,000,000,000 crowns. A great deal of this property doubtless consisted of military stores. The amount has presumably continued to rise somewhat since that date. If this figure is credible—and no better one is at hand—the property thus removed has probably totaled in American terms between $500,000,000 and $1,000,000,000 in value.

The process will presumably be given a sort of permanent form through the direct taxation of the Reich, which is being effected over and above the taxation of the Protectorate authorities. Even before the conclusion of the customs union, a month ago, war taxes introduced by the Reich were bringing in some 600,000,000 crowns a year. Now that the customs barrier has been abolished, consumption and turnover taxes will also, it is understood, flow direct to the Reich treasury, and it is estimated that these will amount to 2,-500,000,000 crowns per annum. Thus some 3,000,000,000 crowns ($100,000,000) will evidently continue to be extracted from the provinces annually in taxation.

Germans will point out that this is only proportionate to the similar burden borne at this moment by the population of the Reich proper. That is one way of looking at it. And if the Czechs were to profit equally with other citizens of the Greater Reich in the triumphs and the conquests which this taxation is designed to assure, the argument would indeed be a substantial one.

What the Germans cannot take, they often borrow. On

October 15, the statement of the Czech National Bank showed under the title of "other assets" an item of 5,600,-000,000 crowns. On March 15, 1939, at the time of the occupation, this item was only 1,200,000,000 crowns. The difference of 4,400,000,000 crowns reflects chiefly the sums loaned to Germany on the so-called "interim account." In return for these loans, the National Bank is understood to hold, for the most part, bonds of the Reich paying about 2½ percent. Credits to Germany and German bonds held by other local banks are estimated at some 1,500,000,000 crowns. While these figures are rough estimates, they indicate a total of some 6,000,000,000 crowns advanced to German interests by the banks of the Protectorate since the occupation.

These exactions have been accompanied—and partly made possible—by the process of inflation. The indications of this process will not be found in the figures on the circulation of the Czech crown, which have remained almost static during the period of German rule. But only the most naïve would look for them there. The crown has been merged with the mark. Promissory notes for German government purchases pass from hand to hand and replace currency. At least 1,-500,000,000 crowns mopped up by the Germans in the Sudeten regions have been placed into circulation again in the Protectorate, making it possible for the Germans to acquire Czech goods and services to this amount at no cost to themselves. Finally, if "inflation" can be described as a relationship between commodities and money, the effects can be produced by a shortage of one as well as by an excess of the other. Thus the growing shortage of goods has aggravated the situation already produced by the increased means of payment.

The authorities have endeavored to conceal the effects of this process, but some of these effects are obvious enough. The price indexes used by the Germans for publicity purposes differ by fantastic figures from those kept by Czech offices which compile such figures for their own use. Both, however, show substantial increases in the cost of living since the occupation. These are shown by the following table:

INDEX OF RETAIL PRICES IN THE
PROTECTORATE

	German figures	Czech figures
March 1939	100	100
December 1939	119	—
January 1940	122.7	155.5
August 1940	132.4	199

Extreme as the Czech figures appear, they are more than borne out by the facts concerning some of the most common products of daily use. A kilo of butter, which cost 18 crowns before the occupation, now sells officially—against ration cards—for 40 crowns, and unofficially on the illegal open market for 100. Clothing prices have shown a similar development, and where the difference is not so extreme in price, it usually becomes so if quality is taken into consideration. With all due skepticism about the Czech figures, it may be assumed that at the present time the increase in cost of living since the occupation amounts to at least 50 to 60 percent, and has been recently rising at a rate of at least 20 percent annually. Now that the customs union has been concluded, the rise in the official prices, which in part reflected a German policy, should stop. Whether the prices on the illegal open market will advance still further remains to be seen.

To offset this rise in prices there has been a rise in industrial wages which amounts to 30 to 40 percent for the lowest paid workers and 5 to 10 percent for the higher income brackets. Salaries to white-collar workers are estimated to have risen 20 to 25 percent in the low salary groups and 10 to 12 percent in the case of the high-paid personnel. These figures reflect the German efforts to win popularity for the new political arrangements among the rank and file of the Czech population and thus to cut the ground out from under the Czech intellectuals and the Czech middle class, who are regarded as the bulwarks of Czech nationalism.

On the farms, gross income is estimated to have increased 10 to 15 percent through the rise in prices. But labor and materials also cost much more and net income probably has been kept fairly close to the former level. Czech sources claim that forced deliveries of cattle and grain have slightly increased farm profits during the present year at the expense of the productivity of future years, so that a diminution of farm income is to be expected. Certainly German policies, while relatively favorable to the farming population, have procured no striking wave of agricultural prosperity and small political gratitude toward the Reich authorities.

Another reflection of inflation can be found in the so-called "giro" account of the National Bank. These are the deposits of the excess reserves of various local banks deposited with the National Bank. These items rose from 1,-300,000,000 crowns at the time of the occupation to 4,522,-000,000 crowns on October 15, 1940. They represent the cash which could not be utilized by the holders because there was nothing to buy with it and nothing in which to invest it. The opposite side of this medal is shown among the credit items of the National Bank statement. On March 15, 1939, bills discounted and loans on collateral stood at 3,560,000,-000 crowns; on October 15, 1940, they totaled only 416,-000,000 crowns. No one wanted the money.

This picture would not be complete without a study of the fate of the national debt of the former Czech state. But here even fragmentary statistical material of any value is lacking. The processes of public finance, already complicated to the point of obscurity in the Reich itself, are almost unfathomable in the Protectorate, where there are two currencies, two national banks, and two state debts to be reckoned with. There are probably not ten men in the world who understand what is being done with government finance in the Protectorate of Bohemia and Moravia, and not all of these would care to admit it.

These inflationary phenomena, of course, affect the entire population of the provinces, without regard to nationality. But what of the relative positions of the Germans and the Czechs?

Accurate population figures are not available. At the time of the occupation, or shortly before, the population of residual Bohemia and Moravia is estimated to have been 6,804,000, of whom only 234,000 were Germans, and 6,570,000 Czechs and others. Czech circles now estimate the population at 7,-200,000. Of the Czechs, roughly 150,000 have gone to the Reich, where they are working voluntarily or otherwise. This would bring the number left in the Protectorate to around 6,420,000. If we can attach any importance to the Czech estimate, there must now be a residue of nearly 800,000 persons, who—in the present circumstances—can only be Germans. This would indicate an influx since the occupation of nearly 500,000 Germans. This estimate is roughly supported by similar estimates for the city of Prague, where the influx of Germans is believed to have been about 120,000, not including the German military forces.

Now what sort of Germans are these? They are for the most part independent, grownup persons who have come to take on influential white-collar positions. They have a tremendous administrative system of their own, most of which is believed to be financially supported by the Protectorate Government. Many of them sit in Czech government offices. Others are representatives of Reich organizations and firms. Numbers of them sit as commissarial directors in local firms which have fallen a victim to the aryanization laws. They have replaced or have been set over Czech officials in firms and institutions which have been bought up by—or otherwise fallen under the control of—interests in the Reich. They are, in the most literal sense of the term, the carpetbaggers of the occupation.

Above all, they are expensive. Where they work side by side with Czechs in government institutions, their salaries are usually double—or more—those which the Czechs receive for exactly the same functions. It is believed that in many instances half of these salaries are paid in the Reich in marks, and the remainder, roughly equivalent to the corresponding Czech salary, is paid in the Protectorate. But most of these Germans are in the higher positions, so that the disproportion becomes even greater. The example can be taken of a small Czech-Jewish-owned hat shop under German commissarial direction, where two German female commissars, who fulfill no function other than that of supervision and who have no previous experience or specialized knowledge in the field, draw down monthly salaries totaling 6,000 crowns, as against a total payroll of not more than 5,000 crowns to the entire regular local personnel, who number about eight.

Now it is doubtful whether the higher-paid white-collar class of residual Bohemia and Moravia, under Czech rule, ever numbered much more than 500,000. It can be established that of a male population between 15 and 59 of about 2,000,000, 1,200,000 were engaged in industry and agriculture alone, and other professions, transportation, domestic service, etc., must have accounted for many more. Thus there are grounds to assume that the provinces have been saddled since the occupation with a new white-collar class roughly as numerous as their own, and at least two or three times as expensive to maintain.

Meanwhile, there is a steady crowding out of the Czechs from the more influential and profitable positions, and a deterioration of the conditions under which they can compete. It is now a year since all Czech institutions of higher learning were closed down completely and without exception by the Reich authorities. The halls of the Charles University have been turned over to the German University in Prague, to which Czechs are not admitted. They teem with the life of

German students from the Reich proper as well as from the Protectorate. Almost no young Czech can at present prepare to become a doctor, a lawyer, a professor, an engineer, or a minister of the gospel. Even the Czech middle schools are being closed in many places, or are being compelled by various factors, such as lack of fuel, to close. The only higher education which young Czechs are now getting is in the little private circles which they form for this purpose; but these academic achievements are ones which will never be recognized in the battle for employment which sooner or later they must face.

Some, of course, have private businesses into which they can step. But these are the fortunate few. Czech industry and business are highly concentrated. Big firms like Bat'a and Škoda and Vitkovice, which employ tens of thousands of workers, have either already fallen or are rapidly falling under German control. They in turn control other and smaller enterprises; and as this controlling German interest spreads, the chances for employment for Czechs in responsible positions become smaller and smaller. Practically no new Czech businesses are being founded. The many Jewish enterprises, now operating under German direction, offer no good possibilities for Czechs. Thus a situation is rapidly being created where a young Czech looking for a start in life has little choice—unless he is so fortunate as to inherit a farm or a small business—but to become an industrial or farm laborer, go into domestic service, learn some handicraft, or seek employment in the Reich.

Czech cultural life still struggles on. It will never be entirely eradicated, as long as any appreciable part of the nation remains. But it is gradually being whittled down to a point where its function will be the quiet cultivation and preservation of the Czech language, literature, and folklore, rather than any active participation in the creative processes—such as they are—of modern Europe. The Czech movie industry is being taken over by the Germans, who find it convenient to make films in a place where there is no bombing. The Czech theatre has become a sort of shrine for the cultivation of historical pageantry. Literature is confined mostly to the newspapers, which are largely translations and are very little read. The decorative arts are ones which few Czechs can afford to pursue, and architecture is almost ruled out. Popular imagination finds its expression mostly in the innumerable bitter jokes and rhymes and plays on words in which the average Czech seeks solace for his plight and which pass from mouth to mouth with a rapidity that even press and radio could scarcely improve on.

The political life of the Protectorate has changed little in the past year. The terms of the Reichskanzler's decree of March 16, establishing the Protectorate, remain in many respects dead letters. Local authority continues to be exerted throughout the countryside by German administrative officials, the Landrat, for whom the terms of the Protectorate made no provision. The fact that the Germans describe the existence of these officials as a war measure and hold out hopes of their withdrawal in the event of a happy ending of the hostilities, is little comfort to the Czechs. Although S.S. uniforms have wisely been withdrawn for the most part from the streets of Prague, German police are still present in other garbs in every community of any size throughout the land, and the prisons are crowded with persons who have run afoul of them. For this, too, the terms of the Protectorate made no provision. Many other similar points could be cited. Nevertheless, the terms of Hitler's decree still remain nominally the fundamental law of the country; a Czech administration of sorts still functions—so to speak—at the bottom; a Czech president and a Czech cabinet, limited as their functions may be, still hold office.

But if German authority in the physical sense is unchallenged, morally it does not exist. Whatever power the Germans may have over the persons and property of the Czechs, they have little influence over their souls.

The Czech nation is probably as solidly opposed to its present form of rule today as it was a year and a half ago. The tiny Nazi groups among the Czechs are now weaker and more devoid of prestige than ever. The leader of the principal group of this sort was recently sentenced to a week in prison by a Czech court for insulting President Hacha, and the court of appeals—probably after taking note of the fact that no protest had ensued from German circles—boosted the sentence to two weeks. The incident caused nothing more than amusement in any quarter. There is simply no real National Socialist sentiment in Bohemia and Moravia, except among the Germans themselves. There is not even any social mingling to speak of between Germans and Czechs. The two groups live side by side in the same cities but yet in different worlds, without real human contact and without inner understanding.

The Germans have tried hard to remedy this, and they have insisted that the Czech officials help them. They have recently installed their own Czech agents at the head of the Czech political organization, the National Unity Party, and have endeavored to use this association, to which 98 percent of the Czechs nominally belong, as a propaganda instrument through which to "sell" the advantages of German rule to the Czechs. They have threatened the Czech authorities that the preservation of the entire Czech administrative apparatus might be dependent on the extent to which it could be made useful in this respect. Delegations of Czech journalists have been escorted through the Reich and required to fill their papers with reports which could not conceivably, in the circumstances, be anything less than favorable. In other words, the Germans have drafted the services of the Czech "autonomous" administration in order to make the rest of the Czechs like them.

But all these efforts are of no avail. The Czech nation respects its own leaders but—appreciative of the situation in which the latter find themselves—it does not believe a word they say. Every utterance by an influential Czech is greeted sympathetically by the population as a statement extorted by the Germans, and the only serious attention given to it is the invariable search for the double meaning, the existence of which no good Czech would ever doubt.

Actually, the Czech nation today lives without moral guidance from any quarter. It is simply not accessible to any influence which it suspects of emanating from German circles, and it prefers to rely entirely on its own instincts. In these instincts it enjoys an amazing unity. It has shifted gears with little difficulty back to the psychology of an unpopular, uninfluential, and mistrusted minority under German administration. It feels itself thoroughly at home in this position, and needs no guidance.

If President Hacha and his associates carry on with their jobs, it is no longer for the purpose of preserving moral discipline and unity among the Czechs; for this is no longer necessary. The aim of the Czech leaders today is to preserve at least a representative head through which Czech grievances can be voiced and Czech aspirations promoted; to defend the conception—still nominally recognized by the Germans and useful to the Czechs in many respects—of the Czech people as a nation rather than as a mere racial relic like the Wends of the Spreewald; finally, to preserve as much as possible of the Czech autonomous administration as a field of employment and experience for individual Czechs and as a bulwark to the self-respect of the people at large.

The future of this Czech administration, provided the Czech leaders continue to show the same adroitness and tact in their exercise of it, depends on the Germans. The latter are still not agreed or even united in their attitude toward the Czechs. The moderates, still headed by Neurath, would like to give them something in the nature of a real autonomy and make a serious attempt to reconcile them to German rule by concessions. The radicals, still headed by Frank, would like to smash them completely as a nation, destroy their intelligentsia, and make Bohemia and Moravia into German provinces. Supremacy between these two groups can be decided only on the mat of Nazi party politics. Prague pundits say that the first round in the battle was won by Frank, that the second was a draw, and that the third is about to be fought out. They imply that the conservatives still have a chance to come out on top.

That may be. But meanwhile the Czechs have been thrown at least 50 percent of the way back toward the status of a nation of peasants, servants, and laborers; and if the liberal views of Baron von Neurath finally carry the field, his conservative followers will have the dubious satisfaction of locking the stable door a good year after most of the horses have been stolen.

Slender as the hopes may be which the Czech nation can place in German moderation, they are, for the moment, the only hopes that most responsible Czechs dare to nurture; and the West has little right to condemn them for attempting to build on this foundation. The problems of this area are not new and they are not susceptible, even in the best of circumstances, of any early or complete solution. The Czech nation, which was only imperfectly prepared for its independence, did not cope entirely successfully with the responsibilities which this independence involved. With all its excellent achievements in other lines, it failed to produce leaders with the requisite realism and vision and self-assurance to solve the questions of the relations between Czechs and Germans within the boundaries of the Historic Provinces or the relationship of the Republic as a whole to the German world around it. The complaints of the Czechs today bear a distressing resemblance to those of the more reasonable Sudeten Germans four or five years ago, and the main difference is that the Germans of that time were more free to air their grievances. Much of what is going on at present is only a chronic expression of the national rivalries of the area; and it will probably continue to go on for many years to come, either in one direction or another, depending on what foot the shoe is on.

Meanwhile, the Czechs are not alone in their misfortunes, nor are their complaints the most grievous ones. Their lands and cities have been spared, and their youth, contrary to the gloomy forebodings which prevailed just after the occupation, has not been forced to fight for Germany. Even the extent to which their labor has been mobilized for service to the Germans has not been as great as was feared. In the government of the Protectorate and its subordinate administration, boss-ridden as these may be by the Germans, they have an institution which they would scarcely have dared to dream of in the Austrian days. And those of their citizens—mostly students, intellectuals, and public figures—who continue to languish in confinement, are not the only foreign guests of the Gestapo. They are merely sharing the fate of a good part of northern Europe. It was probably this which President Hacha meant to convey when he recently remarked to his people, with a gloomy irony, that sovereign states of small nations were a thing of the past and that the small national states were now being replaced by large territorial units of leading nations "which take small nations under their protection."

Irresponsible Czechs, both within and without the confines of the Protectorate, find it easy to dream of dramatic liberation and revenge. But the more realistic and more responsible leaders are sincere in their efforts to combat this line of thought. They can conceive of changes which might ease their relations with the Germans; but they cannot conceive of changes which would suddenly relieve them of the immediate neighborhood of these 80,000,000 German people. They are aware of the sympathy of the West; but they will always appraise this sympathy at precisely the value which it had for them on the day of Munich. They have no illusions as to the extent of the catastrophe which has befallen them; but they are bound to concentrate their attention on what can be recovered from the wreckage. They feel that the cornerstone of any long-term Czech policy must be a modus vivendi with the Germans, and that any national gains based not on such a modus vivendi but on the favor of more distant powers are bound eventually to prove illusory.

Their task is a difficult one. They have to contend not only with German harshness and German stupidity. They also have to contend with the psychological shortcomings of their own people: the nationalistic and linguistic prejudices, the narrow horizon, the social uncertainty, the lack of realism, and the tendency to romanticism in political thought.

In all their efforts, they can hope for some measure of success only if they are able to disarm German distrust. But if they are to do this, they must not be encumbered with too much advice and solicitude from the West. The heroics of irredentism are all very well from a distance. But the problems of these Czechs who must today take responsibility for their people before the Germans are already too burdensome, too pressing, and too delicate to permit them to assume any additional strain. Their tasks leave no room for the glories of martyrdom; and those who wish their people well will think twice before embarrassing them with their censure or their sympathy.

Epilogue

BY FREDERICK G. HEYMANN

When in the fall of 1938 George Kennan, who had just been appointed Second Secretary of the American Legation in Prague, began sending his despatches to the State Department in Washington, probably nothing would have been further from his mind than the expectation to see these reports published as sources to one of the most exciting—and most depressing—chapters of Central European history. Yet for anyone interested in this crucial area ("Who controls Bohemia controls Europe," Bismarck said) this belated publication is of great value indeed. For this is the report of an eyewitness who, highly gifted for and thoroughly trained in the political analysis of developments in Central and Eastern Europe, could look at those critical happenings in Czechoslovakia's "Second Republic," followed by the so-called Protectorate Bohemia-Moravia and the supposedly independent Slovak Republic, with a clear and sensitive, yet also detached, eye. Kennan, after all, represented what was at the time a neutral power, a nation which, even toward the end of his Prague assignment, was still far from ready to enter a second world war. Nor had the mind of the American policymakers, whether in the State Department or in Congress, acquired any feeling of responsibility for what was then occurring—or was allowed to occur—in Central Europe.

It is largely just this measure of detachment and cool examination and evaluation of facts and events which makes these reports so valuable as source material. Nothing else like it exists. The few works in English on the same places and phases are either semiofficial publications of the Czecho-

slovak Government in Exile[1] or works written by authors
who to a considerable degree identified themselves emotion-
ally with the Republic of Masaryk and Beneš,[2] people whose
own sources (while they did not disregard German publications) came again from the London-based government. As
such these publications were good, but they could not and
would not in any sense be neutral.

To some extent those other publications, although most
of them appeared before the end of the war, had the advantage of hindsight in their judgment of what happened in
1939. Their authors wrote under the impression—and ad-
dressed themselves to readers aware—of the full measure of
all the horrors which the Nazi regime would let loose upon
all the nations, large or small, whose territory they had invaded and occupied. In the years 1938 and 1939 civilized
people of the Western and especially the Anglo-Saxon world
who had met many equally civilized Germans in many walks
of life could not, or not yet, easily believe what eventually
they were forced to believe about the murderous policies
practiced in the name of Germany. It is good to keep this in
mind when reading these despatches.

The Czechoslovakia where Kennan began his diplomatic
activities in October 1938 was not the country, or the nation,
at its best. Dr. Beneš later[3] made the point that his government had decided to accept the more than painful Munich
"solution" as a sacrifice for world peace, and that in a sense
this acceptance was a more heroic deed than a bloody and
in the outcome pernicious military resistance would have
been. There may be some justification for this argument,

[1] *Czechoslovak Sources and Documents*, vols. 1-4, The Czechoslovak Information Service, New York, 1942-1943; *Four Fighting
Years*, published by the Czechoslovak Ministry of Foreign Affairs,
London, New York, 1943; also in Czech: L. K. Feierabend, *Ve
vládách Druhé republiky* and *Ve vládě Protektorátu* (*In the Governments of the Second Republic* and *In the Government of the Protectorate*), New York, 1961, 1962.

[2] Sheila Grant Duff, *A German Protectorate*, London, 1942; E. V.
Erdely, *Germany's First European Protectorate*, London, 1941.

[3] In *Czechoslovak Sources and Documents*, vol. 2, pp. 28-29.

yet no one—least of all the Czechs themselves—would dare to claim that this policy could be described as "their finest hour." That widespread and fierce eruption not only of hatred for Beneš and his friends but of something like hate and contempt of the nation for itself—this attitude that swept the country in the fall of 1938 and that Kennan described so well in his early despatches—must have made almost any Westerner shudder, even though Americans did not have as much cause for a bad conscience as had, admittedly or not, the French and the British. George Kennan, with his extraordinary flair for the psychological substance of a political atmosphere, characterized with almost prophetic accuracy the regime of the "Second Republic" as ominously resembling that of the Schuschnigg regime in Austria which had fallen just half a year before Munich. At the same time the contradictions and complexities of political trends in Bohemia and Moravia throughout that winter are often caught in these reports with photographic fidelity.

The situation was in many ways different in the two eastern provinces: Slovakia and Ruthenia. Kennan undertook repeated and prolonged trips there, and his reports, based on fairly broad contacts but above all on abundant information from the people who had newly acquired power, throw a cold and far from flattering light on both these territories. The stories from Ruthenia—in all its poverty and many-sided intrigue a rather sordid little land—read almost like a political comedy, though with tragic background. Kennan's description shows his splendid gift for quick perception and analysis of even the darkest and most unusual scenes and developments. Indeed we have here in his reports probably the last and best accounts of what went on in this tiny country until it was swallowed up by its greedy neighbors—Hungary first, the Soviet Union later—and thereby practically disappeared, perhaps for all time, from the pages of history.

Kennan's reports on Slovakia are, however, of more abiding importance. So far we have had almost nothing but fiercely partisan treatments of what might well be considered the central question of Slovak history in those fateful years. Was this, as Slovak Separatist refugee writers, especially, claim to this day, the shining liberation of a cruelly oppressed Slovak nation from what they call "the Czech yoke," and were the years 1939-1945, in spite of some German interference which the Slovak government manfully resisted, an age of glorious freedom for all Slovaks? Or was it rather a time when, under ever-present German supervision and pressure, a radical minority (not even identical with the majority of the former autonomist Hlinka party) enjoyed a domestic power which the Germans decided to leave relatively unrestricted as long as its openly Fascist protagonists glorified and imitated, to the greatest possible extent, the example given by Nazi Germany? As elsewhere in his observation of Slovak conditions, Kennan had no axe to grind, no old prejudice to defend. Nor was he uncritical in his judgment of the mistakes made, during the preceding twenty years, by the Czechs in their attitudes toward the Slovaks. He also gave full credit, where it was due, to the attempts of some Slovak officials to "run their own show," at least internally. Yet his detailed reports show quite convincingly that of the two existing interpretations, in essence only the second is historically correct. It is a pitiful and shameful story, the story of a government utterly dependent on personal favor, for its leading men, from Hitler and his henchmen, the story of a movement that began with the claim to be a crusade and ended, as Kennan says, "as a racket." Indeed the government was finally hated, as no Czechoslovak government had ever been hated, by the majority of the Slovak people, and this in spite of the support that, especially at the beginning, a considerable part of Slovakia's Catholic clergy gave to it. (It was only in the rebellion of 1944 that this hatred became obvious. In spite of everything that later apologists for the Tiso-Tuka regime wrote in order to prove that the majority of the Slovaks had never wanted it, this rebellion was the one redeeming feature in the history of Slovakia in those years.)

Mr. Kennan's report on the events and immediate consequences of March 15, 1939—the date of the military occupation of Czechoslovakia's remaining territories and the transformation of its western part into the Protectorate Bohemia-Moravia—almost sounds like entries in a personal diary, sketches of an impressionist character. He was clearly in a strange position, as were the other foreign, and especially Western, diplomats. They had to witness the political annihilation of the country to which they had been accredited; whatever their basic feelings were, they had to remain observers and as such essentially neutral, even in a chain of events which might have seemed more atrocious than military conquest would have been. Sometimes the tale of Kennan's impressions sounds as if he had had to force himself to remain cool and almost rigidly detached in order not to be overwhelmed by the dreadfully depressing atmosphere of time and place.

During the first days and even weeks of the occupation, the German element most conspicuously visible everywhere was the army (although the Gestapo, if less in evidence, did not wait a single day to get into action with political arrests). The officers and soldiers of the army, at this stage, generally avoided doing anything that would antagonize the Czech population of Prague, and the worst that could then be said about them was the eagerness with which they bought and greedily consumed or sent home large quantities of food (and other goods) which at this time were in better supply in Czechoslovakia than in many parts of Germany. Kennan states correctly that a good many people immediately arrested by the Gestapo were soon released. He would, if he had planned to write a cohesive story, have had to add that not a few of these were rearrested before long. Kennan reports that of the arrested a large proportion were politically active Jews and anti-Nazi German refugees. He was probably right, especially at the very beginning. Soon, however, as one can see from his own despatches and other sources, the Jewish arrests were no longer limited to those who had taken a stand against the Nazi regime. Often it was sufficient that they were wealthy; before too long all that was needed was that they were Jews. The development toward more anti-Jewish brutality is clearly predicted in Kennan's report of March 30, although with a little note of hope (it would perhaps not turn out quite as awful as in Germany) that did not stand the test of time. The story of the fate of the Jews and specifically of the anti-Jewish legislation was bound to play a role in Mr. Kennan's reports from both Prague and Bratislava. He makes it very clear that under the Protectorate there was practically no anti-Semitism noticeable among the Czech people (although there had been some anti-Jewish propaganda in connection with the anti-Beneš agitation immediately after Munich). In consequence the Czech government, though it could not possibly refuse a steady measure of cooperation with the German masters, was extremely reluctant to extend collaboration to anti-Jewish measures of the type that the Germans would have wanted. The legislation in question, on which there had been negotiations between Czechs and Germans, was eventually simply issued by the "Reichsprotektor," even though, as an internal issue, on the basis of the constitutional fiction of the Protectorate, it should have come from the Czech government. The Czech ministers thus escaped (as did the vast majority of the Czech people), both in contemporary public opinion and in the judgment of history, the blame which rests heavily upon some other governments acting under German guidance —the blame for a more or less willing participation in the genocidal destruction of European Jewry. Among these the Slovak government—in spite of the resistance of decent people on various levels, in spite also of efforts coming from the Vatican—carries an especially heavy responsibility. This becomes quite clear from Kennan's report, even though the decisive steps in the annihilation of Slovak Jewry with German methods were taken only in the years 1941 and 1942.

It is quite obvious that, when faced with a country and a period subject to such tremendous strains as was Czechoslovakia from 1938 to 1940, observers will have different impressions, if for no other reason than that they could not help looking at things from different vantage points. I myself, apart from my historical studies, had during my stay in Czechoslovakia from 1932 to 1939 looked at the political and socioeconomic development there from the viewpoint of a newspaperman of originally German background. But during the time on which Kennan reported, my own immediate information came, to a higher degree than his, from representatives of the replaced Beneš government and other Czech friends. Nevertheless, my own picture is on the whole remarkably similar to that gained by Kennan, and I would have to quote far too much of the material presented here if I were to use every opportunity to express my admiration for the splendid accuracy and three-dimensional quality of his reporting.

In addition to the issues which I have mentioned, I should like to add a few more. I think, for instance, that Kennan was right in his judgment about many of the unfortunate leaders of the Czech government who most reluctantly but often out of true patriotism stayed in office after March 15, 1939[4]—right even in some cases where in the long run the term "collaborator" was bound to blacken their memory inside and outside Czechoslovakia.[5] That their cautious and yet not ineffective policy, aimed at maintaining a measure of political and moral cohesion among the masses of the Czech people, was at the same time an extremely daring and

[4] See the above quoted works by Feierabend, note 1.

[5] I myself owe my life and that of my family to the help of a seeming "collaborator," Dr. Zdeněk Schmoranz, head of the Press Department of the Czech Prime Minister, whose true position the Germans discovered soon after I had left the country in July 1939, and whom they killed in 1940.

dangerous game emerges frequently from Kennan's reports, but it became even more obvious when in the fall of 1941 "Butcher" Heydrich began his bloody rule by arresting the Czech Prime Minister himself, General Eliáš, who was sentenced to death by the notorious "German People's Court" in Prague and soon afterward executed, together with hundreds of other Czechs from all walks of life. (The figures rose to the thousands in 1942.)[6]

Mr. Kennan's descriptions of the mood of the nation during the German occupation often show an almost photographic exactitude. This is just as true regarding the grim and desperate hate that prevailed in the time immediately following Munich as it was for the infinitely more united feelings of the great majority during the occupation. There was a short period following Munich when a good many Czechs would have been willing to support a German action against Poland—an understandable reaction to the absurd and brutal policy of Poland's Foreign Minister Beck against Czechoslovakia late in 1938. But this anti-Polish feeling evaporated on the day of the German occupation. From then on, as Kennan emphasizes, probably no European nation nursed such an intense wish and hope for the outbreak of war as did the Czechs. This can hardly be considered a selfish and irresponsible attitude. The Czechs assumed—and rightly, as it turned out—that war was not only the one way to their liberation but that the destruction of their state was merely the beginning of a determined process of violent German expansion. War, they felt, was inevitable in any case, and they feared that, if it was too long delayed, Germany would have a chance of destroying more than merely the superficial structure of the Czechoslovak state.

How dangerously far this process of destruction—economic, social, and cultural—had gone after a relatively short period of occupation, emerges clearly from the report

[6] See Sheila Grant Duff, *op.cit.*, pp. 288f., and *Four Fighting Years*, *op.cit.*, pp. 122, 133.

which, after a long pause presumably resulting from a time of absence from Prague, Mr. Kennan sent in October 1940. By that time a full year had passed, a year during which all Czech universities and all other institutions of higher learning had been closed completely, and with it not only all opportunities for a substantial education for the young, but also most chances for scientific work in almost all fields. All intellectual and cultural freedom was thus effectively suppressed. True, the destruction of the Czech intelligentsia never quite reached the measure of systematic mass murder that it achieved in Poland, yet it went far enough to become a terrible burden for the survival of one of Europe's finest, most highly developed national civilizations; even now, after a quarter of a century, it is not easy to judge whether some of its indirect effects are yet overcome.

In this same highly informative summary of the fall of 1940, Mr. Kennan differentiated between "irresponsible" Czechs who "dream of dramatic liberation and revenge," and the "more responsible leaders" who "feel the cornerstone of any long-term Czech policy must be a *modus vivendi* with the Germans." This, of course, was written in a very particular historical moment when Hitler had imposed his rule over most of Europe west of Russia without as yet giving any distinct indications that before long he would follow the example of Napoleon's suicidal policy. It was a moment in which none of the great world centers except London thought or acted as if there were much hope of defeating Hitler—perhaps least of all Moscow and Washington, even though luckily Ambassador Joseph Kennedy's judgment did not prevail upon the decisions of the White House. In any case it probably took a Churchill to look ahead from late 1940 with any confidence in final victory.

Today we can perhaps say with the wisdom of hindsight that the first group of Czechs, somewhat harshly condemned by Kennan as being limited by a narrow horizon, a lack of realism, and a tendency to romanticism in political thought

—a characterization more frequently applied to the Poles than to the Czechs—that these Czechs represented the overwhelming majority of the people from all social and political levels, people who would live to see their dream come true, at least as far as liberation from the Nazi incubus was concerned. Looking back we can also say that the other Czechs, those who expected from collaboration even the most modest national gains beyond mere physical survival, were perhaps the ones who lacked realism and who believed, or at least pretended to believe, in what could never be more than hopeless illusion. But here, again, the diplomat could not be independent from his sources. He could talk, albeit cautiously, with the men around Hacha, but he could not achieve, could hardly dare seek, any substantial contact with those who, if they were politically active or even well enough informed about what was going on under the surface, could easily be on, or get on, the black lists of the Gestapo and in any case could only be harmed by contact with a Western diplomat.

The only objections of any significance to which Mr. Kennan's reports seem to me to be open are a few remarks by which the situation under the German occupation is compared in some way with what appeared to him previous historical parallels. Thus he finds, in one instance of Czech complaints, "a distressing resemblance to those of the more reasonable Sudeten Germans four or five years ago." I would certainly not deny that reasonable Germans in the Czechoslovakia of the Thirties had cause for complaints. But a real resemblance appears to me, on the basis of years of personal experience, almost nonexistent, for one main reason: if, before 1939, any country of Central and Eastern Europe was wholly free of anything like an atmosphere of terror, then it was the Czechoslovakia of Masaryk and Beneš—and she was really the only country in that part of the world of which this can truly be said. This atmosphere of terror, perhaps less noticeable in the beginning of the Protectorate to a foreign diplomat than to a defenseless private individual, was literally present from the very first day of the German occupation; indeed it seems to me that Kennan did notice and describe it. Without going into the complex issues of the more or less justified demands and complaints of the German minority (with all its cultural and political liberties, its huge system of free schools at every level, its publicly supported theatres and operas, its utterly free press), we can perhaps say, using a well-known expression, that the Germans of Czechoslovakia could and did complain about unnecessary and sometimes silly pinpricks. What the Czechs had now to complain about was that the hand of the killer was around the throat of their nation.

The political parties of the Sudeten Germans had not only their free, and often enough screaming, say in Parliament, but, beginning in 1926, regular representation in the cabinet, often as heads of ministries which, like the Ministry of Justice, had considerable influence. Altogether, Czechoslovak parliamentarism, while indeed sharing some of the shortcomings of all the European multiparty systems, was not without a measure of dignity and competence. Above all, it was almost the only parliamentary system which quickly achieved, and long maintained, a remarkable degree of stability, not only in comparison to the many nations which soon slipped, as did Poland and Germany, ever deeper from democracy into dictatorship, but even in comparison to the country that had largely served as a model for both Czechoslovakia and Poland: the Third Republic of France.

There is one other comparison with earlier developments which may need questioning: the impression, in the report of May 15, 1939, as well as in the later report of October 1940, that the political arrangement of the Protectorate was one "which the Czechs would have been overjoyed to receive, even on paper, during the last years of Austrian rule." This statement is based on the assumption that Habsburg rule in Bohemia and Moravia-Silesia in the beginning twentieth century was exclusively or at least predominantly German rule, and a harsh one at that. In fact, in the three lands of the Crown of St. Wenceslas, the German element was in those years already strongly on the defensive and even on the retreat, trying hard and often desperately to maintain its old strength and influence against the steadily growing pressure of the economic and political power of the Czech majority. In the Habsburg Empire as a whole, or at least in the Cisleithanian (Austrian) half, and even in its capital of Vienna, the Czech element, especially in many branches of the imperial administration, played an increasing role (though a relatively modest one in foreign policy). The Germans, although a majority in the Alpine provinces, had to try to hold their own in the Vienna Reichsrat against an ever-growing non-German population which was no longer—as were the Slavs in Hungary—subject to systematic denationalization. Thus the Czechs in the late Habsburg Empire were energetic but also, and justifiedly, confident fighters for a still better, at least still more autonomous and more influential, future for themselves and their Slav brothers. Surely they would never have accepted, let alone been overjoyed by, a paper-autonomy which would have deprived them of large stretches of their land, of any substance of national self-determination, of their strong economic and precious cultural institutions, and, last but not least, of anything like a future of hope.

There are other historical parallels which Kennan uses with much more justification. He is right, for instance, when he describes the attitude of many Czechs in the early phase of the Protectorate as akin to the attitude of the "Good Soldier Švejk" toward his Austrian officers in World War I. For a while, indeed, some Czechs felt that their famous sense of humor would put them on a level or even above their German oppressors. Perhaps the creation, originally upon German suggestions, of one united "National Community" instead of the previous parties, and the well-nigh unanimous enlistment of all Czech adults into this organization—thereby making monkeys of the Germans—belongs in this category. But in the long run the situation became too serious and deadly to be the subject of any but the most bitter humor. Czech solidarity did indeed remain strong throughout those years and far beyond the period of Kennan's Prague assignment. It showed the very first, as yet indistinct, signs of splintering only when, much later, the Communists tried to gain a leading position. Kennan was surely right when he described the way in which the Czech-German relationship led, on the side of the Czechs as well, to a cynicism and indeed a measure of corruption that could not bode well for the postwar situation.

All in all, of course, this is a sad chapter, if only one of many in a totally sad story. The final history of the years of the German occupation of Czechoslovakia has not yet been written; it will be hard to write at any time and anywhere, if indeed it can ever be written. But for an understanding of what went on, in some detail, in the two then separating and separated parts of Czechoslovakia during the first two years after Munich, Mr. Kennan's reports help us substantially in giving us a clear picture, never distorted by emotional ties or prejudging partisanship. His account makes some of the later developments more understandable: the regrettably indiscriminate eviction of the great majority of Germans from postwar Czechoslovakia, the surprisingly strong showing of the Communist party in the postwar elections. Above all, Mr. Kennan offers a source work, the result of first-class observation, combined with careful political analysis and interpretation, from which the historian, the political scientist, and the general reader will profit in equal measure.

Glossary

(This glossary has been compiled from the limited information available to me in Princeton at time of writing. It may well be inadequate or inaccurate in one detail or another; but it may be helpful to the reader to whom the names are wholly unfamiliar.)

Beck, Colonel Jozef, 1894-1944. Polish Foreign Minister 1932-1939.

Beneš, Dr. Eduard, 1884-1948. President of Czechoslovakia 1935-1938 and 1945-1948.

Beran, Rudolph, 1887-195?. Prime Minister of Czechoslovak government from December 1, 1938 to March 13, 1939, and, until April 1939, of the provisional government under the Protectorate. Tried in 1946 as a collaborator and sentenced to 20 years imprisonment, to include 10 years of hard labor. Reputed to have died in detention.

Brody, Andreas. Hungarian born Ruthenian leader, reputedly a protagonist of the Russian, rather than the Ukrainian, cultural orientation in Ruthenia. Became, briefly, first Premier of the autonomous Ruthenian regime, in October 1938, but was soon removed and replaced by the pro-German and pro-Ukrainian Vološin.

Buerckel, Josef. Prominent Nazi official. After having supervised the incorporation of Austria and the Saar into the Reich, took a very active part in the secession of the Slovaks in March 1939, then became first Gauleiter of Moravia in March 1939. Died by his own hand in 1944.

Čatloš, General Ferdinand, 1895-1944 or 1945. Minister of Defense in government of independent Slovakia from March 1939 to September 5, 1944. Deserted to insurgent territory and was arrested there in 1944. Tried and condemned to five years penal servitude after the war.

Černy, Josef, 1885—. Czechoslovak political leader. Minister of the Interior from 1934 to December 1, 1938.

Chvalkovsky, František, 1875-1944. Czechoslovak Foreign Minister October 4, 1938 to March 13, 1939. Minister without portfolio in interim government of the Protectorate from mid-March to April 27, 1939. Then, Minister of that government in Berlin until his death in an air raid there during the war.

Čipera, Dominik, 1893—. A high official of the great Bat'a shoe concern. Served as Minister of Public Works in both the Beran and Eliáš cabinets from December 1, 1938 to September 28, 1941.

Durčansky, Dr. Ferdinand, 1906—. One of the leading members of the autonomous and independent Slovak regimes. Served as Minister of Railways and Transport in the autonomous regime (1938-1939), and as Foreign Minister (March 1939 to July 1940) and Deputy Premier (1939 to 1944) of the independent regime. Reputed originally to be close to the Germans; later fell out with them and was removed from the position of Foreign Minister, in 1940, at their insistence. Was reputed to be living, in the 1950's, in Argentina.

Eliáš, General Alois, 1890-1942. Minister of Communications in the Beran government from December 1, 1935 until April 27, 1939, at which time he became Premier and (for a time) Interior Minister in the Protectorate government. Removed from office by Heydrich in September 1941. Executed in Prague, apparently by the Germans, in 1942.

Feierabend, Dr. Ladislas, 1891—. Minister of Agriculture in the last Czechoslovak and the late Protectorate governments, from October 1938 to February 1940. Understood to have been living, as late as 1964, in the United States.

Fenčik, Stefan. Ruthenian politician. After serving, prior to Munich, as a Ruthenian deputy in the Prague parliament, became an official in the autonomous Ruthenian regime in

1938, but fell out with his associates and fled to Hungary even before the final Hungarian occupation of Ruthenia.

Fischer, Dr. Ottokar, 1883-1939. Minister of the Interior in the provisional Protectorate government in March-April 1939. Dropped out when the regular government was formed, in late April, and apparently died the same year.

Frank, Karl Hermann. 1898-1946. Assistant to the Reichsprotektor and leading German political representative in Bohemia-Moravia after March 1939. Executed in Prague in May 1946.

Fritz, Dr. Geisa. Minister of Justice in the independent Slovak government from March 1939 to September 1944. Condemned after the war to five years' penal servitude as a war criminal.

Gajda, General Rudolph. Czech fascist leader. Active as senior military leader in the uprising of the Czech Legion in Siberia in 1918. Headed various fascist political undertakings in Bohemia in the 1938-1939 period, but never won any extensive popular following or German support.

Hacha, Emil, 1872-1945. Originally an Austrian official and then a judge of the highest administrative court in Czechoslovakia, Mr. Hacha consented reluctantly to serve as President—first of the rump Czechoslovakia, after Munich, and then, until 1945, of the Protectorate government. Arrested in May 1945, he was fortunate enough to die in prison the following month, and thus to escape trial as a war criminal.

Havelka, Dr. Jiri, 1892—. Previously an associate of Hacha on the highest administrative court. Served as minister in the governments of the rump Czechoslovakia and then of the Protectorate until September 1941, when he was dismissed and arrested by the Germans. Tried in 1946 as a collaborationist, he was acquitted, and is understood to have been living, as late as the 1950's, in communist Czechoslovakia.

Henlein, Konrad, 1898-1945. Leader, before Munich, of the

Sudeten German Nazis. Served, after March 1939, as Gauleiter in Bohemia, but did not play a major role. Arrested after the war, he committed suicide before he could be tried as a war criminal.

Hlinka, Mgr. Andrej, 1864-1938. Founder (1918) of the Slovak People's Party, of which were formed the autonomous and independent Slovak regimes of 1938-1944. Died in 1938 on the eve of the breakup of the first Czechoslovak Republic.

Hruby, Adolph, 1893—. Formerly a parliamentary deputy of the Agrarian Party. Served from 1942 to 1945 as Minister of Forestry and Agriculture in the Protectorate government. Although this was a relatively minor job, he seems to have been heavily involved with the Germans, for the sentence pronounced upon him when he was tried in 1946 was the heaviest (life imprisonment, to include 15 years of hard labor) levied against any member of the Protectorate regime.

Ježek, General Joseph, 1884—. A senior gendarmerie officer. Long in the Austrian military service before 1918. Reputed to harbor fascist sympathies, he served as minister in the governments of both the rump Czechoslovakia and the Protectorate, holding the Interior Ministry in the latter from July 1939 to September 1941.

Kalfus, Dr. Josef, 1880—. Finance Minister right through from 1936 to 1945 in all the successive governments centered in Prague. He was thus more consistently a member of the post-Munich regimes than any other person. It must be assumed, however, that he either kept his contacts with the London government-in-exile during the war, or that he used his official position in a manner agreeable to that government, for when brought to trial, in 1946, he was exonerated and acquitted.

Kapras, Professor Jan. Minister of Education in the final (rump) Czechoslovak, and the Protectorate, governments December 1938 to September 1941.

Klumpar, Dr. Vladislav, 1893—. Minister of Health in the final (rump) Czechoslovak, and then Protectorate, governments December 1938 to September 1941.

Krejci, Dr. Jaroslav, 1892—. Minister of Justice in the final (rump) Czechoslovak, and then the Protectorate, governments. Took over as premier after Eliáš' execution, and served to May 1945. Tried in 1946 as a collaborationist, he received the severe sentence of 25 years imprisonment.

Mach, Alexander, 1902—. Prominent member of the leadership of the Slovak independence movement. Served first as propaganda chief and then as Interior Minister of the independent Slovak regime, 1939-1945. Caught in Germany, together with Tiso, in 1945, he was returned by the American military authorities to Slovakia, tried there, and—rather surprisingly—let off with a sentence of 30 years penal servitude.

Neurath, Baron Constantin von, 1873-1956. Reichsprotektor in Bohemia-Moravia from April 5, 1939 to September 27, 1941. Formerly (1932-1938) German Foreign Minister. Sentenced at Nuremberg to 15 years imprisonment as a war criminal, he died in 1956.

Osusky, Dr. Stefan, 1889—. Czechoslovak Minister in Paris at the time of Munich. Holder of ministerial posts in former Czechoslovak governments. Although a Slovak, he at once disassociated himself from the post-Munich regimes both in Prague and Bratislava. Has resided, in recent years, in the United States.

Prchala, General Lev. Czech general. French-trained. Former officer of the Czech Legion. Previously military commander in Ruthenia. Sent to Ruthenia in January 1939 to try to keep the autonomous Ruthenian regime in line. When the Republic broke up, in 1939, he apparently fled to Poland.

Pružinsky, Dr. Nikolaus. Minister of Economy in the autonomous Slovak regime (January-March 1939) and then Finance Minister in the independent regime throughout its entire existence. Tried as a war criminal in 1946-1947, and sentenced to seven years of penal servitude.

Revay, Julian. Former Social-Democratic deputy in the Prague parliament. A born Ruthenian. Served as minister in the autonomous Ruthenian regime, 1938-1939, with Vološin. At the time of this writing, Director of the Ukrainian Institute of America.

Ritter, Karl. German career diplomat, formerly ambassador in Brazil. Charged, March 1939, with liquidation of the Prague Foreign Office. Generally regarded as a specialist on the liquidation of the diplomatic affairs of conquered countries. Sentenced at Nuremberg, in 1949, to four years imprisonment as a war criminal.

Šadek, Vlastimil, 1893—. Minister of Commerce in the two post-Munich Prague regimes from December 1, 1938 to February 3, 1941. Never very popular with the Germans.

Sidor, Karol, 1901-1953. One of the leaders of the Hlinka People's Party in Slovakia. After serving as Deputy Premier and virtual representative of the autonomous Slovak regime at the Prague government in the weeks after Munich, Tried unsuccessfully to head, during the March 1939 crisis, a Slovak government that would retain the tie to Prague. Soon displaced by Tiso and Tuka, who had German support, he found himself in disfavor in both Berlin and Bratislava and was given an honorable exile as Slovak Minister to the Vatican, where he remained throughout the war. Said to have died in Canada.

Sivák, Josef, 1896—. Minister of Education in the independent Slovak regime, down to September 1944. Tried after the war as a war criminal and sentenced to three years penal servitude.

Stříbny, Jiri. One of the founders of the Czechoslovak Republic and minister in several of the early cabinets. Always a political rival to Beneš, he was soon eclipsed by the latter in the leadership of the Czech National Socialist Party, and never regained, in later years, the influence he had enjoyed in the 1920's. Reputed to have died shortly after World War II.

Stuckart, Dr. Wilhelm von, 1902-1953. German administrative official. Charged with the general supervision from Berlin, in 1939, of the administration of the Protectorate. Tried at Nuremberg, in 1949, as a war criminal, and found guilty, but given no sentence because of critical illness.

Syrový, General Yan, 1888-19??. Variously Minister of Defense, Premier, and Acting Premier in the post-Munich Prague regime. Appears to have dropped out of political life as early as April 1939, but was nevertheless tried, with Beran, after the war, and sentenced to 20 years of penal servitude. Said to have died in prison.

Tiso, Mgr. Jozef, 1887-1947. One of the leaders of the Hlinka People's Party after Hlinka's death. Became the leading figure in both the autonomous and independent Slovak regimes, serving the first as premier, and the second first as premier (1939) and then—to 1945—as president. Tried after the war as a war criminal, and executed in April 1947.

Tuka, Dr. Voitech, 1880-1946. Leader of the Hlinka People's Party after Hlinka's death and after his own release (1938) from long incarceration by the Czechs. Served variously as Premier, Deputy Premier, and Foreign Minister in the autonomous and independent Slovak regimes after Munich, he and Tiso being the two leading figures in German-dominated Slovakia. Tried and executed in Slovakia in 1946.

Vološin, Mgr. Augustin, 1874-1945. Premier of the autonomous regional Ruthenian regime from December 1938 to March 1939. Spared by the Hungarians (under German pressure), he was evidently overtaken somewhere by the Soviet advance in 1944, and is said to have died or been murdered in prison, in Galicia, in 1945.

Index

Index

of Jesuit Order, Slovakia, 51-52

Moravska - Ostrava (Mährisch - Ostrau), 131-134, 147, 162

Munich Agreement, xi-xiv, 15

Munkačevo, 62, 65

Nachod Incident, 194

National Unity Party (National Community), 11, 45, 99, 144, 157-158, 168, 174-177, 192-193, 236

Nemsova R.R. Junction, 110

Neurath, Baron Constantin von, xix, 97, 111-112, 114, 119-120, 145-146, 174, 179, 188-190, 196, 218, 237-238. *See also* glossary

Oderberg, *see* Bohumin

Olfredi, Head of German minority in Ruthenia, 67

Olomouc, 133, 147

Osusky, Dr. Stefan, 180. *See also* glossary

Pieštany, 78

Plzen (Pilsen), 133, 147

Poland, xii-xxi, 109, 131-132; relations with Slovakia, 15-16, 19-20, 38-39, 41, 120, 161-162, 202; relations with Ruthenia, 41, 62

Prchala, General Lev, 65-66, 68, 180. *See also* glossary

Přerov, 36

Prešov, 69

Protectorate of Bohemia and Moravia, establishment of, 94-102; delay in putting into effect, 119-120, 172-174; appointment of new government, 143-148; German disappointment with, 167-168; in jeopardy, 177; abuse by Germans, 188-190; condition in 1940, 226-240

Pružinsky, Dr. Nikolaus, 156, 199. *See also* glossary

Reichsprotektor. *See* Neurath, Baron Constantin von

Revay, Julian, 55, 60, 67, 88-91. *See also* glossary

Ribbentrop, Joachim von, German Foreign Minister, xv, xvi

Ritter, Karl, German Foreign Office representative in Prague, 1939, 97. *See also* glossary

Ruthenia, xii-xxi, 9, 40-41, 58-74, 88-93

Šadek, Vlastimil, 38, 145, 148. *See also* glossary

Schuschnigg, Kurt von, Austrian Chancellor, to 1938, xvii, 9

Schwedler, General von, Commander of German Fourth Division, Prague, 1939, 129-130

Sebekovsky, Dr., German administrative official in Bohemia, 1939, 174

Sidor, Karol, 19, 38, 54, 78, 81, 139, 205. *See also* glossary

Sigmund Pump Works, 227

Sivák, Josef, 156. *See also* glossary

Škoda Plant, 184, 227, 234

Slovak-German Agreement of March 23, 1939, 107, 120, 137, 140-142, 164

Slovakia, xii-xxi, 9, 12-27, 39-41, 75-83, 104-110, 120, 122-128, 135-142, 149-156, 160-164, 173, 198-206; new constitution, 212-216

Slovošovce, 162

Spisska Nova Ves, 106

Šramek People's Party, 60

Střibny, Jiri, 210. *See also* glossary

Stuckart, Dr. Wilhelm von, official of German Ministry of Interior, in charge of Protectorate affairs, 1939, 97, 173. *See also* glossary

Sudeten Area, xi-xii

Sychrava, Dr. Lev, Editor of *Narodni Osvobozeni*, 35